Gambler Way

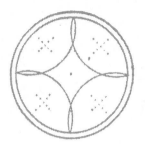

Gambler Way

Indian Gaming
in Mythology, History, and
Archaeology in North America

Kathryn Gabriel

Johnson Books

BOULDER

Published in the United States by Johnson Books, a Division of Johnson Publishing Company, 1880 South 57th Court, Boulder, Colorado 80301.

9 8 7 6 5 4 3 2 1

Cover design: Margaret Donharl

Library of Congress Cataloging-in-Publication Data
Gabriel, Kathryn.
    Gambler way: Indian gaming in mythology, history, and archaeology
in North America / by Kathryn Gabriel.
            p. cm.
    Includes bibliographical references and index.
    ISBN 1-55566-160-2 (alk. paper)
    1. Indians of North America—Games. 2. Indian mythology—North
America. 3. Indian philosophy—North America. 4. Gambling—North
America—History. I. Title.
E98.G2G33 1996
394'.3—dc20   96-7872
                                                           CIP

Printed in the United States by
Johnson Printing
1880 South 57th Court
Boulder, Colorado 80301

 Printed on recycled paper with soy ink

Contents

For Sri Gurudev,
Master of the Game

Here the point is that, one turn of the wheel—and everything changes, and these same moralists would be the first (I am sure of this) to come and congratulate me with friendly jest. And they would not all turn away from me as they do now. Yes, to hell with them, with all of them! What am I now? Zéro. What can I be tomorrow? Tomorrow I may rise from the dead and start to live again! I may find the man in me, before he is lost for ever!

—Fedor Dostoevsky, *The Gambler* [1866]

INTRODUCTION

Way-Winning:
A Sacred Rite

Lo! and of Chance and Fate were they the masters of foredeeming, for they carried the word-painted arrows of destiny (shóliweátsinapa), like the regions of men, four in number. And they carried the shuttlecock of divination (hápochiwe), like the regions of men, four in number. And they carried the tubes of hidden things (íyankolotómawe), like the regions of men, four in number, and the revealing balls thereof (íyankolote tsemak'ya móliwe), like the regions of men, four in number. Yea, and they bore, with these, other things—the feather bow and plume arrow of far-finding, tipped with the shell of heart-searching; and the race sticks of swift journeys and way-winning (mótikwawe), two of them, the right and the left, the pursuer and the pursued of men in contention. All these things wherewith to divine men's chance, and play games of hazard, wagering the fate of whole nations in mere pastime, had they with them.
　　　　　—Frank Cushing, "Outlines of Zuñi Creation Myths" [1896]

Raising Capital

In 1895 the Puyallup and Black River tribes of the Puget Sound area in Washington State held a "sing gamble" against each other in Jake's big barn on the Puyallup Reservation. The sonorous beat of the drums could be heard half a mile away as the songs began, the men shouting "hi-ah, hi-ah, hi-ah," the women chanting "mm-uh, mm-uh, mm-uh, mm-uh." The pot opened with twelve Winchester rifles, eleven sound horses, seven buggies, one hundred blankets, forty-three shawls, an uncounted pile of mats and clothing (mostly worn), and forty-nine dollars in cash. Gamblers clad in bright blankets squatted around two mats, seven to a side. The dealer shuffled ten wooden chips, one of which was marked differently from the others,

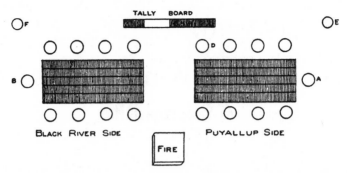

Diagram shows position of the players around the mats in the Sing Gamble between the Puyallup and the Black River reservations. Sketched by the Tacoma correspondent for the *San Francisco Examiner*. (Culin, 1907)

and deftly hid them under one of two piles of shavings. Opposing teams took turns guessing the location of the distinctive chip. The game would go on until one team lost all that they had owned.

The Black River tribe was on a losing streak, but Captain Jack, their leader, would not quit. He held out in the hope that every moveable thing, except what belonged to the government, would be transferred from the Puyallup Reservation to the Black River Reservation. He put up his big knife (his principal ornament), his shiny brass rings, all his money (sixty dollars), his watch, and his rifle. He advised his companions to likewise bet everything but their canoes, which they would need for the return trip home. Failing to follow his own advice, Captain Jack bet his big horse, harness, and buggy, and ended up walking home. In the words of a *San Francisco Examiner* reporter, "Poverty is intense this year at Black River and the Puyallup is having a boom."[1]

The events in Jake's big barn, while perhaps surprising to the modern reader, were not unusual in either their scale or in their drastic consequences. Native Americans in general have a strong tradition of raising capital through gambling. Historically, "gambling and games of skill were informal and voluntary mechanisms by means of which possessions circulated through a community and often allowed booty or newly acquired trade goods to pass to new owners." Horse racing and dice games permitted informal redistribution of goods and food. Most southwestern Indians, for example, preferred trade and such other modes of exchange as gambling versus "raiding and the expensive and unpredictable results of warfare."[2]

Gambling continues to be of great economic and social significance to Indian peoples—presumably a four to six billion dollar annual business.[3] Since the Seminoles opened their first bingo parlor in Florida in 1974, roughly 200 tribes in twenty states have banked on gambling ventures in the attempt to gain economic independence. These enterprises have proven to be a bonanza for most groups, and a sign of their success is that gambling has surpassed baseball as a national pastime. Why? Americans live closer to reservation casinos than to Las Vegas or Atlantic City.

Success has not come without struggle, however, and the battle is far from over. The opening of reservation casinos has been embroiled in controversy, locked up in courtrooms, and argued in Congress. The main conflict has been between individual states and the reservations within them. In part, it is a battle between sovereign entities, each determined to decide for itself what is to take place within its borders. It is also an economic struggle involving the redistribution of goods. Yesterday, horses, blankets, rifles; today, hard cash.

Through their casinos, many tribes are today turning the tables on their historical adversaries, and the irony has not been lost on them. The once-feared Mashantucket Pequots, for instance, were down to 280 members before they began operating the richest reservation casino in the country. Shakopee Mdewakanton Dakota tribal members went from earning $1.95 an hour stripping copper to netting nearly a million dollars *each* since opening their Mystic Lake casino at Lake Prior, Minnesota. The casino itself was named after the tribe, "dwellers at spirit lake," but the holding company for the tribe's casino is named after Little Six, the Sioux leader hanged in 1862. Pojoaque Pueblo in New Mexico named its casino Cities of Gold after the search for the fabled Seven Golden Cities of Cíbola (Spanish for buffalo) conducted by Spanish conquistadors of the sixteenth century. Early in 1996, the governor of Pojoaque was the first to threaten to close down state highways if the state legislature failed to ratify gaming compacts with the tribes. If this action were joined by the other reservation casino operators who line the major freeways, the state could virtually be shut down, a possibility reminiscent of the 1680 Pueblo Revolt against the Spanish.

The logo for Sandia Pueblo's casino just north of Albuquerque, New Mexico, depicts a buffalo suspended inside a half hoop. Perhaps this is an allusion to the game of hoop and pole played by Plains Indians prior to a raid or the spring bison hunt. The hoop symbolized the buffalo in mythology. Today, the Indian gaming movement is referred to as the New Buffalo, a chance to revitalize the tribes and establish economic and political independence.

Gaming has always been a serious business among Native Americans, but profit has not always been the primary motive. Anthropologist James Mooney in 1897 noted that he had witnessed the games of many North American tribes and, yes, he "had seen groups of men or women wager their ornaments and all their personal goods, even to their articles of clothing, until their bodies were nude."[4] Indeed, the play did not stop for meals or sleep until one or the other of the parties had lost everything. But most Native games originated in "sorcery" and were "founded on universal concepts," for "everywhere in this stage of society they are rooted in divination or the universal longing of mankind to know the causes of things and how effects may be controlled."

The tone of sorcery is evident in this gaming story reported by Mooney.[5] A Kiowa leader, Pa-tepte, or "Buffalo-bull-coming-out," challenged Dävéko, an Apache chief, to a hand game called *dó-á* (tepee medicine game). The Kiowa leader possessed a reputation for his ability to pass the "button" unnoticeably between wide-stretched hands and even to suspend it invisibly in the air until he was ready to catch it. The Apache leader was not only a medicine man but, apparently, could kill an enemy

Logo from the National Indian Gaming Association depicts the traditional game of "hoop and pole."

with invisible darts from a great distance. On this occasion he boasted his superiority, but it was not to be so. The winter of 1881–82 was named for the Kiowa victory, and a picture of two males playing the game was commemoratively etched into their religious calendar.

An important and overlooked aspect of traditional Indian gaming is that gambling has nearly always been a sacred activity, inextricably bound together with myth, legend, and ritual. Since the sixteenth and seventeenth centuries, white observers of Indian culture have casually noted the connection between gambling and religion, but it was not until the end of the nineteenth century that the academic community realized the supreme importance of that connection in the understanding of Native gaming. It came about as a result of a chance meeting.

Hand game depicted in a Kiowa calendar. (Mooney, 1898)

Games Study

As ethnologist Frank Hamilton Cushing (1857–1900) browsed through the booths of the 1893 Columbian Exposition in Chicago, a collection of Oriental and European games caught his eye. Cushing had served as field collector under Major John Wesley Powell, a famous explorer of the American West, and was intimately acquainted with the Zuñi of western New Mexico. Fascinated by the uncanny resemblance of Old World games displayed in the booth to those of the Southwest, Cushing struck up a conversation with the curator, Stewart Culin (1858–1929). Excitedly, he described to Culin the dice, wheel, moccasin, shinny, and dart games the southwestern Indians played and the elaborate rules, rituals, and myths that attended each one. Cushing suggested they look into these apparently parallel phenomena.

Culin was intrigued. He, too, possessed a profound interest in games and the mysteries of their origins and cross-connections throughout the world. He had already trekked to the Orient on several field expeditions and had written papers on Chinese and American games. Culin and Cushing resolved to collaborate on an exhaustive study of games, starting with North American Indians, then moving on to the rest of the world.

During the next decade, volumes of material were produced as other scholars such as James Mooney, inspired by Culin and Cushing's ambitious project, paid particular attention to Indian games in their field work. George A. Dorsey, curator of anthropology at the Field Columbian Museum in New York, mobilized the museum's resources and for five years in a row marched his assistants out to various reservations in search of games. Culin himself amassed countless journal entries, letters, and reports by scores of scholars, missionaries, military officers, explorers, and traders who had witnessed or heard testimony of Indian games since the seventeenth century (mostly excluding Spanish documents). The result, after fourteen years, was the 846-page *Games of the North American Indians*, published by the Smithsonian's Bureau of American Ethnology (BAE) in 1907. No one could have known, until all the material had been compiled, just how widespread gambling games were or how Native people's fascination with them equaled, if not surpassed, that of the European newcomers. The book still serves contemporary scholars as a primary source, since Culin printed verbatim hundreds of documents.

Culin gathered gaming material on 229 tribes in North America and Mexico. He identified thirty-six different kinds of games and divided them into two categories: games of chance and games of dexterity. He further divided games of chance into two subcategories: (1) games in which dice-like pieces are thrown at random to determine a score tallied with sticks, pebbles, etc., or kept track of on an abacus, counting board, or circuit; and (2) games consisting of players guessing the places where a particular lot is concealed, with success or failure resulting in the gain or loss of a counter. Games of dexterity included archery in various forms, sliding javelins or darts along hard ground or ice, shooting a netted or stone wheel or a ring (called "hoop and pole" or *chungké*[6]), ball games in highly specialized forms, and racing games more or less related to ball games. Culin also noted the adoption and adaptation of many European games by Natives, thereby extrapolating that most traditional games predated the arrival of Columbus in the New World.

Nearly every tribe played several versions of these games, but not all games were played by every tribe. All games could be gambled upon, however, and it is safe to assume that every game was. The games Culin classified were played only by adults (children had a variety of their own amusements), and most games were restricted to one gender or the other and were usually played at a fixed time of the year during certain festivals and religious rites.[7]

Frank Cushing died in 1900 halfway through his grand collaboration with Culin. One can only guess what his intuition, artistry, and personal experience with Zuñi religion would have brought to the study's conclusion. After Cushing's death and the publication of the Indian games book, Culin's interests changed to costume, fashion, and furniture. Perhaps fourteen years on such a vast subject simply exhausted his impulse to conquer the world of games. During his career, however, he wrote papers about the similarities of games among the Chinese, Japanese, Koreans, Africans, Egyptians, Hawaiians, Siamese, Philippines, Syrians, New York Italians, and Brooklyn streetboys.

Culin was a games diffusionist; that is, he believed that worldwide similarities in games proved direct or indirect contact between cultures. In 1948 Alfred Kroeber, who wrote *the* book on anthropology, reached the same conclusion about gambling.[8] His list of gambling cultures included native Australians, the Papua-Melanesians, most of the Poly-nesians and Micronesians, and Indonesians not too heavily influenced by the Hindu, Chinese, or Malay. In Asia, the chief nongamblers were the more remote nomadic hunters of "Farther India" and Siberia; in Africa, they were primarily natives from the upper Nile to Capetown, although tribes in West Africa and the Congo Basin gambled. Most of the northern continent of Native America gambled, with the excep-tion of scattered hunters in parts of the transcontinental subarctic belt (although I found two gambling myths from the western portion of this zone). South American gamblers included natives of Peru, highland Bolivia, Chile, Argentina, and Paraguay. The strongest addiction, Kroeber believed, was west of the Mississippi, where wealth was the outstanding symbol of success in life. The areas of gambling and non-gambling are both large and compact and, he wrote, "we must there-fore conclude that they are both due to consistent diffusions."

Diffusionism in any field of study has its harsh critics who say that diffusionists concentrate on parallels and ignore important differences. Scholars of games today maintain that cultural traits can only be under-stood within their context and that they most likely develop indepen-dently.[9] While not the primary subject of this book, the controversy is important to keep in mind as we examine the gaming rituals and myths, for to entertain a single origin is compelling.

Diffusionism aside, Culin's study transformed the academic attitude toward the role games have played in human culture, not only in social life but also in spiritual life. "In general," he wrote, "games appear to be played ceremonially, as pleasing to the gods, with the object of secur-ing fertility, causing rain, giving and prolonging life, expelling demons, or curing sickness."[10] BAE Chief W. H. Holmes, in his introduction to the volume, summarized the connection between gambling games and the sacred: "Although engaged in by both men and women, apparently as a pastime, and played persistently and with utter recklessness as to the wagers laid, games of all classes are found to be intimately con-nected with religious beliefs and practices, and to have universally a devotional aspect and cases of divinatory significance."

Early chroniclers often observed the gambling fervor among indige-nous peoples, sometimes with shock and moral indignation, noting especially the high stakes and dreadful consequences to the losers while missing or ignoring the sacred element entirely. The observations almost say more about the observers than about the events themselves. Words like "obsession," "addiction," and "intensity" resound in their historical texts. In 1775 Captain Bernard Romans, apparently opposed to gambling by both Natives and whites, described a hoop and pole game among the Choctaws of what is today Mississippi. He saw it as "plain proof of the evil consequences of a violent passion for gaming upon all kinds, classes, and orders of men." Captain Romans noted several cases where the loser, having bet and lost everything, went home, borrowed a gun, and committed suicide.[11] The governor of Washington Territory reported that tribes of the upper Missouri River (Montana/North Dakota) devoted all their leisure time, both day and night, to gambling in various ways.[12] Their infatuation was the cause of much distress and poverty in families. A reputation as a desperate gambler formed an obstacle in obtaining a wife (for who would want to be gambled away?). Many quarrels arose, and a man once was murdered for refusing to stake his wife after already winning everything.

Some of Culin's sources sensed the sacredness of the games they observed without delving into it. A missionary to the Iroquois, for instance, reported in 1794 that during an eight-day dice game between two rival groups, the townspeople made offerings at night, dancing and singing and tossing potions into the fire.[13] An 1872 report noted that the Kailtas of California, if unsuccessful in gambling, frequently slashed themselves from the ankles to the knees in crisscrossed strokes with bits of flint and glass to appease whichever bad spirit was preventing their good luck.[14] Sometimes observations were filtered through religious biases. At a California mission, church fathers forced the Indians to abandon their games known to be "heathen worship."[15] These observers entirely missed the underlying religious and ritual significance of the games.

A few scholars, Frank Cushing among them, were able to discover the actual ceremonies associated with the games. Lewis Henry Morgan noted in 1851 that the Iroquois played an ancient betting game called *gus-kä'-eh* with a bowl and peachstones as dice on the last day of the Green Corn festival and the Harvest festival and during the New Year's jubilee. Players reportedly believed they would be enjoying the game in a future life with the Great Spirit.[16]

The Hurons played a dice game to heal the sick. This ritual became quite elaborate, as Father Lalemant reported in 1639 (and not without an element of ridicule). On behalf of a sick person, the medicine man—usually upon the dictates of a dream—organized a preliminary match among the seasoned players to determine which two men had the best luck. Afterward, they slept in the lodge together, having previously fasted and abstained from sex with their wives. The next morning they collected the lucky charms revealed in their nocturnal visions. If they dreamt that a certain old man's strength and virtue would be efficacious to the game, they carried him to the gaming place on their shoulders. They even went to the priests for prayers, if deemed necessary. At last the selected players squared off beneath a canopy in the cabin while assistants stood by with the charms. The crowd made wagers, chanted for good luck, and gestured wildly to drive away the evil demons that might have caused the sickness. Having gambled everything away, the losers often left naked, but they were heartily thanked by the sick people who believed their health recovered. Father Lalemant added that the patients often died shortly thereafter.[17]

Luck Casting

No historical period or culture on the globe lacks dice games, and they rarely stray from hallowed ground: Antelope ankle bones, presumed to have been used as dice, are often found in prehistoric tombs and burial caves, perhaps for after-life recreation. A Sumerian board game was found in a royal cemetery dated to circa 2600 B.C.E. A mural in an Egyptian tomb depicts two figures playing odds and evens on their fingers. In ancient Chinese temples, the patterns made by a handful of tossed reeds corresponded to the intricate diagrams of yin and yang in the I Ching, The Book of Changes. From Greek historians we know that Zeus and Aphrodite, among others, were consulted with the toss of dice, and the Iliad describes how the Olympian gods were beseeched in lotteries held by soldiers to select a champion. Later Greek vases display Homer's heros, Achilles and Ajax, playing a sort of backgammon.

The Jews in ancient Israel gambled at an ancient form of craps, and the Bible tells how the Urim and Thummim, possibly the names of a pair of stone dice, helped determine Divine will. These are the universal concepts of "sorcery" gaming Mooney had spoken of.

Far back in prehistory, idle humans began carving and painting bits of bone, shell, stick, arrow, or halved reed, inventing a little game around the number of two-sided dice falling solid-side, black-side, or convex-side up. The binary quality of these pieces began to be associated with "yes" or "no," and decisionmaking could be aided by a rattle of the bones. Before long, players attempted to appropriate the future by risking something of value against it. The two activities passed into one another and in many cultures were practiced as one and the same. The magician drew lots to learn of the future and the gambler to decide the future; the difference between them was that of "will" and "shall."[18] Gambling and praying were two sides of the same coin. Even today, a gambling addiction is often treated as a disease of the spirit.

Johan Huizinga, a historian of play in human culture, assigned dice and other gambling games to the domain of "sacred play," which aided groups in maintaining cosmic order.[19] We see this illustrated by most of the tribes in the Western Hemisphere, from Alaska to Peru, from California to Florida—many of which are listed in Culin's study—and in the ritual and mythological documentation by a number of other ethnologists. For example, dice and other gaming equipment were often sacrificed on Hopi and Zuñi altars associated with specific ceremonies to dramatize war or the chase, to gain success over the enemy, or to promote the reproduction of animals and the fertilization of corn.[20] It is likely that the rites were performed to discover the probable outcome of human effort, representing a desire to secure the guidance of the natural powers that dominated humanity. But Culin had no direct evidence that the dice were thrown for purposes of divination. In historical times, the Zuñi game was simply played in hopes of receiving rain.[21]

Playing boards or fields are themselves altars of the sacred. Huizinga said that the magician, priest, and gambler all begin their work by circumscribing the consecrated spot.[22] There is no distinction between marking out a space for a sacred purpose and marking it out for purposes of sheer play. The turf, the tennis court, the chessboard, and the

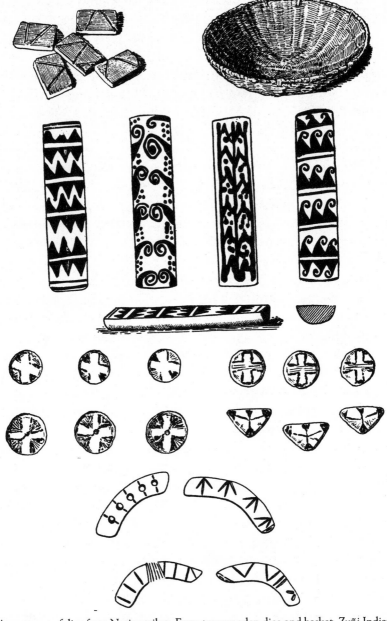

Assortment of dice from Native tribes. From top: wooden dice and basket, Zuñi Indians; stick dice, Yuma Indians; bone dice, Shoshoni Indians; beaver-teeth dice, Thompson Indians. (Culin, 1907)

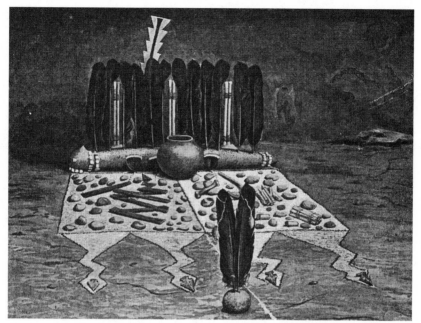

Gaming reeds displayed on a Tewa Kiva altar at Hano, a Hopi village in Arizona.
(Culin, 1907)

pavement hopscotch cannot formally be distinguished from the temple
or the magic circle. Game diagrams were built into roofing slabs of a
temple in Thebes in ancient Egypt, carved into the cloister seats of
medieval English churches,[23] and pecked into survey markers for the
grid underlying the pyramid city of Teotihuacán.[24]

Native Americans also made no distinction. Their playing fields were
mandalas—literal maps of the universe. The circuits on which the
Navajo and Pueblos played stick-dice, for instance, were often circles
of pebbles in the dirt with a striking stone in the center. The stone symbolized the island through which the ancestors emerged from the
underworld. The ring of pebbles, usually arranged in four groups of ten,
represented the sacred mountains in the four directions, and inside the
ring lay the great body of water that flowed away through the breaks in
the circle. Contenders struck the center stone with four sticks, black
on one side for thunder and red on the other for lightning. The very

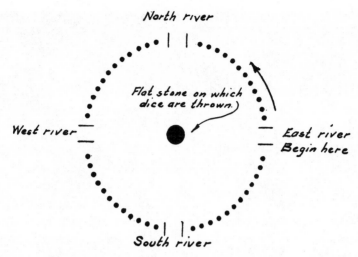

Sketch of a San Felipe Pueblo dice game called "The Horse Race" shows the center stone symbolizing the Place of Emergence surrounded by the waters of the four directions. According to many Southwestern myths, First People emerged from the underworlds through a hole in the ground on an island. (White, 1932)

act put the players simultaneously in touch with their origin and their ultimate destiny. Just as the object of the Hindu dice game of *pachisi* is to enter the gates of heaven, the object of the Navajo stick-dice game is to return to the underworld through the place of emergence.

Hoop and pole, another game played widely among North American tribes, replaces dice with human players on a three-dimensional field, but the need for control over cause and effect continues. The game, in which opposing teams battle to spear a stone or rawhide-covered ring, was a practical athletic contest as well as an occasion for gambling; it tested a player's fleetness, eyesight, and skill in throwing the stick, and it also served to strengthen the sense of community. A triumph meant salvation for the victor as well as for the group the player represented. To some tribes the hoop or wheel symbolized the eternal circle of day and night.

Duality is inherent in the games, reflecting Nature itself. The processes are composed of opposites seemingly working against each other: day/night, summer/winter, male/female, birth/death. Games were played to bring harmony to these forces continuously fighting for ascendancy. The play, with its constant running, volleying, and bouncing between two goal posts, simulates the perpetual thrust and parry action of the polarities characterized by the Chinese yin as the female principle and yang as the male.

Traditional games epitomized archaic social life shouldered on the antagonistic and antithetical structure of polarities. Tribes tended to divide themselves into opposing halves, called phratry or moiety by the anthropologist, distinguished by directional schemes, totems, seasons, celestial lights, colors, numerology, and even general personality traits.[25] The mutual relationship of the two tribal halves was marked by contest and rivalry, but also by reciprocity and mutual responsibility. The simple dualism encompassing a single clan or tribe developed into an extended system that included several clans or tribes, and the spirit of competition expressing cosmic duality continued. Seasonal contests were devised to promote fertility, the ripening of crops, a good hunt. Every game duly won secured a blessing for the community and assured cosmic integrity.

"The dualism that sunders the two halves extends over their whole conceptual and imaginative world," wrote Huizinga. "Every creature, every thing has its place on one side or the other, so that the entire cosmos is framed in this classification." Light and darkness, for example, is probably the most fundamental aspect of duality in observable Nature, and the sun figures into most games played by agrarian and pastoral societies in the New World.

An essential idea of the "cosmovision" of pre-Hispanic peoples in Mesoamerica, for instance, was that the night sky was the setting for an unending war between light and darkness.[26] Players, impersonating the rain and warrior deities, volleyed the ball, symbolizing the sun or the planet Venus, in ballcourts precisely aligned with symbolic horizons demarcating night and day. The word "recreation" no longer translates into leisure play when a ballgame is played to re-create the daily struggle between opposing natural events such as drought and fertility, and when it ends in human sacrifice.

Pueblo cultures marked the solstices with such "extreme activity" as ritualized role reversal, relay races to give the sun its strength to reverse its journey, and shinny games to renew and regenerate nature. The

The lords of the day and the night in the ball court with their followers. (Codex Colombino)

equinoxes are times when the Pueblo ideals of moderation, order, and the combining of opposites are given full symbolic rein.[27] This is when new songs for ritual are composed, and when song contests, games, or races end with opposing groups joining forces.

Winning in games of any type was naturally of great importance, and that hasn't changed to this day. I witnessed this firsthand when my son's middle-school basketball team played the team from Santo Domingo Pueblo—and lost. It was standing-room only, mostly Pueblo spectators who came to see their five champions mop the floor with our twenty or so players. The zeal with which they supported their boys rivaled Major League fans and Little League parents, and I've been both. The cheering and jeering had an intimidating effect on the visiting team, and rocks were chucked at their bus as it slowly pulled out of the parking lot in defeat. Huizinga said, "Serious play, fateful and fatal play, bloody play, sacred play . . . raises the individual or the collective personality to a higher power." Gaming ritual as sacred play is "indispensable for the well-being of the community, fecund of cosmic insight and social development but always play in the sense Plato gave to it—an action accomplishing itself outside and above the necessities and seriousness of everyday life."[28]

Lest one thinks this is overintellectualizing a middle-school basketball game, Maria Allison, in her study of Navajo basketball, recognized that the game was converted into a religious form. She reported that Navajos called basketball the "oval game" after the shape the court took once the spectators crowded in. Medicine men performed "sings" to ward off a losing streak possibly caused by witchcraft. Basketball has replaced last century's baseball, called "run-around-ball" by the Navajos. They learned the game from the whites when they were forced to live on the reservation at Fort Sumner after 1863, and it remained popular to the end of the 1890s. The bases were placed at the four cardinal directions and were run sun-wise (clockwise). The run became a chase, and the runner could jump, circle, dodge, or knock the ball from the enemy's hand to reach the base.[29] Interestingly, the Navajos considered baseball a game of the mythological Great Gambler.

Gambling Mythology

Native American traditions abound with myths and legends that reveal the sacred significance of gambling and the divine origin, power, and symbolism of the games. The Navajo, for example, called these accounts *bási hané*, "legends of games," and gave not only the origin of the games but also the rules for play.[30] The gambler figure is an important element of the gambling myths of all the tribes who have them. He—and occasionally, she—is a thoroughly frightening supernatural authority who upsets the balance of nature. These figures are challenged and defeated by "good" gamblers.

The core plot of most gambler myths plays on the often real consequences of ordinary people who gamble too much, and then takes the plot to the extreme. Typically, the people live near an ominous gambler whose gaming challenges are irresistible to the people. They systematically lose their possessions, a piece at a time, until they are naked and destitute. They lose their families, village/tribal members, and finally themselves. In the worst case, losers go into slavery or forfeit

their body parts during one play after another, working up to decapitation, and then they may be burned or eaten. The losers' heads, eyes,
hands, and ears are strung up as trophies or made into a soup and fed
to the hero(s) in order to thwart the rescue mission.

Through gambling contests of all kinds, the divinely sanctioned hero
usually overcomes the dangerous opponent with superior skill, cunning,
or magic. Equipped with covert schemes and special gaming implements (which often serve the dual purpose of hunting and warring) the
divine representative, be it human, animal, or natural medium, helps
the hero beat the bad gambler. The bad gambler tries to renege on his
wager, but the hero calls him on it, and the same misery the gambler
dispensed to others is visited upon himself. The people are then
restored to life and freedom.

The protagonist is often the culture hero, who is born to a nonhuman,
matures quickly, and is prone to wander. Like the trickster, the culture
hero has a fierce appetite for sex, food, and gambling. He or she is
frequently responsible for conditions in nature and culture and can
transform living things into animals and change the shape of the land-
scape.[31] When a culture hero beats a bad gambler, usually some natural
or cultural phenomenon is occasioned or explained: The rains come,
the crops grow, the buffalo return, the world is recreated, a new game
is introduced.

A frequent theme among gambling myths involves testing the identity and parentage of the protagonist. Most often, this involves hero
twins or sets of siblings, usually brothers. Twins aid in uniting the dual
forces in many gambling myths. These scenarios are also played out in
many myths through animal characters who have both human traits
and superordinary powers and are often thought of as protohumans.
Coyote, Raven, Crow, Caterpillar, and Gull, among many others, are
all known to wreak havoc through gambling.

In addition to the gambler myths, gambling also occurs in many
myths as a footnote rather than as the central activity. Gambling isn't
explicitly involved in all stories about games, either. Mythic characters sometimes enter contests or play games without wagering against
the outcome, but their stories are included in this book because the
gambling is implied or can be presumed. Most of the games portrayed

in the myths—such as the various forms of dice, hoop and pole, stick or hand game, and the moccasin game—are those described by Culin's study, and no one game is unique to myths told by any particular cultural or regional group. The myths are possibly told to establish the sacred context of the games and gaming equipment, to deliver playing instructions, or to teach a moral message.

* * *

Across the wide range of scholarship devoted to anthropology, mythology, and religion in all world cultures, there is a great deal of latitude and ambiguity in the use of the terms *myth* and *legend*. Legends, according to classical historian G. S. Kirk, are "of a historical or historicizing nature—tales, that is, that are founded, or implicitly claim to be founded, on historical persons or events. . . . [They] are always in some sense rooted in actuality."[32] They are stories passed down through the generations about a person, event, or place popularly believed to be historically true. Legends are not obliged to have anything to do with the sacred, although they may.

The gambler traditions of the Navajos are exclusively considered legends. Indigenous peoples tend not to include history in their oral traditions, yet the Navajo gambler legends are linked to specific thousand-year-old archaeological sites and allude to the Spanish Conquest of five hundred years ago. When matched to the historical record, the Navajo gambler legend is uncanny. Yet, when we compare the Navajo gambler legend to the constellation of myths among disparate Indian nations across the continent, we see that the gambler is not necessarily an historical figure, but an archetype, one who has so far been overlooked.

Myth, as opposed to legend "narrates a sacred history; it relates an event that took place in primordial Time, the fabled time of the 'beginnings.' . . . [It] tells how, through the deeds of Supernatural Beings, a reality came into existence, be it the whole of reality, the Cosmos, or only a fragment of reality—an island, a species of plant, a particular kind of human behavior, an institution." Historian of religions Mircea Eliade, the author of this definition, cautions us that since "myth is an extremely complex cultural reality" his definition is personal and "seems least inadequate because most embracing."[33] Thus defines the myths in this book, and a closer look at the Southwestern narrations will show them to be included in this category.

Kirk argued that myth doesn't necessarily have to be about gods, be associated with ritual, or even be religious.[34] Anthropologist Clyde Kluckhohn said myths can be intimately affiliated with ritual even when they appear to be independent.[35] We need not become involved in this controversy because the myths can often demonstrably be tied to gaming ritual, which is encompassed in ceremonies dedicated to other purposes. Historian of Native American religions Åke Hultkrantz stated unequivocally that myths are primarily religious and deal with gods.[36] In most myths, the adversarial gambler possesses invincible and often supernatural power. Sometimes the hero beats the antagonist gambler with supernatural aid. In many myths, traditional deities like Thunder or Sun pose as gamblers, benevolent or tyrannical. To my knowledge, however, the Navajo Great Gambler is the only gambler to be considered a god.

Eliade would say that all myths are sacred. The native or archaic world knows nothing of profane activities. Every act has a definite meaning—hunting, fishing, farming, games, conflicts, and sexuality in some way participate in the sacred, and these acts are synthesized with religious symbols into narrative form.[37] Myths form the symbolic base of a culture; they explain the creation of the universe and natural phenomena, the origin of humanity, the evolution of society, and the cycle of agricultural fertility—that is, birth, death, and resurrection of vegetation. Gambler myths fit into this scheme. They speak to the chaos of weather, the randomness of life, and the divinity of chance.

One shouldn't be surprised at the extent to which gambling myths reflect the events surrounding real-life gambling as recorded in historical documents. Obsession, addiction, jealousy, revenge, exploitation, victimization, and sudden poverty are a few of the dissonant chords. Other more disturbing negative tones include mass murder, mutilation, and cannibalism—all historically unfortunate realities in various North American societies.

Most of the myths explored in this book reflect the religious beliefs and environment of the host culture, and this is why they are presented according to region. Whatever their unique characteristics, they share an attempt to understand and control cause and effect in nature and society. Sometimes evidence of intertribal conflict is detected in the myths, particularly among the Northwest *potlatching* groups and the Northeastern tribes. The gambling rituals of the Plains Indians, particularly the Pawnees, changed in response to their near extinction, and although their gambling myths did not change, they supported the new rituals. Only the Southwestern myths respond to conflict between nations; even then, history is used as an object lesson for maintaining personal harmony. We will investigate the effect of historical conflict within the myths as they progress.

Classical Gambler Versus Native Gambler

"The oral tradition is more than a record of a people's culture," said Paula Gunn Allen, a Sioux/Lauguna writer, "It is the creative source of their collective and individual selves." The problem in interpreting Native American myth is in racial bias, she wrote. Anglo versions of Indian myths are often distorted because they are given a formal plot structure that makes them seem like narratives, but "whites do not think like Indians." Some translations reveal "more about American consciousness when it meets tribal thought than it reveals about the tribe."[38] If translated from the original format, as in a storytelling session, the ritual nature would be much clearer. Allen was referring to the work of her Caucasian uncle, John Gunn (whose gambling myths are cited in this book), but her opinions can be extended to all gambler myths recorded by whites, the prominent sources cited in this book.

Alas, for the purposes of establishing the gambling myths in a cultural context, it became necessary to further abstract the myths into vignettes with a somewhat linear storyline and to condense or omit the long and repetitive play-by-play narratives. The original narrations are often lengthy and would have been otherwise difficult to follow without a cultural blueprint. I have retained most characters, numerology, ritual, and other symbolism and unique cultural traits whenever they were recognizable. Furthermore, I am non-Indian, although my life has been thoroughly steeped in the native cultures of New Mexico since infancy.

But we can heed Allen's advice somewhat by not contaminating the Native American gambling myths with Western mores. Old World civilizations have always had a conflict with gambling, and most religious texts, while recognizing the sacredness of chance, denounce gambling as inherently evil. Chaucer, in the opening of "The Pardoner's Tale" (in *The Canterbury Tales*, 1380), captures the viewpoint held by most classic authors. He wrote of young champions in Flanders who were given to riot and gambling, brothels and taverns. They played at dice both day and night:

> Thurgh which they doon the devel sacrifyse,
> Within that develes temple, in cursed wyse,
> By superfluitee abhominable.

Western literature does have a gambler archetype (whom I will call the classical gambler), and he is present in Plutarch's *Cato the Younger*; Dickens's Sydney Carton in *Tale of Two Cities*; Tolstoy's Captain Iashvin in *Anna Karenina*, and Dolokhov in *War and Peace*; and Aleksy Ivanovich in Dostoevsky's *The Gambler*. The classical gambler is invariably connected with such words as "notorious," "inveterate," "jackal," and "rake," yet he isn't unambiguously evil. He usually drinks like a fish, but his clearheadedness and gaming prowess commands respect from his peers. He is a man without principle, yet he possesses strength of character. What would be regarded by some as manipulation is finesse to others. Many gamblers, like Lew Wallace's Messala in *Ben-Hur: A Tale of the Christ*, exhibit an incomparable intelligence.

Classical gamblers also have their own ethics. In Crane's *Blue Hotel*, the gambler preys on reckless and senile farmers and so is "judicious in his choice of victims." He is a thoroughbred, a "thieving card-player . . . so generous, so just, so moral, that, in a contest, he could have put to flight the conscience of nine-tenths of the citizens of Romper." In London's *Call of the Wild*, Manuel has one besetting sin, Chinese lottery; and one besetting weakness, faith in the system, and "this made his damnation certain." The character flaw as a risk-taker turns to virtue in London's Wolf Larsen in *Sea Wolf*, who says, "Man is a natural gambler, and life is the biggest stake he can lay." The sentiment is the hallmark of the stereotypical American frontiersman.

The Native American mythical gambler is equally complex and dubious. Sometimes it is difficult to determine a good gambler from an evil one, and the confusion varies from story to story. Bad gamblers may be gluttonous, tyrannical, shrewd, and violent, and they are frequently cannibals, witches, abductors of women, breast grabbers, or shape-shifters. In the Southwest, the gambler transforms into the benevolent prophet. For that matter, the ambivalent gambler is often none other than the culture hero.

Allen explained that there are no good guys and bad guys per se in Native myths. The social function of traditional tribal myth is to distribute value evenly among all the elements "providing a model or pattern for egalitarian structuring of society." This is not easily understood by "hierarchically inclined westerners." Traditional American Indian stories "work dynamically among clusters of loosely interconnected circles," shifting the focus from one character to the next "until all the pertinent elements in the ritual conversation have had their say."[39] In this way, there are no heroes, no villains, no chorus, no minor characters. In the gaming myths, all characters have equal weight. Although heads and necks are wagered and lost by lesser opponents, the gambler himself is not always killed but sometimes whittled to a more manageable proportion.

In classical gambling literature, characters who gamble have a mixed heroic value. Their purpose is to turn life on its head. Dostoevsky's literary technique in *The Gambler* harkens back to a medieval carnival which temporarily reverses hierarchical roles.[40] Kings become paupers and paupers kings. The roulette table is a symbol for a reversal of fortune—one turn of the wheel and a rich man becomes poor, and vice versa.

The turn of the hoop in Native gambler myths is the turn of the sun and the seasons. Indeed, the myths offer an archetypal template for struggle, conflict, and revenge. Gambling is the great equalizer; in stories where body parts are wagered, an eye for an eye literally applies. The reversal of fortune, however, is deeply primordial; it means resurrection of the dead, revival of the old ways, transformation of the obsessed.

Native gambling myths all contain an element of violence and border on the macabre. They explore the predator-prey cycles, territorial rights, body functions and fluids, slavery, sacrifice, and violent death—

the usual human fixations. Some versions are equipped with a kind of voodoo ritual. Others are associated with witchcraft and ceremonies that ward off the enemy. Still, many others are invoked to heal the sick, call forth animals, or beseech the gods for rain during drought. In short, Native gaming myths give a sense of the dark as well as the light side of the cosmic drama. Their raw aggression almost seems contradictory to Allen's declaration of an egalitarian scheme, but a closer look at the myths proves that she is right. Although the stories are about conflict, they are not adversarial plots that set protagonists against antagonists in the Greek sense (*agon* is the Greek root for contest), but restore the détente of nature. While Westerners might see the battle between night and day as a battle for dominance, Native Americans see the battle itself as a striving for homeostasis.

Ways and Means

Since gambling myths are sacred, there is the danger that significant portions or symbols were purposely obscured or omitted when they were relayed to white recorders. This was certainly true for the Navajos. The Navajos are the largest tribe in the United States, yet they voted against opening gaming facilities in 1994, turning down a potential source of massive income.[41] One reason is the tribe's taboo against gambling,[42] which may have less to do with moral strictures and more to do with religious restrictions that may extend to storytelling protocol.

David Aberle, as a field school student, found that the Navajos he interviewed didn't like talking about their games, rules, gaming rituals, or myths.[43] "A white person would tend to differentiate between the rules, the more elaborate good luck methods, and the myths, and would think that information on such different subjects would be differently regarded," Aberle said. But as one informant told him, "They hate *all* these questions about this old game, both about the rules and the stories. They *hate* them!"

Aberle's storytellers frequently changed the origins of a particular game or the symbolic meaning of the equipment and games with each telling. Some informants denied knowing the story or that there was a story at all, "a typical Navajo evasion." Those who talked sometimes claimed convenient memory loss of certain passages or omitted what they didn't want to tell. "This story and the names are what I've been hiding all the time you've been asking me for the story," one Navajo woman said. "My grandfathers and father told me how this game started, but I still keep that." One source for the Navajo Great Gambler cited in this book admitted to capsulizing the legend because he was not being paid for the three nights it would take to tell it.[44]

The Navajo taboo against telling gambling stories is complex. To talk about stick-dice, seven card, hoop and pole, and racing—all summer games—in the summer, was not as dangerous as talking about the winter moccasin game in the summer. Such a transgression invited "lightning disease" or snakebite for the tellers, their families, and their stock. Some story sections were more dangerous than others, particularly if the material was formally taught to the teller. The more the teller knew, the greater the danger. One Navajo man who traveled around all summer telling forbidden stories would offer a couple of pieces of turquoise and sing a couple of songs when he got home to propitiate the Holy People. Others thought they should be paid for the risk, since they themselves had paid dearly to learn the myth. They feared that the whites would carry away the stories and that telling the story would diminish the protection one received from it; some kind of remuneration eased the risk.

The Navajo penchant for omission and their resistance to retell stories assumedly apply to all gambling myths. Moreover, we cannot know for certain that we are accurately interpreting the myths with the information at hand. We can guess by comparing elements to the endless ethnologic studies painstakingly compiled by scholars of different tribes. There is no way to be sure of the internal meaning.

Although the gambler motif is ubiquitous in most Native American mythological storehouses, this book conveys more detail on the gambling myths and legends of the Southwest than from any other region. Not only do the myths from this region more profoundly relate to history than those from anywhere else, but they also are more complex and more heavily influenced by the mythologies of Mexico. These myths exist in multiple versions and benefit from the sheer volume of ethnological study. The Southwestern and Mexican mythologies consequently serve as a template for myths from other tribes. This in no way implies that the gambler originated in this region. On the contrary, certain elements are so universal they would be difficult to trace.

My expertise, admittedly, lies in the Southwest, specifically in the archaeological site of Chaco Canyon, the location of ancient sandstone cities where I first encountered the Navajo Great Gambler mythology. Bone dice have been found in a related 1,500-year-old ruin near my home along the Rio Grande, 150 miles away from Chaco. Just up the road is a gambling casino owned and operated by Santa Ana Pueblo, who are among the descendants of Chaco Canyon. Many other casinos line the major highways of New Mexico, and all have fought long court battles over the legality of their facilities. If the Navajo gambler legend is to be believed, Indian gaming politics have persisted in New Mexico for more than a thousand years. The continuity of Indian gaming through time is intriguing.

I started out to solve the mystery of the Chaco Canyon gambler and discovered a global phenomena. My Southwestern studies led me farther and farther afield into the world of Native American gambling as a whole and its place as a sacred activity at the root of nearly all cultures. No general study of gambling and its religious significance in Native America exists nor has anyone introduced the Great Gambler as a possible archetypal figure. The attempt to cut a path through a pristine field resulted in a rather unusual combination of survey and detective story.

Chaco archaeologist Thomas Windes, author Paul Zolbrod, and mythology expert Janet Cliff provided comprehensive references to the Navajo gambler myth/legend.[45] For Pueblo references, I turned to Franz Boas, Leslie White, Matilda Coxe Stevenson, John Gunn, and Elsie Clews Parsons with good results. Outside of the Southwest, the task became more difficult. Sometimes Culin mentioned a profitable source in his games catalog, such as the works of Mooney or Dorsey. Most of the time, though, I was reduced to pulling books from library shelves and scanning the pages—I depended on chance, in other words. Gambling references in indexes and tables of contents vary in quantity and quality. Particularly vexing was Stith Thompson's *Tales of the North American Indians*. Buried under "miscellaneous" is a brief Chicoltin gambling myth, which cross-referenced some forty other citations in coded italicized fine print in the back of the book. A good and easy source was Sam Gill and Irene Sullivan's *Dictionary of Native American Mythology*. To date I have accumulated more than a hundred gambling myths.

Many traditional Native games have been lost to the past. The Pueblo calendars of public activities still include rooster pulls, grab days, and races, but there is no way of truly knowing whether dice or stick-and-hoop games are still played and with what frequency and meaning. Some traditional games are now played only by children, their religious value lost.

I informally surveyed a few Native Americans in the course of researching the book, although I was reluctant to do so. To ask about such religious material is considered poor manners, especially in the Southwest, but I eschewed etiquette to test the validity of gambling mythology in modern Indian thought. The response was not surprising. A man from Sandia Pueblo said that the games were no longer played there, but he also said he wasn't the best person to ask. A Santo Domingo woman

Taharumara demonstration of the game generally known as shinny. (Photo by Kris Gudmunson, courtesy Aspen Evans)

denied a known mythical gambler existed at her pueblo. Maybe at Jemez Pueblo, she said. A park ranger in Arizona, who was a descendant of Pima and Tohono O'odham,[46] told me he remembered the old men playing stick-dice when he was a child and had heard stories about a cruel, bitter man who ruled over one of the ancient Hohokam sites. Neither the Sioux law student nor the Mohawk public relations manager for Indian gaming I spoke to recalled any gaming myths on the "rez." A white woman who had traveled widely had come across traditional games being demonstrated by a tribe in North Dakota and the Tarahumara in Mexico. A Hopi woman selling little stick and ball ornaments at an Indian market told me the game was played only by children, but a Hopi research assistant told me the game was still played in association with winter solstice ceremonies. He added that the major ceremonial activity his people retained was running. His young Hopi companion jokingly added basketball and was quickly dismissed with a wave of the hand, but I, of course, already knew basketball was sacred.

This work cannot possibly be a systematic or complete study—the subject is too vast, the myths buried too deeply, and the feeders rooted too intricately into the cultures. Furthermore, interpretation has for the most part been left up to the anthropologists whose methodology was simply to record and publish. Kirk said nearly all modern anthropological work on myths suffers from its smallness of scale, which prevents adequate classification and definition. The scale could be the result of anthropologists' propensity to write short papers as opposed to books. But Culin's games study was no small project—it was rather like an encyclopedia. Although Culin did compare gaming rituals between tribes in his introductions to the different games, he did not compare gaming myths, perhaps because those reports were not yet all in.

The other problem with anthropologists, according to Kirk, is their understanding of mythology. Kirk found it paradoxical that they would continue to compare Native myths to Greek myths even after recording many different sets of myths from other cultures and showing how they fulfill functions not exemplified by Greek materials.[47] Be that as it may, we owe the preservation of what myths we have to anthropologists. The gambler has been lost to many tribes, probably for want of an anthropologist to record his story. This book could not have been written without the work of all the field anthropologists listed in my bibliography.

To my knowledge, none of the Native American gamblers have been compared to Greek models or to any other figures in any Old World mythology, and, to my knowledge, few analogues exist. This is not to say that gambling did not thrive in Old World history or that gaming contests or gambling were not mentioned in the literature. We'll look at gambling in Greek historical texts, in Homer's *Iliad*, and in the Bible and compare and contrast what we find there to Native American gambling. The one remarkable parallel to the North American gambler myth is in India, where it is said that the world itself was conceived as a game of dice between the deities *Shiva* and *Shakti*. An important part of one text, the *Mahābhārata*, written beginning in 400 B.C.E., is a Brahmic-style gambler myth and includes many features that are strikingly similar to the Navajo legend.

I do not wish to glamorize, condone, or condemn gambling at Indian casinos or anywhere else. Instead, it is my intention to probe its sacred aspect, while raising the possibility that it is at the origin of nearly all ancient religions. Non-Indian readers may be uncomfortable with the ambiguities of the gambler myths, the inability to fit their contents into black-and-white slots. Native storytellers know the gray areas represent paradox, the meat closest to the bone. The paradoxes draw one to the murky waters of the underworld where the images first emerged. And that is their purpose.

ONE

Reversal of Fortune:
Gambler Myths of
the Northwest and West

Take care of yourself—shoot well, or you lose.
You warned me, but see! I have defeated you!
I am one of the Great Spirit's children,
Wa-konda I am! I am Wa-konda!
    —Iowa Song of Ing-kee-ko-kee (Moccasin Game)[1]

The chess board is the world, the pieces are the phenomena of the universe,
the rules of the game are what we call the laws of Nature. The player on the
other side is hidden from us. We know that his play is always fair, just, and
patient. But also we know, to our cost, that he never overlooks a mistake, or
makes the smallest allowance for ignorance.
    —Thomas Henry Huxley, *A Liberal Education* [1868]

The North American continent is large and complex, geographically, historically, and ethnographically. In a general study like this, one takes on a subject that includes—in the words of Carl Waldman, author of the *Atlas of the North American Indian*—"hundreds of different tribes, both extant and extinct, each with a unique history, demography, and culture," and that involves the disciplines of "history, archaeology, anthropology, sociology, geography, politics, religion, linguistics, and more." Furthermore, he wrote, "Native American studies can be difficult emotionally in that Indians as a race have been victimized by what has been traditionally represented in public education as progress."[2] Every generality has an exception; there is no universal American Indian.

Commonalities in religious viewpoint do exist, however, and they are reflected in the gambler myths. Traditionally, Native American beliefs and practices stemmed from an acceptance of a universe controlled by supernatural beings and forces, with humans as subordinates. Most cultures believed that spirits occupied nearly everything in nature, including rocks, trees, unusual landforms, insects, animals, birds, weather elements, and celestial lights. Beyond those were powerful, distant, usually expansive creator beings as well as numbers of other, more-immediate godlike beings. Activities and rituals, both elaborate and simple, were associated with times of passage (birth, puberty, marriage, death); war and other crises; or with staying in harmony with the sun, moon, rain, animals, and other natural phenomena.

In most cultures the supernaturals of greatest importance were the good and evil spirits capable of influencing hunts, fights, love, health—and gambling. The souls of the dead (ghosts) were often believed to be the most malignant of spirits, except in societies where ancestors were worshiped. Spirits lived in dark caves, forests, canyons, or atop sun-drenched mountains, and in beasts or other people. Success in all human endeavors depended upon maintaining a constant balance between the spirit forces and human needs, a balance made difficult by the actions of evil spirits. Native Americans generally acquired spirit allies or guides who could bring them power or "medicine" through vision quests and ceremonies. If one offended the inhabitants of the spirit world embodied in animals and natural objects, this same power could cause negative effects, including bad luck in gambling.

Besides vision quests and ceremonies, most Native American cultures possessed supernatural techniques with which to face most of life's unpredictable events, such as self-privation or mutilation, drugged states, and dreams. To effect cures, religious leaders (shamans) were usually consulted. They massaged, danced, sang, smoked tobacco, or ingested drugs and otherwise induced spirit helpers to search out the cause of a misfortune, generally considered to be the result of either the loss of the soul or the intrusion of a foreign object. As discussed previously, a shaman sometimes prescribed game playing and gambling to heal the woes caused by evil spirits. The source of an illness was almost always believed to be witchcraft, despite the fact that in practically no Native cultures were there individuals who attempted to practice sorcery to harm others. These commonalities can be applied to the gambling myths in the following regions examined in this chapter: Subarctic, Pacific Northwest, California, Great Basin, and Interior-Plateau.

Subarctic Hunters and Fishers

Hide tepees and bark-covered wigwams provided mobile shelter for the inhabitants who huddled in small nomadic family groups against the harsh climates of the Subarctic region, which encompasses most of Canada. Snowshoe, toboggan, and canoe were the only modes of negotiating the deep winter snows and the endless chains of lakes and streams in the tundra and forest. People subsisted on vast migrating herds of caribou, as well as moose, bear, deer, and fish. Interband conflict was slight, although—as is common among nomadic peoples—each band was suspicious of its neighbors.

The hundreds of groups who lived in the Subarctic region can be divided into two major linguistic blocks: the Athabaskan speakers of western Canada and the interior of Alaska and the Algonquian speakers of eastern Canada. We will look at the myths of the Chilcotin and Carriers tribes, both Athabaskan speakers. Algonquian gambler myths exist, but they have been found outside the Subarctic region and so are discussed in the Eastern Woodlands section of the book.

Religion in the north was essentially informal, with few commonly held beliefs except those concerned with guardian spirits or witchcraft. Many people, particularly among the Algonquian speakers, believed that the forests harbored *windigos*, thirty-foot monsters who could turn humans into cannibals. The Chilcotin believed that *desini*, unseen strangers, stole their women, and the loss of women (apparently a high commodity) through gambling is a typical theme in their myths.

The following gambling myths are somewhat pragmatic, however, and do not deal with ghosts. But one can almost sense the isolation the tribesmen in this region must experience. The gamblers are ordinary men who are too obsessive in their behavior. They seek salvation near a lake or a hilltop—both common sacred places among Native Americans—and the counsel of the supernatural, thereby becoming somewhat powerful themselves. If they abuse the gambling power as seen in the second myth, it turns against them. We will see this theme repeated throughout the regions. Mention of the seasons is important, because it hints at natural cycles and the times when certain games are played.

In the Chilcotin (British Columbia) story, a bankrupt gambler discovers he can see through rock.[3] After stockpiling furs and hides all summer, he challenges the winning gambler to another round at salmon time, staking his cache against the return of his wife. His X-ray vision enables him to see where the gambler has hidden the bone every time. He wins the gambler's wife, then wins back his own wife, one half at a time, thus achieving spiritual wholeness.

The following Carrier (British Columbia) myth isn't a conflict between man and gambler but the gambler against himself[4]: The villagers abandon a penniless gambler to freeze to death. He treks, without snowshoes, to a hilltop called *Yihta* (the constellation Ursa Major), the home of an old man named *Ne-yer-hwolluz*, "he who carries his house on a sleigh." The man invites the naked youth to sit by one of two fires, clothes him with fine fur robes and moccasins, feeds him the grease of two whole bears, and gives him his daughter as a wife. After a few months the old man, sensing the younger's craving, sends him to gamble with his people. He gives him four highly polished bonesticks and four counter rods and specifically tells the young man that when he is finished gambling, he must throw the rods over the roof and return home immediately. The youth is victorious and throws the rods over the roof, but he stays to play the bonestick game some more and is soon stripped to his original impoverished state. Upon further rejection from the village and his former wife, he fails to find his new house and new wife.

Northwest Coast Fishing Cultures

In the bountiful Pacific Northwest—one of the richest sources of Native myths in North America—the denser population is more tightly organized into communities as is reflected in the myths. Salmon-spawning streams endowed the Northwest coast—the narrow strip along the Pacific from southern Alaska to southern Oregon—with an abundant annual harvest, and the sea provided a wealth of fish, shellfish, sea lions, and whales. Caribou, deer, and other wildlife combined with numerous roots and berries to provide a rich and varied diet. The abundant environment likewise gives rise to a collection of gambling myths.

Villages in this region traditionally consisted of autonomous kinship groups of one hundred or more individuals. Each village ranked its members according to their closeness to the headperson or chief. Only war captives and debt victims, who formed an outcast or slave category, were excluded from this strictly hierarchical ranking system. Great emphasis was placed on individual and group wealth, measured by the stockpiles of cedar-bark blankets, shells, dried fish and fish oil, dugout canoes, native copper shields (named, and allotted a set value), resources, and slaves.

Characteristic of the status-conscious Northwest Coastal tribes is the *potlatch*. The term comes from traders' Chinook jargon, although each Northwest Coast language had its own term. Originally it was thought that potlatching was a means of gaining prestige and that it was up to guests at a potlatch feast to reciprocate on a grander scale or face economic ruin. Now it is believed that the potlatch was an institutionalized method of reassigning the social rights and property—honorific names, crests, ceremonial paraphernalia, songs, and dances—of the deceased.[5] The inheritance had to be claimed during a lavish feast where guests were presented gifts. At a subsequent feast, guests validated claims by reciprocating gifts and ritualistically seating the heir at a table according to the new place on the totem pole. Lesser potlatches were given to rid the stigma of a slight to a chief or heir. Potlatches surface in some gambling myths of this region, and in this context they connote superiority.

The myths are otherwise heavily laced with elements of the people's religious practices. Based mainly on faith in mythical ancestors, the religion often took on a dramatic flair in public dramas involving spirit quests and encounters. Highly stylized representations of these ancestors were everywhere, not only on totem poles but also on house facades, boat prows, masks, bones, and blankets. The Kwakiutl, with their Heiltsuk kin, originated the most spectacular ceremonials of the Northwest Coast culture area. These included a chief's dramatic reenactment of the capture of an ancestor by a monstrous spirit. Believed to be possessed by the spirit, the chief performed its violent and macabre acts, pretending to devour human flesh until cured by rites of exorcism. These ritual events preserved the formal ranked statuses valued by their society. In all these stories, sea otters or bears tend to be potent religious symbols when it comes to gambling.

The following Haida (Queen Charlotte Islands) myth expresses elements of encounter, exorcism, and status.[6] It tells not only how the seaward-Sqoā'ɫadas, a Raven family, obtained the names of their gambling sticks, but how they obtained a family crest and the right to a certain style of house pole, all of which would be considered potlatch property. No doubt this myth was considered property as well. Note the duality in the story and the typical quest for supernatural help.

Poor-Chief's-Son, who despite his name was actually wealthy, gambles away all his father's potlatch property while his father is away inviting the Tsimshian to a potlatch. The son goes into the woods and fasts, eating only leaves, then defecates on a rotten stump. He continues traveling and later passes the mossy bones of two humans near two streams flowing from a mountain, one red, the other blue. The first represents the mountain's manure, and the second its medicine. He drinks from the blue stream and loses consciousness.

When he awakens, he finds himself standing in front of a house with a two-headed pole. He enters the house of the chief who has heard of his gambling mistake. The "grandfather" sticks a hawk feather in the corner of the youth's eye and extracts blood and moss. He then squeezes blood from the youth's gambling sticks. He kisses his hands and cuts around the middle of one stick with a fingernail, naming it "counting-out-ten-times." He repeats the process with variations on nine more sticks, naming each one separately ("thing-always-carried-along," "always-running-off," "bloody nose," etc.). He then gives the youth elaborate instructions for defeating the Tsimshian in the game and sends him home.

Poor-Chief's-Son takes the same route home and finds a sea otter at the stump where he has defecated. He also finds a small copper coin in a gambling-stick bag on the left side of the red trail. Upon reaching his home he sees that the Tsimshian have arrived in ten canoes. The next day, following the grandfather's predictions of which sticks he would lose or win, he wins everything from the Tsimshian while wagering only the copper coin and sea otter. His father's potlatch now over, the canoes are returned to the Tsimshian. His father tatoos him with a beak on his breast, wings on his shoulders, and tail on his back. He is the only member of the Raven clan with the cormorant for a crest.

"Rivalry potlatches" occurred when, with no living direct heirs, remote relatives claimed the right to the vacant status. In this Chinook (Washington) story, gambling serves as a rags-to-riches potlatch.[7] Three brothers, who are greedy "gambling fools," ridicule and antagonize their impoverished, lice-ridden cousin and steal his sea otter. Stranded by their antics, the boy is forced to swim home, during which time he encounters four bears, and faints. *Itc!x'ia·n*, a supernatural being, carries the youth to his house where he gives him three different languages, four wives, and a bird-bone arrowhead that would mark him as a chief. He then goes to Mythtown where people are playing disks for arrowheads and wins ten of them. One by one, he wins all the people, chiefs, slaves, and property. He becomes a chief, and the people are now in his house. He then beats all the cousins, "all the Chealis, the Quenaiult, Tillamook, and Cowlitz." If his cousins had not stolen his sea otter, he would not have seen Itc!x'ia·n and become a chief.

In its more modern form at the end of the nineteenth century, when intertribal conflict escalated, the potlatch was used to bankrupt an enemy. Potlatch exchanges were prohibited by Canada's much-amended Indian Act of 1876 (repealed in 1951). Many of the gambling myths in this area reflect the sentiment of the nineteenth-century potlatch. In these myths, groups of one tribe rove around the countryside to economically wipe out whole villages.

In an Alsea (British Columbia) myth, for instance, four adolescent boys go on a gambling spree.[8] It may be that females are seen to have more power than their counterparts, for the mother of the boys sends her daughter along as protection. The boys stake their sister at shinny and the guessing game and win the women of the villages. At the fourth village, the boys are encased in a house turned to rock. The girl fetches their mother and is ridiculed by all the villages on her ten-day round trip. The mother declares, "I am cyclone" and splits open the house, freeing her sons. They gather all their new wives, now pregnant, on their way home. The woman touches her cane to the ground and each village collapses into the earth. At home she turns her children into winds and says she will travel to the ocean as cyclone. "Those who dream of me will possess the powers I possess." This is a case where Nature seeks her own balance.

In another Haida myth, the chief's son, Sounding-Gaming-Sticks (a guessing game), gambles with the son of Great-Moving-Cloud, who appears as hands extending from a cloud.[9] The chief's son loses and is taken underwater to see his powerful grandfather, who performs an exorcism on his bloody eyeball, decorates mats and clams for betting—five each—makes new gambling sticks with sea otters on them, and instructs him in winning the game. In the new game, the boy gives tobacco seeds to the spectators to keep them quiet while he cheats. The sea otter sticks become animated and coach him from his shoulders in the complicated scoring. The boy wins back the village from Great-Moving-Cloud's son.

A footnote to this myth says that Great-Moving-Cloud's son owns the dog salmon and lives within sight of the Land of Souls. When a gambler dies, Great-Moving-Cloud's son gambles with him, staking souls for dog salmon. If the cloud spirit wins, there will be many deaths, but if the gambler wins, there will be a great run of dog salmon.

The Tsimshian (of British Columbia) myths recovered are about gambling birds, including Raven (Giant), Gull, Heron, and Crane. Gambling is used as deception for stealing fish from another's gullet.[10] In a game between Thunderbird and Gull, Thunderbird's hoop is fire, and Gull's is fog. Gull wins four times.[11] In another version, the heavenly birds of Thunder Place play against the earthly birds of Crooked Beach. The gambling stones of the heavenly birds are fog, rainbow, cloud, and Carrier of the World.

There's a tale among other, related tribes—Comox, Nootka, Kwakiutl (British Columbia)—in which Thunderbird looses a game of rolling the hoop and steals the wife of another bird.[12] The birds send out a fake whale to take revenge. In the southern versions we learn the reason why Thunderbird abducts the wife who belongs, in this case, to Woodpecker. Woodpecker has invited players to his house, and his salmonberry bush produces salmonberries when Thrush, wife of Woodpecker, sings. Thunderbird wants her so much that after he is beaten in the game, he breaks

up the party with a storm and carries away Thrush. Thunder, personified in this case as Thunderbird, is a recurring figure in gambler myths
across the country. Storms are a typical tactic in the games.

The following Chinook myth is an introduction to the macabre
events and bouts with the supernatural so common to other regions.[13]
The trickster, Blue Jay, pits Thunderer's son-in-law against a village
chief. Now, Thunderer, in a test-theme sequence, has put the son-in-
law through the hoops, including having him steal hoops and targets
from the supernatural people. Although the myth doesn't say so, one
gets the impression that the youth is tired of the run-around and leaves,
ending up at Blue Jay's village. But the young gambler loses to the chief
in a shooting contest on the beach. Little by little, the young man loses
arrows, arms, legs, and head. His hair is hung up in the smoke of a fire
tended by two old lady mice.

A year passes and the gambler's sons (Thunderer's grandsons), having searched high and low, are brought to their mutilated father. Blue
Jay arranges a shooting match on the beach, but this time one look from
the boys sets his hair on fire. Blue Jay warns his chief of their power. The
boys replace the chief's targets with the ones their father has stolen from
the supernatural people. When the chief shoots, the targets move and
the chief loses. They win back their father and the village people and
perform a lengthy mutilation on the chief. With a bit of green mud and
paint, cinquefoil, and pieces of flint, they transform the chief into a
green sturgeon, whose song will forever be a bad omen.

Another frequenter of gambling myths is Coyote. He emerges as the
tricky culture hero gambler in an Alsea gambling myth called "The
Universal Change."[14] He organizes a sort of Olympics that involves the
entire gambit of games and ends up solidifying all the different animals
in their present form. We'll see Coyote often in the myth descriptions
of other regions.

California Foragers

The California culture area covers approximately the extent of the present state minus the southeast section along the Colorado River. More
than two hundred independent dialects existed among its aboriginal

population. The single village (tribelet) of one hundred or more people, bounded by its own dialect, was often the largest unit of political integration. The village was divided into groups to permit marriage. In the south localized patrilineages were the common residence type. Headmanship, inherited in some groups, served to organize social and ceremonial life but carried little political power. Organized conflict between villages was rare. Curing ceremonies were frequently held; drug cults and male puberty ceremonies were especially important. All Californians were primarily foragers who relied heavily on acorns, grass seeds, cattails, and other plant foods. Shellfish and fish were important along the coast, as were deer, wapiti, bears, rabbits, and other animals in the interior.

Gambling myths in California do not overtly reflect the social and religious culture. They tend to involve the mythological animal kingdom, including Coyote, Prairie Falcon, Meadow Lark, Gopher, and Rabbit, with one or two exceptions similar to those we've discussed. The following Shasta myth is one such exception.[15] A bankrupt gambler jumps into a lake and is swallowed by a rattlesnake. After five days, the snake spits out the man, who is found on the sixth day by his brother. When he gambles again, he wins back as much as he has lost. As usual, adversity enhances gambling luck.

Thunder shows up in another Shasta myth to beat Silver Fox, Black Fox, and Red Fox and his nine brothers in a gambling race.[16] The foxes hire Wolf to race Thunder. Wolf knows that Thunder usually wins races by ripping up the earth in front of his opponent, so Wolf, praying silently, runs directly behind Thunder and then stops Thunder by throwing a "pain" from his tongue at him.

Coyote is the preeminent trickster among most Native American groups. He represents "the evil aspect of the demiurge, that aspect, that is to say, that keeps things going by keeping them going wrong."[17] Yet he is also the inventor of cultural objects. He can emerge in gambling myths on either side of the fence. One of his talents is the ability to change forms.

Coyote is the underdog in a Shasta myth where he loses his tribe to the Rogue River people.[18] His aunt teaches him how to use rattles, water, poison, singing, and dancing to dodge the gambling sticks. She sends him downriver to marry two fine women to use as gambling stakes, for the Rogue River people will only gamble for people. He then enters the Rogue River camp disguised as a Klamath Indian and challenges them to a game. A little bird concealed in his hair coaches him in dodging the sticks, and after five days he wins back all his people. The Rogue River people try everything they can to kill Coyote through a series of tests, such as burning him in a sweat bath, but his gambling only grows stronger and more prosperous. Coyote and his women escape successfully as he turns himself into various forms: old woman, salmon, stem of grass, fog, rain, and hail.

In a Yana myth, Coyote invents a stick game to play with Rabbit as a rite of Spring.[19] The game is to be played at the time when leaves appear on the oaks, but if the game were played in the summer, there would be no acorns. In another Yana myth, Gopher tells Cottontail Rabbit they would always gamble when they met.[20] Through a series of games, however, Gopher loses everything, including his body, to Rabbit.

The Western Mono, Southern Sierra Miwok, and Yokuts bring Prairie Falcon into their gambling myths, which are even more gruesome. In the Western Mono myth, Prairie Falcon's wooden shinny balls keep breaking.[21] He finds that his Cormorant sister's freshly laid egg works as a ball. He takes it down to the gambling place to play shinny with Meadowlark. Prairie Falcon's people have already forfeited their lives in an earlier contest to Meadowlark and have been skinned by the winner's people. Flies buzz the area. Coyote, who calls Prairie Falcon "nephew," accompanies him to challenge Meadowlark. Along the way, they pick up Owl to blind the opponent, Gopher to make holes to trap the balls in the ground, Skunk to spray Meadowlark, and Swan to cause confusion with its trumpeting. Meadowlark, "the fat chief of the Plains tribe," takes the bet, and they drive their balls all the way to the coast and back. Prairie Falcon wins with the help of the animals, and they burn Meadowlark's people. The Cormorant sisters burn fires around the skins of Prairie Falcon's people, and they are restored to their original form. They pound acorns, which distracts Coyote from turning into an eagle and flying away.

Coyote is the hero in a succession of Southern Sierra Miwok myths, and his gambling game precipitates an apocalypse.[22] He avenges his grandson, Prairie Falcon, thought to have lost his life to *Ki'lak*, an unknown being, in a dodge-ball kind of contest. When Coyote beats and kills Ki'lak, the world bursts open and burns for a month. Falcon is restored and helps create human beings and change the animal and bird people into the forms they are today.

Among the Yokuts, Prairie Falcon is at the mercy of Coyote. In one myth, Coyote transforms into Prairie Falcon in a game to avenge the death of his son, Hummingbird, due to gambling, and loses his eyes to Eagle.[23] In another myth Coyote helps Rabbit win everything from Weasel, Fox, and Magpie, all known gamblers, in a game of hoop and pole. Prairie Falcon then wins everything from Rabbit, including Rabbit's ears.[24] Coyote stops the game, goes to Prairie Falcon's wife for a gambling hoop, and mates with her. Prairie Falcon then begins to lose, and Rabbit wins everything back. Prairie Falcon drowns himself, making Coyote so sad that his heart comes out of his mouth, but he catches it and puts it back. He follows seven underwater trails and finally finds Falcon in a large communal house.[25] Coyote revives Prairie Falcon through a series of rituals, including smoking tobacco, rubbing his body with blue rock paint, and sticking a sharp grass up his anus. This is the only myth of this region thus far that seems to closely reflect religious aspects of the culture.

A Southern Sierra Miwok tale proves that the hero doesn't always win.[26] Falcon's father, *Yayil*, a great gambler, journeys to the south country to gamble with *Kū'tcū*, a type of buffalo. He loses and is burned to death. Death by fire is a typical wager in many myths belonging to tribes in the Great Basin and the Plateau.

Great Basin Desert Foragers

Directly east of California is a vast, dry, upland expanse of mountains and basins with interior drainage and sharp extremes of temperature in winter and summer. Small foraging bands or single families, speaking mostly Numic (Shoshonean) languages, were spread over this inhospitable land resulting in population densities as low as one person per fifty square miles. Summer foods included seeds, roots, berries, cactus fruits, and pine nuts; ants, locusts, snakes, lizards, and rodents (particularly mice and rabbits); and occasional pronghorn antelope and deer. Pioneers called the basin dwellers "diggers" because of the way they scavenged for their food. Coyotes were not eaten because they were believed to be endowed with supernatural power. In winter, foods were minimally available; stored summer foods were relied upon, and the threat of starvation was ever present. Many basin peoples pursued bison herds in the Great Plains after obtaining horses from the Utes in about 1680.

People traditionally gathered together in larger bands during the barren winter months and during brief periods of plenty. Leadership was informal and in the hands of respected elders, usually males. Interband conflict, although rare, occasionally occurred as the result of witchcraft accusations or disputes over women. Little existed in the way of formal religion, although spirit guides, contacted through dreams or visions, were believed to lend power not only to heal but also to hunt pronghorns and to gamble.

Gambling stories become more thoroughly ghastly in the Great Basin, and we begin to see an element of gambling witchcraft.[27] The bones of women who have been dead for thirty or forty years were considered to be powerful gambling medicine. Gamblers would disinter their graves and remove their middle or upper finger bones. They would wash the bone while talking to it about their planned use of it. While they slept with the bone, it might say, "Keep me for two years and you'll always win, but if you don't return me to the grave after two years, you will die."

Stories of gambling animals would be appropriate for people who turned to them for spiritual guidance. We aren't so easily rid of Coyote. In a Shivwits Shoshone tale, Wolf, who lives with Coyote, helps his father-in-law win back everything he has lost in a gambling game.[28] Unfortunately, Wolf looks upon the scabbed face of a bad person and jumps into a stream. After his grandfather rescues him, Wolf tells his grandfather that he wishes to return to gamble with the person who has scared him. Warning Wolf that these are wicked people, the grandfather cuts a cane four inches long, saying that it will hold Wolf's body while his spirit gambles.

Wolf returns to the village in spirit, but forgetting that his real form is inside the cane, he places it on the hut. He returns to his grandfather but disappears as soon as the bad people pitch the cane into the fire back at the gambling camp. Grandfather recovers the charred cane but becomes so angry that he causes a storm fierce enough to rip up the trees and throw the gamblers into the air. He boils the cane in water and restores Wolf to life. Wolf gives Grandfather all his winnings, then he cuts off the head of one of his wives, who is pregnant, and squeezes out all of his babies. Keeping one, he takes it and his wife to the village of the wicked gamblers who are playing with their genitalia, throwing them in the air and laughing. The story continues into a passage about cannibalism.

Among the Southern Paiute (Maopa), gambling myths involve the creator beings *Cunawabi* and his brother, *Tobats*. Cunawabi creates disease and the night, and he names the mountains, waters, rocks, and bushes. He is characterized as a gambler and trickster.

Cunawabi's failure at gambling is a mystery to him until his brother tells him that the food given him by his opponents drains his power, so he refuses to eat and his success increases.[29] In fact, he wins all the property, including pine nuts, which he plants on Big Mountain near present-day Las Vegas, Nevada. He gambles with Turtle for a sheepskin hide by seeing who can jump over the sheep. He wins the hide, but Turtle makes off with the whole sheep. Furious, Cunawabi asks his sons to dream up a flood to kill Turtle. But turtles can swim. Turtle makes his children dream of heat, and Cunawabi becomes so uncomfortable that he jumps into a pail of boiling water and dies.

In another Shoshonean myth, Cunawabi purchases a woman, and he and all his followers have their way with her.[30] The young woman's husband, *Qosabi*, a whippoorwill or bluejay, becomes so angry that he decides to gamble himself away. (He has already gambled away all his relatives.) The woman doesn't want to live without him, so she tells him he'd better gamble her away as well. They discover that they can fly through solid objects. At the camp, Qosabi races another gambler to the ocean and back, using a stick to push the egg his wife has given him in place of a ball.[31] His opponent never sees the egg. Here the myth turns surrealistically dual. Two Cunawabis, one for each opponent, wrestle over who is going to win. Qosabi's opponent barely makes it to the tree, the designated goal, but Qosabi runs through the tree and wins. Cunawabi on Qosabi's side kills the loser, then tries to cut off the head of the other Cunawabi, but fails. Qosabi does the task, thereby releasing the people.

Cottontail,[32] a member of Cunawabi's party, and a bug named Mu'qwa'mbi [33] also gamble in separate myths, but the most grisly gambler of all is Centipede (A´qonidza'Ba), who belongs to the Paviotso people. Centipede gambles well at handgame and football (a race with a ball), and he keeps all the people he defeats in gambling games.[34] The only members left of the tribe who have not gambled with Centipede are two girls and a boy. While hunting one day, the boy is told by a little bird that a bad man has killed all of his people, cut out and dried their hearts, and strung up all their hands together, burning the rest of their bodies. The bird instructs the youth in how to beat the gambler and gives him two eggs—one owl and one gopher—to aid him in football. Don't sit on Centipede's red robe or let him get his arms under you, the bird advises. Choosing to gamble at football, Centipede leads the youth into a place where it is always night.[35] Owl appears from one of the eggs to shine a light for the youth, and gopher digs a hole to trap Centipede's ball. The youth wins, and instead of receiving his payment in hands and hearts, he throws Centipede into the fire with the help of Crow. They plant the dried hearts in the damp earth, and his people are restored on the third sunrise.

In another version, the boy is the son of Chickenhawk, who has lost to Centipede at two-balls. Woodpecker, Owl, and "another person" aid the game in much the same way as in the previous version. Instead of hands and hearts, Centipede has strung up the eyeballs of his victims, which the youth frees after winning. In both myths, Crow has been maimed by Centipede, hence his propensity to hop, and the youth must heal Crow before the bird can help him burn Centipede.

Interior-Plateau Foragers

The Interior-Plateau culture area, spreading east from the Northwest Coast to the Rocky Mountains, is a high, relatively well-watered, wooded region that was peopled by numerous small groups of peaceful, foraging village dwellers. They subsisted on an abundance of game, fruits, and salmon, and after horses reached the plateau region beginning around

1740, many Plateau tribes began to participate in the great bison hunts. Culturally, the Plateau people resembled their Northwest Coast, Great Basin, and California neighbors, and gambling myths are likewise similar.

The theme of the bankrupt gambler gaining mystical prowess after a retreat resurfaces among the Lillooet of British Columbia.[36] Note the heavy duality in this myth: An old woman tells the self-pitying loser to go to the mountains and train himself for four years. At the end of that period, he goes to a lake where, on the other side, stand two underground houses. Good people live in one house, cannibals in the other. *KalEnüxxwa'* is the chief of the bad people; *Asüxxwa'* is the good chief. A loon appears (answering a telepathic call) to ferry the gambler across the lake in a copper canoe and is surprised that the gambler does not want to see KalEnüxxwa' like everyone else. Instead, he enters the house of the good Asüxxwa', who whips him four times to make him "right" and gives him two daughters. The gambler washes himself four times. He then enters the other house, where he stakes his two wives against the two daughters and property of KalEnüxxwa' and wins. The gambler returns the property to KalEnüxxwa' but keeps the daughters as wives. Now he has four women who each bear him a daughter. He returns home and enjoys infamy as a great gambler. Another man who loses everything begs to learn the gambler's secrets. The gambler tells him he trained in the mountains for four years, then gained vast knowledge from KalEnüxxwa'. The man foolishly does everything as the gambler directs him to do, and KalEnüxxwa' eats him and throws his bones on the pile of his other victims.

Considering the proximity of some Plateau groups to those of the Northwest region, it is not surprising to see similarities in gambling myths. The following myth echoes the Chinook myth of the Thunderer's grandsons.[37] Multiples of five and two are strong in this Wasco myth about Eagle. Eagle gambles and wins against Crow, Hawk, Crab, and Raven, but eventually his luck turns against him and he loses one half of his body, piece by piece, before losing his head. His two sons seek help from supernatural powers. Younger brother gets power from twenty-five grizzlies and the elder brother from five double fires. They track their father for five years. At last they come to the gambling village (on the Dalles River in Oregon) where they find an eagle's head stuck on a pole.

They enter the house of two old women, to which the village chief sends five messengers, one at a time; each is burned by the stare of the brothers. The chief invites them to gamble, the brothers win back all the pieces of their father, and they put him back together by stepping over him five times. With the twenty-five grizzlies on one side of the village and the five double fires on the other, the brothers fight, kill, and burn the people. They scatter the bears over all the mountains and go home.

Antelope joins Coyote in the following myth of the Thompson Indians of British Columbia—despite the fact that antelope are not naturally found in the area.[38] Antelope is a great friend to Coyote, and in this myth the two covet a golden fireball (sun) owned by the people of Lytton. They quarrel over whose sons would be instrumental in obtaining the ball, and Coyote wins. Their sons station themselves at intervals along the Thompson River, with Antelope's sons nearer to their lodge and Coyote's sons closer to Lytton. One of Coyote's sons goes in for the ball as the Lytton people play with it on their field. He grabs the ball and runs, but is killed as he throws it to his brother. Relay fashion, the Coyote brothers are all killed just as each throws the ball upriver to the next one. The Lyttons turn back out of fear or exhaustion as the Antelope son catches the ball from the last Coyote brother. Antelope says to Coyote, "You see what comes of putting your sons before mine." Coyote gains revenge by trampling the Lyttons and returning the ball full of his excrement.

The sun, in another Thompson gambling myth, once lived nearer to the earth, and when he traveled from east to west everyday, he killed people, hung them up to dry at home, and ate them the next night.[39] An unlucky gambler of Lytton, after taking a sweat bath and speaking with his manitou or protecting spirit, dreams of turning his luck around by traveling. The next day, he sets out and is delivered on a cloud to the sun's house where he meets Sun's son dressed in rainbow garments. The gambler witnesses Sun's eating habits from his hiding place and decides to go home. Son of Sun gives him a bundle to carry home on his back, which turns out to be an endless supply of blankets for the village. Loon and Goose give the gambler their daughters for wives. He presents the daughters to Sun and his son. Sun is so pleased he promises not to kill any more people.[40]

* * *

In this chapter we have witnessed the gambling myths of five regions, all of which appear to be culturally pristine. Although many themes know no boundaries, the setting almost always remains true to the group telling the story. Nowhere is there evidence for tale-tampering from non-Indians, nor do the myths address conflicts with the dominant culture. The Indians would have had plenty of opportunities to do so.

In western Canada and interior Alaska many bands were left relatively undisturbed until well into the nineteenth century, but disease, alcohol, trading posts, missions, and other manifestations of Western influence brought cultural dissolution. When hordes of Americans arrived in California during the Gold Rush of 1849, many Indians were ruthlessly overrun and often wantonly massacred. By 1900 fewer than 15,000 survived, and Native American cultural traditions were largely destroyed. The Northwest Coastal area was visited by at least a hundred foreign ships between 1774 and 1794, and disease, guns, conflict, and alcohol took a rapid toll. By the end of the nineteenth century, the traditional economy and culture were increasingly undermined in that region, although the people survived by remaining on or near their ancient lands, developing their world-renowned artistry, and working in forestry. The gambler myths do not reflect the cultural devastations of these regions, although they do touch on gambling addictions and their cure by going back to traditional and spiritual values.

Fur trappers arrived in the Plateau region during the early nineteenth century, followed by missionaries and tens of thousands of pioneers. Disease and bloody conflict led to loss of life, culture, and land, and by 1860 little remained of the traditional Plateau way of life. Pioneers freely dispossessed the natives of their lives and land, and the impoverished culture quickly succumbed. And here also, history is not reflected in the gambling myths.

In the Eastern Woodlands cultures, the gambler myths pick up bits and pieces of the former, more ancient cultures, yet, again, much of the horror of more recent history is absent from the myths.

TWO

Rolling Stones, Birds' Eyes, and *The Song of Hiawatha:*
Gambler Myths of the Eastern Woodlands

I am walking amid all the beautiful goods,
A white bead gambling stick is in my hand.
It is tied with the white bead string.
I am walking amid all the beautiful goods,
With the white bead stick in my hand.
The white bead ring is on top of the stick.
Today luck is on my side.
—Song of the Gambler during the Rolling Ring Game[1]

Hiding it, with it they gamble. Into a tent they go. Half on one side sit down, half also are inside on the other side sat down. Then bets they make. Robes, beaded robes, other things many they bet. After that they put down their stakes. Then the to-be-hidden (elk tooth) they take. Then they sing; they hide it; these on the other side guess. (If) they find out, then they hide it. Tally sticks ten; these ten all (if) they take, then they win. If they win, they get up and dance. This is the end.
—Crow Hand Game Song[2]

Evergreen and hardwood forests extending from the Mississippi River to the Atlantic Ocean and from southern Canada to the Gulf of Mexico have supported many large populations since prehistoric times. Various ancestral tribes of the peoples later living in this vast region constructed more than a hundred thousand earthen burial and temple mounds, geometric earthworks, and walled cities between 1500 B.C.E. and 1500 C.E. Classified as Mound Builders, these cultures possessed priest-temple-idol complexes and highly stratified classes and castes, all of which may have been derived from the high cultures of Mesoamerica, such as the Olmec.

These ancient sites yielded a crop of what archaeologists call gaming or *chungké* stones: highly polished flat disks, bowls, or pulley-shapes with perforated centers.[3] Figurines exhumed from Mississippian mound complexes show players on their knees rolling the bowls. Many historical tribes across the continent played with similar stones, which explorers from as early as the eighteenth century thought had been preserved by the generations since prehistoric times. Culin classified chungké as a hoop and pole game in which the objective was to spear or knock the hoops, whether of stone or rawhide-covered wood. The addiction to the game was remarked upon as early as the seventeenth century, and of course, gambling away everything at the game, even one's liberty, was inevitable.

John Ax, the oldest living Cherokee at the turn of the twentieth century, was the only remaining tribal member who had ever played the game. He had been coached in the sport as a boy by an older man interested in keeping the ancient rites alive. "The sticks used have long since disappeared, but the stones remain, being frequently picked up in the plowed fields, especially in the neighborhood of the mounds," he

Rings wrapped in rawhide and often decorated with beads and feathers may have evolved from stone rings used in the traditional game of hoop and pole. (Culin, 1907)

said.[4] Some observed the games being played on or near ancient fields in the Southeast region.

John Lawson said in his 1701 history of Carolina that the Eno played "upon a smooth place, like a bowling green, made for that purpose."[5] The Hidasta of North Dakota, like most historical tribes, played on a field bordered by a picket fence, grass beaten as smooth and hard as a floor. In more recent Cherokee villages, there were signs of these greens near ancient mounds, but the modern game was played in a different place prepared for the purpose. The old yards, though not built or used by current residents, were swept clean and kept up by the locals.

William Bartram described in 1849 more hideous chungké yards among the Creeks and Cherokees. The public square and the rotunda or great winter council house stood at opposite ends of a rectangular field. Some of these "chunk" yards were as long as two or three football fields end to end and were sunk two or three feet below the embankments or terraces surrounding them. The terraces served as spectator seats. In the center of the yard was a low circular mound, in the middle of which stood a chunk pole, a thirty-foot-tall, four-sided pillar of wood that tapered to a point. Some sort of object was fastened to the top of the pole as a target. At each corner were twelve-foot-tall poles, called slave posts, to which captives were bound for burning. The tops of the posts were crowned by a dry skull and decorated with scalps of slain enemies, suspended by strings.

"It thus appears that this area is designed for a public place of exhibition, for shows, games, etc.," Bartram wrote. The traders told him the chunk yards were used for torture, but he thought it a lame story. "I observed none of these yards in use in any of the Cherokee towns. . . . [I]t must be understood that I saw only the remains or vestiges of them among the ruins of ancient towns."[6]

The Eastern Woodlands region is commonly divided into two subsections, Northeast and Southeast, and we'll look at the myths in the context of each section. Although ancient mounds and the game of chungké and hoop and pole were widespread among both regions, I found mention of chungké stones only in Cherokee, Alabama, Koatsi, and Natchez myths of the Southeast.

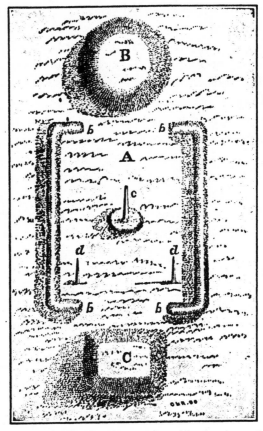

"Chunk yard" where the Mound Builders presumably played a prehistoric game of "chunkey" or chungké, or hoop and pole. (Culin, 1907)

Northeast Cultivators

Cold weather and a short growing season in the Northeast and around the Great Lakes limited horticulture and forced heavy dependency on fish, game, maple syrup, and wild rice. Among cultivators, men generally cleared the fields, and women did most of the farming. The Northeast subsection was peopled by numerous societies that can be classified into two principal divisions: Algonquian and Iroquoian speakers.

The majority of the Algonquian-speaking peoples lived in small, semi-sedentary villages along the eastern seaboard, extending north and west to the Great Lakes. A few other tribes lived along the south Atlantic coast and were strongly influenced by their southeastern neighbors. Farming was less developed along the coast, where foraging was excellent. Group leadership was generally weak, territory ill-defined, and political organization similar to that of tribelets elsewhere. Algonquian groups were among the first native North Americans to suffer destruction at the hands of Europeans; the cultures of many effectively ended before the eighteenth century began.

The most famous Indian gambler myth in print comes from this area: Longfellow's 1855 epic poem, *The Song of Hiawatha*. Although Hiawatha is borrowed from Iroquois history and mythology, background for the poem's gambling myth was provided by Henry Rowe Schoolcraft's ethnological materials on the Ojibwa/Chippewa Algonquian-speakers of the Upper Great Lakes region.

The gambler antagonist is *Pau-Puk-Keewis*, called the Storm Fool, who has the power to form the dunes of Nagow Wudjoo. Setting forth on new adventures in Chapter 16 of the poem, he comes to Hiawatha's village and enters a lodge where old Iagoo is telling a story about how the animals broke open the sky and climbed into heaven to let the summer weather out. Tiring of the older man's stories, Pau-Puk-Keewis challenges those present to a game of bowl and counters.

Pau-Puk-Keewis plays until dawn, stripping all the young and old men of their deerskin shirts, ermine robes, wampum belts, feather crests, war weapons, pipes, and pouches. Declaring that he is in need of a companion, Pau-Puk-Keewis ventures all his winnings against Iagoo's sixteen-year-old nephew, Face-in-the-Mist, whom he wins handily. He orders his new slave, or *Meshinauwa*, to carry all his winnings to his wigwam in the far east. Then, "with eyes hot and red from smoke and gambling," he enters Hiawatha's lodge. Hiawatha and Minnehaha are absent, so Pau-Puk-Keewis strangles the raven he finds there, ransacks the house, and then proceeds to kill the birds of the mountains by the hundreds. At the close of the chapter, the birds sing for Hiawatha's return.

Pau-Puk-Keewis, who is a nearly perfect archetype of the destructive Native gambler, is derived from *Paup-pu-ke-nay*, the Ojibwa/Chippewa trickster grasshopper who has the ability to shape-shift. Iagoo is a mythological figure with a reputation for telling extravagant tales of all that he sees, hears, or accomplishes. The story he tells of the animals cracking open the sky is reminiscent of Southwestern emergence myths where the people come up through the watery underworld through a hole in its ceiling. Even the sand dunes Pau-Puk-Keewis creates, Nugow Wudjoo, is a legendary chief named for his birth place on the shore of Lake Superior.[7] Hiawatha was a legendary prophet.[8]

The Passamaquoddy Algonquian-speakers of Maine believed the aurora borealis was the dead playing ball.[9] Dice games were played with incantations to drive away evil spirits. A run of bad luck brought on a phrase like, "I know there is a Micmac squaw around." One legend tells of a dice game between Youth and Old Age. The old man of magical powers has regained his youth several times by inhaling the breath of youthful opponents. Having grown old, he selects another victim. The young man is also powerful and consequently knows the old man's scheme, but he consents to the match anyway. The old man uses the eyes of his former victims as dice and a human skull as a tossing bowl. The young man's spirit in the air elevates the dice and makes them disappear, thus breaking up the game. The legend says the old man still waits for the dice to fall, and the young man still outwits him.[10]

The Seneca Iroquoian-speakers, who traditionally occupied a territory in what is now New York State, had an abundance of gambling myths. They were intensely committed to raids, warfare, and the taking of captives, with torture and cannibalism inflicted upon the noblest male captives. The Senecas were among Iroquois nations (along with the Cayugas, Mohawks, Onondagas, Oneidas, and later the Tuscaroras) united in the powerful Iroquois League that exerted a formidable military and political influence until the end of the eighteenth century. Guardians of the strategic Western Door of the longhouse, symbolizing the Great League, the Senecas were among the most respected and feared North American Indian tribes.

They lived in scattered villages organized within a system of matrilineal clans. Men hunted, cleared fields, traded, and made war. Women gathered various wild plant foods and tended gardens in which were grown several varieties of maize, beans, and squash. A calendric cycle of ceremonies reflected their agricultural and hunter-gatherer way of life.

One Seneca mythological figure is *Géha* (or *Gaha*), the wind who often befriends humans and aids them on their quests.[11] In a story that might be told as a model for social humility, Géha gives supreme hunting powers to an abandoned boy by way of a knife. The boy uses it to kill *Nyagwaihe*, the Ancient of Bears.[12] Géha tells the boy that the bear came because the boy was too proud, and that he should not boast about how he killed the bear, but should give the meat to the village anonymously. The supply of meat is infinite.

The chief in the east challenges the boy's village to a race, with losers forfeiting their heads. The boy uses his powers and wins the race, with the typical bloody pay-off. That night, a stranger challenges the boy to another race, staking his own head against the village. Géha tells the boy that he is on his own, since he did not obey and had boasted. "Help yourself, and I will help you," Géha says. When the race begins, the boy runs over the hills without ever seeing his opponent who is so far ahead. A whirlwind pushes the boy up to the heals of the challenger, and the boy wins. He cuts off the head of the opponent, who has resumed his true identity as the bear the boy had killed in the forest, and carries the head home. It takes the village ten years to recover the body from the tenth hill, which the boy had raced to over the course of one year.

Dice are again associated with birds' eyes in a test-theme myth of a Seneca culture hero.[13] A boy hunts in the north despite his grandmother's warning. The boy and his grandmother are the last of their people, and she knows how dangerous it is in the north. He comes across four "uncles" who refuse him passage until he meets a challenge from each of them. The first uncle causes a storm of raining fish, spears, and stones, but the boy kills the uncle with a whirlwind. He is then challenged by the next uncle to race across a field, wagering heads. Halfway, a sharpened deer horn sticks in the boy's foot, tripping him. He throws it into the old man's foot and wins. He cuts off the uncle's head and proceeds to burn it, at which point it bursts open and owls fly out.[14] The third uncle challenges him to a game of hide and seek, agreeing to let the boy keep his head if he finds the old man by midday. The boy turns into a tick on the uncle's neck and cries "found you!"; the old man, however, keeps punching the sun back with a pole to prevent the coming of noon. Eventually the sun moves overhead, and the boy collects his gruesome winnings.

The fourth uncle wants to play dice; same wager. The boy uses the right eyes of six live ducks as dice. He explains to the dice that when the old man throws them, some must fall with their sight down, but when the boy throws, all eyes must be looking up. During the game, the eyeballs fly into the sky when the old man throws, quacking, and landing as instructed. But when the boy throws, the duck eyes fly out the smoke hole of the cabin and can be heard in the distance. "No count!" says the old man, but the eyes return and land sight up. The boy decapitates the old man, sets the house on fire, and returns the eyes to the ducks. When the boy grows into a man, he has the power to call the animals to him. One day the grandmother looks outside, against the boy's wishes, and sees him being carried off in the antlers of a white deer. He is still singing as he disappears into the forest.

Elements of that story are similar to another Seneca myth about a culture hero named *Hodadenon* (also spelled *Hodadeio*), "he, the last."[15] He is the younger brother of *Yenyethwus*, "she, the planter." Hodadenon goes on a quest to cure the illness of his elder brother, *Hadjigwas*, "mush eater." On his adventures, he meets his uncle, *Hodiadatgon*, a powerful and malevolent medicine man who has caused illness to the elder brother. They play a dice game, using owl's eyes, called *hihi ogashoon* (or woodcock's eyes in another version), for dice. The uncle loses his head to Hodadenon, of course.

In the next Seneca story, the gambler is a woman—a rare occurrence.[16] *Híno' Hohawaqk*, the son of *Híno'* or Thunder, is raised by a poor, dirty woman who finds him on her daughter's grave in the forest. When Thunder Boy is old enough, he learns that Thunder is his father and the woman's deceased daughter is his mother. He learns that the heads of the woman's other six daughters have been lost to a gambler woman (Panther) and her son in a game of dice. He sets out to find the old woman gambler in the West. He comes to a bark house with a skin blanket hanging from a pole. Old men are betting on boys playing ball (with a stick) and invite Thunder Boy to play. He plays so well that they ask him to play dice with the old woman, saying they will wager their own heads on the game.

The betting woman sits near the pole on an elk skin. With Thunder Boy insisting she go first, she blows on her stone dice before throwing them from the stone bowl. The dice turn into crows, fly around, and drop back into the bowl, but she doesn't score. Thunder Boy uses his own dice from his squirrel pouch. When he throws them, they turn into ducks and land to score ten. He is about to settle the bet when the woman insists he play ball with her son. He wins that game, too, and removes both their heads. He goes off to find his father, Thunder.

Southeast Cultivators

In the Southeast, horticulture, supplemented by abundant products of the forests, provided the basis for large-scale settlements and political forms characteristic of chiefdoms. Villages with hundreds of inhabitants were palisaded against attack. Fires burned perpetually in the Mesoamericanesque moundtop temples containing elite residences. Chiefs possessed absolute political power over their noble and common subjects and in some cases commanded a dozen or more villages. Raids and wars took place primarily to obtain wealth and honor but also to secure captives for slavery, sacrifice, and group cannibalism. Disease and the effects of war destroyed many of these peoples before any but the most superficial accounts were written by European explorers and settlers.

We have met Thunder and his half-mortal son as supernatural figures in the gambling myths of the Shasta in California, the Chinook in the Pacific Northwest, the Seneca of the Northeast, and personified as Thunderbird among the Tsimshian of the Northwest and as Storm Fool in Longfellow's poem. In a Natchez myth, a young woman enlists the help of thunder, lightning, and cyclone in a ballgame in which she and her husband play against her mother, who often eats sons-in-law, and her mother's husband.[17]

Up to this point, many of the myths involving thunder have been associated with hoop games. In the Southeastern myths, Thunder appears more frequently as a mythical character in association with the chungké stones and the hoop and pole game. James Mooney, however, says that the Cherokee consider thunderstorms to be the Thunder Boys playing ball. The ball would have to be made of stone to make that kind of noise, so perhaps the reference is to a stone disk, bowl, or pulley so common to these cultures.

Mooney reports yet another story of Thunder's son and the gambler, this time from the Cherokee.[18] The gambler's name is Ûñtsaiyi´, which is the ringing sound produced by striking a thin sheet of metal.[19] Cherokee tradition asserts that their wheel-and-stick game of gatayûsti, played with a stone wheel or circular disk, was invented by the mythic gambler. Ûñtsaiyi´ lives on the south side of the Tennessee River at a place called Ûñtiguhi, or "pot in the water." It was known as "The Suck" to Euro-Americans because of the dangerous rapids where the Tennessee met Suck Creek below the Chattanooga. According to Cherokee informants Swimmer and John Ax, the large flat rock on which the wheel was rolled is still on the south side of the river, with the wheel grooves still visible. The wheel and stick are also still there, now turned to stone.

In this story the spiritual quest and the test theme are combined, and Mooney's observations provide a rare commentary on the myths. A boy goes to his father, Thunder, in the west to be cured of sores caused by tuberculosis of the lymph nodes. On the way to his father, the boy runs into Ûñtsaiyi´, who challenges him to a game of stone wheel and stick for the spots all over the boy's body. Ûñtsaiyi´ is good at bluffing and always wins because of his ability to shape-shift. The boy declines, saying he is on his way to meet his father.

Once the boy arrives, Thunder dunks him into a pot of boiling water filled with roots to cure him of his spots. The effect is similar to a spiritual sweat bath. To test the boy to see if he really is his own son—for he has spawned many while on his travels—he asks the boy to select a snake (universally associated with lightning and thunder) from a jar to use as a necklace. The youth selects a rattlesnake from the bottom, which Mooney says is the most unlikely and, therefore, divine choice. Thunder asks him to play a game of ball against the Thunders in the Darkening Place.[20] The boy learns his own identity as Lightning during the game. The father stops the fight for fear Lightning would split a honey locust tree.[21] Thunder then advises the boy how to beat the gambler Ûñtsaiyi´.

Ûñtsaiyi´ is beaten with the help of the magical gourd and war club Thunder gives him. The gambler has staked his life, but he runs away.

Thunder and his son stop an old woman to inquire about the where-abouts of the gambler, but she says she hasn't seen him. A Horned Green Beetle, which the boys refer to as their dog, circles overhead. The beetle strikes the old woman on the forehead with a dart and it rings like brass—Ûñtsaiyi´! The old woman reverts to the form of the gambler and runs away. The boy and his brothers pursue him to the edge of the great water where the sun goes down. They tie his hands and feet with a grapevine, drive a long stake through his breast, and plant him far out in the deep water. They set two crows on the ends of poles to guard the spot and call it *Kâgûñ'yi*, "Crow place."

"But Brass [Ûñtsaiyi´] never died," said Mooney, "and cannot die until the end of the world, but lies there always with his face up." Sometimes he struggles under the water to get free, and sometimes the beavers, who are his friends, come and gnaw at the grapevine to release him. Mooney was reminded of a Cheyenne myth where a beaver, regarded as a great father of all mankind, gnaws the pole supports of the earth, thus threat-ening it. Then the pole shakes, and the crows at the top cry *Ka! Ka! Ka!* and scare the beavers away. In the myths we have examined up to now, it is unusual for the hero to spare the gambler's life.

In a Koatsi myth, Thunder is the gambler, chungké is still the game, and Iron Woman is the spiritual advisor to one of Thunder's victims.[22] Thunder burns a man who won't give up his wife after losing her in a game. Walking along the river, the man meets Iron Woman pounding iron; she sets minnows to eat his dead skin. After he recovers, she instructs him in beating Thunder with her arrows. He wins everything back, but Thunder doesn't want to return the wife. Instead of the Horned Green Beetle, we have dung roller, *Laigatonōhana*, who chases Thunder around the four corners of the earth until the bones split off him. Mooney says that a dung roller is regarded as a horned beetle with the brass rubbed off.

The chungké stone has some interesting properties not necessarily associated with thunder. In a Natchez myth the mischievous brothers Lodge Boy and Thrown-Away (who grew from the navel string), make a chungké stone called a *wagul*.[23] When one of the boys throws it after their father, they can hear what he is saying at a distance. (He was scolding them for their actions.) In this myth, a self-operating ball, one-and-a-half feet in diameter, leads the boys into trouble. In an Alabama Indian myth, two men start off to meet The-One-Sitting-Above (God).[24] One of the obstacles is a black chungké, or *kalaha*, rolling toward them, with malevolent intent. Apparently, this magic stone is also self operating.

The following Alabama Indian myth is not about thunderstones but touches upon the recurring theme of cataclysmic destruction and rebirth.[25] In it, a man of considerable family wagers the water of the world in a moccasin game called *takálu´nka* and loses. All the bodies of water evaporate, and the people begin to die of thirst. Woodpecker pecks a hole into a canoe he has discovered, which is as large as a tree, and all the water comes gushing out and back into place.

* * *

Thunder may have ripped up the land and terrorized people in gambling games, but he paled in comparison to Manifest Destiny. The earliest colonists generally came to North America for the express purpose of settling the land, and since virtually all of it was already in use by the indigenous inhabitants, war was inevitable. Apart from isolated incidents of violence, hit-and-run raids, and intertribal wars, as many as sixty-seven brutal massacres were initiated by whites or Indians beginning with the Pequot War in 1637. Between 1778 and 1871, a total of 389 treaties had been signed and ratified. Many of these treaties were relentlessly broken in the nineteenth century as large numbers of white settlers moved into Indian lands. Beginning about 1815, federal policy supported the forced removal of Indians from their traditional territories to isolated reservations administered as trusts by the U.S. government.

Algonquian-speakers were among the first native North Americans outside of the Southwest to encounter Europeans. The Ojibwa/Chippewa prospered in the fur trade, expanded their population and territory, and developed new tribal-level institutions as an indirect result of contact with the French in the seventeenth century. Many other cultures effectively ended before the next century began. Not that the battles were one-sided. The Algonquian-speaking Pequot (from Pekawatawog, "the destroyers") for instance, were the most feared tribe in New England in the early seventeenth century. Their campaign against New England ended in a massacre by the English militia in 1637. The few survivors were caught and killed, enslaved, or transported to the West Indies. In 1655 colonists removed other survivors to two reservations on the Mystic River in Connecticut. There the Mashantucket Pequot became the richest Indian gaming operators in the country—and not a single gambler legend to show for it, at least not on record.

The Iroquois League originated in the seventeenth century, perhaps as a defense against their Algonquian neighbors. The league had a military and political stronghold in the Northeast until the end of the eighteenth century and consequently suffered less devastation due to European contact. According to Iroquois legend, the prophet Hiawatha (fl. c. 1550), as the earthly spokesperson for a divine leader named Deganawidah, unified the original Five Nations to stop intertribal warfare marked by blood feud and cannibalism. Initially, sporadic warfare and raiding against tribes outside the league were conducted for prestige. Eventually, the league skillfully played the British, French, and colonists against one another and subjugated neighboring tribes for both economic and territorial gains, proving to be a nearly invulnerable political alliance until its eventual collapse during the American Revolution.

Mention of Hiawatha might harken the reader's attention back to the gambler passage in Longfellow's poem. Iroquois tradition indeed romanticizes the historical Hiawatha as a semi-mythical culture hero, but he was a Mohawk, and Longfellow's poem was based, ironically, on the enemy Algonquian-speaking Ojibwa culture. We can't even count Longfellow's poem, whether fictitious or not, as an example of a gambler myth imitating history.

Though it was never mentioned in the gambler myths, the wheel spun continuously between glory and despair for the Cherokees. Iroquoian-speakers, they originated near the Great Lakes; but after defeat by Iroquois and Delaware tribes, the Cherokee migrated to the mountainous region of the Southeast, eventually becoming the largest and most powerful group in that region. Their culture included maize agriculture, settled villages, and well-developed ceremonialism. They aided the British during the American Revolution and continued their hostilities against the Americans until 1794. After the war, they borrowed from the lifestyle of their enemy, including plow agriculture, animal husbandry, cotton and wool industries, and slavery. They invented a syllabic alphabet around 1820, and in 1827 the tribe established a constitutional form of government. A series of land-fraudulent treaties resulted in the tribe's forced relocation to Arkansas and the Indian Territory (present-day Oklahoma) in 1838–39. As many as four thousand Cherokees died along the way on what is known as the Trail of Tears. Some Cherokees escaped into the Great Smoky Mountains and resettled in North Carolina. It is from this group that most of the Cherokee Thunder gambler myths were retrieved, although the myths do not comment on their tumultuous lives.

Many other Southeast tribes drew the same lot. Crippled first by disease and the effects of war during the period of European exploration and colonization, they, too, were forced to move to the Indian Territory in the early nineteenth century. Between 1830 and 1840, more than seventy thousand highly acculturated southeastern peoples were removed to the newly established Indian Territory in Oklahoma, land already in use by other Native American peoples. Many Indians fought bitterly against their forced resettlement on reservations.

By the mid-1800s, as white settlers pushed westward to the Pacific Ocean, tragedy after tragedy was visited upon Indians of the Great Plains and in the Far West, where Pueblos and Spaniards had been clashing for two centuries. The doctrine of Manifest Destiny fueled the frontier people into hostile actions against even peaceful peoples, and massive slaughter of men, women, and children sometimes resulted. The spread of disease also contributed to the defeat of the Indians and the suppression of their traditional ways of life.

The gambler myths we have examined up to this point have generally reflected the environment, Native lifestyle, and the religious beliefs of each region's peoples. Important components such as numerology, spirit-like birds, status-marking poles near gambling places, and culture heroes continue to cross cultural borders. Themes have centered on human nature, the propensity for conflict, holocaustic weather, and the supernatural reversal of fortune. Even cannibalism and slavery displayed by gamblers have some basis in fact.

* * *

My intention in these first two chapters has not been to emphasize the oppression of one society over another, but to explore whether the Native peoples used myths to express or affect the outcome of the conflicts. (Certainly, the horrors of historical reality far exceeded anything the mythical gambler could inflict upon his victims.) The collected myths so far have presented no outright evidence for a Native attempt to comprehend the violent clashes with whites.

The Pawnees of the Great Plains are a different story. Their gambler myths do not describe their political ordeal, but they were merged with ceremonies and games meant to revitalize a culture driven to near extinction by the white tide.

THREE

Tribal Revivalism:
The Pawnee Ghost Dance Hand Game

*Where Fleur's cabin stands, a parking lot will be rolled out of asphalt.
Over Pillager grave markers, sawed by wind and softened, blackjack
tables. Where the trees that shelter brown birds rise, bright banks of slot
machines. Out upon the lake that the lion man inhabits, where Pillagers
drowned and lived, where black stones still roll round to the surface, the
great gaming room will face with picture windows. Twenty-four-hour
bingo. I see the large-scale beauty of it all, the thirty-foot screens on
which a pleasant-voiced young girl reads the numbers of balls, day in and
day out. Auditorium seats, catered coffee, free lunch. State-of-the-art
markers, electronic boards. I see the peach and lime interior, the obedient
lines of humans all intent on the letters and the numbers that flash on the
twin screens telling how near, how far, how close to the perfect dreamstuff
they're coming.*

—Louise Erdrich, "A Little Vision," *The Bingo Palace* [1994]

The Vision

In January 1889 a monster began devouring the sun. Nevada
Paiutes, frantic by the total eclipse, shot their guns into the
sky to kill the demon while a thirty-three-year-old Paiute
named Wovoka collapsed with a severe fever. His near-death experience brought about a series of reversed fortunes far more dynamic than
anything a cannibalistic gambling centipede could ever cause.

Wovoka "died" and was taken to a village in another world where
all the ancestors lived in a happy, youthful state while engaged in all
the old games and occupations. God told Wovoka to return to his people and tell them they must live in peace with each other and with the
whites; they must work and not lie and steal or inflict war. If they
obeyed his instructions, they would be reunited with friends in the old

world without disease or old age. Wovoka was to take a dance back to his people that promised to hasten the reunion. The dance was to occur at intervals and last for five days. On each day, he was to sing songs designed to bring about certain kinds of weather: rain, clouds, snow, hard rain, and sunshine. Wovoka returned to his people, preached the prophecy, and organized the dance.

The people of various Nevada tribes quickly put their own spin on Wovoka's intent and technique. Obviously impressed by, but not totally sold on, the God of the white missionaries, they believed that Christ himself had come to tell the people to dance. Wovoka never claimed to be the Son of God, but he wasn't an accidental prophet, either. He was the son of Ta'vibo, the Paiute Prophet whose doctrines had been the stimulus of the Ghost Dance that swept through the tribes of northern California (1871–74). Wovoka absorbed the practices of the great medicine man, earning a reputation for being one himself.

Within months, the new Ghost Dance spread like prairie fire through the tribes of the Great Basin, Plateau, and northern Plains, many of them sending out spiritual reconnoiters to Wovoka to validate the vision dance. Northern Plainsmen sent delegates to southern kin in 1890, and by that fall, an Arapaho Ghost Dance prophet named Sitting-Bull was holding clinics in Oklahoma.[1] This prophet introduced peyote-induced trances to the Ghost Dances and hypnotized the dancers so that they could fall into their own visions. He set the stage for the Ghost Dance organization in these regions, and also for the politics. At the time, he was instrumental in persuading the southern Cheyenne and Arapaho to sign an agreement with the government by which they would relinquish much of their reservation land for payment. He told them they needed the money and the Messiah would soon restore the land to them anyway.

Life on the Great Plains, an undulating sod-covered belt extending from Canada to the Gulf of Mexico, was in massive transition by the time the Ghost Dance movement took root there. Bison hunting had been a way of life, revolutionized by the introduction of the horse in the early 1700s. But all that changed in the 1830s when a tidal wave of disease-carrying, gun-toting white immigrants and transcontinental travelers invaded the Plains. Traders encouraged the stepped-up slaughter of buffalo, railroad tracks later cut the herds off from their feeding and water supplies, and the increased population of people effectively reduced the buffalo population and free ranges where they grazed. The horse also played a role in the speedy communication of the dance from the Paiute center to the Plains.[2] Those who rejected the dance were still operating under old values in an aboriginal state, or under the new religion brought by missionaries, or, like the Navajos, were relatively too well-off to take interest. Alexander Lesser, author of *Pawnee Ghost Dance Hand Game*, said those tribes who accepted the dance were at a cultural impasse and they danced to retrieve their old way of life, their land, and their buffalo. They also danced to make white people go away.

The most tragic outcome of the Ghost Dance was the Wounded Knee Massacre. The dance reached the Dakota Sioux by 1889, and soon some twenty thousand Sioux began ghost-dancing. Wovoka's intent was for peace, but the Sioux transformed the dance from hope to war. They were embittered by reduced rations and were in despair over disease and natural disasters. The rapport with the supernatural achieved in the dance not only guaranteed a resurrected life but shielded the body in battle. In December 1890, hundreds of Sioux warriors, women, and children were massacred at Wounded Knee because of that belief. Many had worn "ghost shirts" emblazoned with eagle, buffalo, and Morning Star icons. On December 15, the legendary Sioux warrior Sitting Bull (not to be confused with the Arapaho prophet) who had helped to defeat General Custer, was killed during an attempted arrest by the U.S. military hoping to make an example of him for participating in Ghost Dances. Thereafter, government officials worked to stamp out the practice.

For the Pawnees, the Ghost Dance merged with old gaming ritual and myth to rescue their lost heritage.

The Pawnee Ghost Dance

The Pawnees first became known to the United States after it gained their territory as part of the Louisiana Purchase in 1903. One of the oldest Native American cultures of the Great Plains, these Caddoan speakers had entered the plains from east of the Mississippi River and settled near the Platte River in present-day Nebraska around 1200 C.E. After the Treaty of 1833, three of their four bands moved to the north side of the Platte, where they became more vulnerable to their ancient enemy, the Sioux. Since they were not given guns or allowed by treaty to retaliate, their numbers were halved by raids—and disease—twenty years later, despite government protection. In 1857, they accepted a reservation and for giving up their lands were to be paid handsomely in money, industrial equipment, schools, and lumber mills, but the hostilities visited upon them didn't stop. They finally joined their relatives the Wichita in Indian Territory (Oklahoma) in 1876, where they were further acculturated.

By 1892 the Pawnee culture of a century earlier had been profoundly altered. They had been accustomed to living in earth lodges and tepees; to digging-stick cultivation of corn, beans, and squash; and to hunting buffalo twice a year (once after planting and once after harvesting). The Pawnees were being mainstreamed into the farming industry and, consequently, they had become a loose mixture of people living in small family groups on separate farm tracts. Chiefs, no longer the governing power, maintained their status by reputation only. Ceremonies, religious societies, pottery-making, and the decorative arts became extinct. Nothing could fill the void, not even Christianity. Introducing any but the old ways would have been like throwing seed onto rock. One seed took.

The Ghost Dance came to the Pawnees in fall 1891 by way of a self-styled Pawnee prophet named Frank White who had participated in dances among the Comanches and Wichitas and had been initiated by the northern Arapaho prophet Sitting-Bull. At home, White advised tribe members to stop working at white man's jobs because the white men would not be present in the new world. He told them that if they danced, the white people would be wiped out by a great wind. The promise was similar to the book of Revelations in that at the end of the world, only the pure of heart would rise in the sky to Jesus.

The Pawnees embraced White's new dance. With painted faces and feather adornments, they formed a circle and joined hands. Many shook and fell in a peyote-induced trance, now the goal for every dancer. During one of the first dances, the clouds in the western sky resembled people sitting in a row; White told the participants that these were their dead fathers, mothers, and grandparents, and most believed it. It was in the west where the dancers would unite with the ghosts at the end of the world.

The dances came in rapid succession through the winter, and by 1892 most of the Pawnee people came under White's control. An Indian agent reported that two-thirds of the tribe believed in the second coming of Christ, and that He would destroy all the whites and bring back the buffalo and the wild game.[3] Since the end of the world was near, the people indeed deserted their plows in the cornfields as if they planned to return the next day. But that day was not to come for a long time.

The Indian agency in Ponca City got word the Pawnees were ghost-dancing and dispatched a clerk to put a stop to it immediately. After interviewing White, the clerk called him an imposter and told him to leave the reservation. Two hundred Pawnees "painted in high colors" came to the agency in an aggressive and defiant mood. For two hours, the agent spoke of false prophets and told them to return home to raise something to eat. They professed their loyalty and did go home. Thereafter they continued the Ghost Dance in secret.

The government continued its plan to persuade every last Pawnee to take out allotment tracts to finalize the program of civilizing them. Upon hearing that resisters were still ghost-dancing, a United States marshall arrested and held White for a couple of weeks. With him out of the way, the agents told the Pawnees they could keep their dance if they took allotments. The fracturing of the land was in direct violation of the dance itself, which promised a return of the land to its holistic state. A new agreement was drawn up with further fiduciary appeasements and was ratified on March 3, 1893. As a result, the lands ceded and opened to white settlement were scattered all over the Pawnee Reservation as if growing in between planks of a picket fence.

In the meantime, the Pawnees became free U.S. citizens, no longer subject to the dictates of the agents. The agents believed their actions had wiped out the dance, but the Pawnees soon learned of their freedom and flouted authority. The dance continued, by this time metamorphosed into the Ghost Dance hand game ceremony, practiced regularly until the turn of the century.

Throughout the development of the Ghost Dance movement, White had positioned himself as sole prophet and proprietor. All sanctions came through him, all visions were reported to him, all costume changes were approved by him, all dancers were trained by him. The people lavished gifts and money on him in return for his training. A small face painting earned him five dollars, for instance. At the same time, his conduct was not up to the standards of ancient code. The peyote may have made White wise, but the whiskey made him drunk, and the two didn't mix. It soon killed him in 1893, but not before the Pawnees had taken charge of their budding ceremony.

An Old War Game Converted

It was not a Pawnee who salvaged the ceremony from White, but an Arapaho named Joseph Carrion who had danced beside White for nearly a year and had even supplied him with his own sister for a wife. When the Pawnees began to revolt against White out of suspicion and jealousy, Carrion went to his own people to seek answers through their ceremonies. The Arapahos obtained a two-day Ghost Dance permit from the agency. They then painted a rainbow on Carrion's forehead, a crow on his right cheek, and an eagle on the other to give him the viewpoint and power of both birds. He fell into a five-hour trance, during which he saw a big circle of people above him. The next day, it was decided to stop ghost-dancing and to play a hand game for four days.

Carrion fasted during the entire game and on the fourth day went to the top of a hill. He could see many things in the sun: crows, an eagle feather, a black background with white streaks, the head of a bull buffalo. Just before sundown he saw Jesus standing in the western part of the sun with His hand extended toward Carrion. The Arapahos later interpreted the vision as the gift of the hand game presented to Carrion by Jesus. He took the vision of the hand game home to the Pawnees.

A new feeling of liberation and creativity shot through the Pawnees. Many conducted their own visions, which produced more hand-game sanctions and embellishments from Christ. The Ghost Dance hand game circumvented White's copyright. Furthermore, it was not owned and sanctioned by priests in the typical Pawnee style of the ancients, but was brought forth through visions embarked upon by new spiritual entrepreneurs, Arapaho-style. Therefore, it had the freedom to evolve into a new cultural form that mixed the old ceremonies with the revival Ghost Dance.

Other factors went into the swift development of the game. Tribal conditions had greatly improved during the Ghost Dance era. The Pawnees leased land lots to whites and they could even hire the whites to do any work that was required. There was plenty of time to practice the new game rituals, and that became the primary preoccupation.

Key Pawnee revivalists went back to three sources for their materials: bundles and bundle rituals, religious societies, and games. Fostered by mandates from visions and inspirations, they resuscitated the old ceremony and play, renewed and re-created the old paraphernalia, and transformed the old symbolism and concepts into new forms.

Take bundles, for instance. They enshrined the history of a group and a covenant of the gods. Contents of a bundle were dictated to priests during encounters with the supernatural and might include such items as tobacco wrapped in the pericardium of a buffalo, pipes, braids of sweetgrass, paint, corn, skins of birds or animals, and scalps. Bundles belonged to a village or band or were designed for a doctor or warrior, and ceremonies were conducted through the bundle. However, the secrets of the bundles were only passed on to apprentices from the priest's deathbed—and if there was no one to accept the secrets, the unidentified contents were to accompany the final owner in death. The bundles remained on the surface but atrophied and were only opened for repair of the contents or renewal of their expression. Although much of the original meaning had been lost, partially disintegrated bundles became centerpieces on the altars for the new gaming rituals. As we shall see later, the bundles were formerly associated with the Human Sacrifice to Morning Star and the Creation Ritual of the Evening Star, among others.

For their new ceremonies, the people were forced to rely on their collective memory of the nonesoteric aspects of their religion. Anything that had been public could be recalled and woven into the new ceremonies. The most obvious activity of the former culture was game playing. These included the large hoop and pole game, hand game, and moccasin games for men; and for women, the plum-seed dice game, shinny, and double ball. During the Ghost Dance period, the games were played with renewed enthusiasm. People began making gaming equipment in the old ritualized ways, which became the sources of visions used in ceremonies. As the ritual hand game developed, other game objects, like hoops, shinny balls, and dice, were carried in the dances and used to embody symbolic concepts.

There was precedence for incorporating the games in the dances. Mooney reported the presence of the wheel from the hoop and pole game in Sioux ceremonials.[4] At a dance at No Water's camp near Pine Ridge, South Dakota, four arrows were shot into the air from the center of the dancing circle, then gathered up and hung in a tree with a gaming wheel and sticks. At Pine Ridge and Rosebud, South Dakota, a young woman generally stood in the center of the circle holding a pipe toward the Messiah in the west, and another woman stood beside her holding out a *bäqati* wheel in the same way. A medicine man carried such a hoop with him in his flight from the north and displayed it at every dance held by the band until the fatal day at Wounded Knee.

The Arapahos used a befeathered hoop decorated with two crosses and two thunderbirds in the Sun Dance. The hoop represented the four directions, and the four old men, or deities, were represented by humans who were addressed in the ceremony. The game using the wheel had nearly become obsolete but was born again for the dances. A great many songs founded on trance visions refer to the game, and the wheel and sticks were made by the dreamer and carried in the dance as they sang.[5]

The hand-game doctrine, said Lesser, was based on stored images of a past way of life. In their visions, dancers saw the old people bustling about in the awakenings of spring. With the first clap of thunder came the opening of the bundles and the reciting of the creation ritual (Thunder Ritual of the Evening Star bundle). The men and women made ready for war, patching old moccasins and garments and making new ones. They began playing games as the war societies performed their dances, then the men went off to war.

In the Great Plains, gambling and making war were parallel, and each had a dualistic property in the constant shifts between victory and defeat. Conceived of as a warpath and dramatized as such, the hand game was played as a challenge game between boys, between Pawnee bands, and against other tribes. Tribes would enter the camps of the others, announcing, "We've come on the warpath for the hand game." Other war-party metaphors in the old game included animal imitations by players, the dramatization of concealing the trail of the warriors, dramatization of seeking the trail of an enemy, and the counting of coup by the winners. Rituals included a war-pipe ceremony, burning a long fire, orientation of players determined by how the war party entered the camp, and the dancing of war-society dances and songs. These elements of the hand game faded as the occupations of hunting and war turned to politics, cultural survival, and peace. The long fire became round, the pipe was smoked on behalf of everyone present, and war songs became Ghost Dance songs.

In the new hand-game ritual, players and spectators sided with either the eagles or crows. This is one element of the old hand game that carried over to the new, but the idea also carried over from the Ghost Dance proper. At the suggestion of the Arapaho prophet, the Arapahos and Wichitas selected a panel of singers, called the Seven Brothers, who danced inside the revolving circle of ghost dancers, entrancing them with feathers so that they could see their dead relatives in the other world. People began to feel an affinity for the bird of the particular feathers that caused their visions. Crows were supposedly able to find everything they were looking for, and those under the influence of the crow had the ability to read minds. Eagles flew high, could see all, and could find things; in a sense, they were omnipresent like the sun. When White brought the Ghost Dance to the southern bands of the Pawnees, he organized the Seven Brothers of the Crow. Of the four Pawnee bands, the only one that did not completely buy into White's doctrine were the Skiri Pawnees, who toward the end of White's tenure organized the Seven Brothers of the Eagle. These affinities held over to the Ghost Dance hand game.

The Pawnees attempted to reconcile the dual forces on earth and in the heavens. The ancestral ceremonial circuit of the dance represented the perceived movement of the stars around the North Star, which dictates that everything on earth must move synchronously with it.[6] In the sacred bundle rituals, the female western powers were dominated by

Evening Star, and the male eastern powers were dominated by Morning Star. The relationship between the two defined earth; the space
between the central fireplace and the western altar became a sacred
pathway which could not be crossed anywhere but at the ends. Thus,
dancing was conducted in a large circle moving clockwise.

The heavy star symbolism and orientation is evident in the following
gaming myth about the origin of the dice basket and twelve dice. The basket represents the moon and the dice the twelve stars, as well as earth and
its contents.[7] The myth is reminiscent of others explored in this section.
During the creation, the gods make a boy and girl out of mud. They give
the boy a bow and arrow and tell him to shoot a (buffalo) cow at random
in the dark to determine the division between night and day. He shoots
a spotted cow, hence the light and dark would be approximately equal.

Then, the boy and girl hear people singing in a lodge. Moon Woman
invites them in. Four old men daubed in red clay sing at the altar (presumably in the west). They are Wind, Lightning, Thunder, and Clouds.
Moon's many children, all girls, are present. The boy and girl are taught
many songs, dances, and games, and afterward they are given the basket game.[8]

The dancing in the myth comprises many intricate movements, only
summarized here, which seem to serve as a model for the dancing and
the gaming circuits described later. Evening Star, the female god of
storms, dances in the west in front of the four men, holding the basket
representing the moon and giving them permission to create. The four
men are also dancing. Four other women stars dance in a line in the
east and move west. They are the daughters of the Big Black Meteoritic
Star who stands in the northeast heavens and who in time gives bundles to the medicine men. They each dump two swan necks and two
fawn skins into the baskets. Basket Woman (Moon) gives her permission to the gods to make the earth (basket) out of willow, water, and
mud, so that the earth will be filled with timber. Big Black Meteoritic
Star puts everything into the earth for mankind's power.

The girl (now called a woman) is told to gather plum seeds and mark
them with stars.[9] The basket is to remind them that *Tirawahat* (the creator) sent the stars in the basket to prepare the boy and girl for earth.
The twelve sticks represent the twelve stars in a circle above the heav-

ens who sit as chiefs in council. By moving the sticks, they count, and when done, they win the game. When the stars are finished with their teaching, they ride the basket back to the heavens. The final line of the story discusses Spider Woman's role. She helps Big Black Meteoritic Star anoint the medicine men to cure and do mysteries. She sits in the south-west corner of the lodge, and the people in the south call her sister, while the people in the north call her wife. In other myths, she is referred to as a witch and is a bad gambler. In Pueblo myths, Spider Woman is the creator, and she often helps the divine twin gamblers in their task.

The new hand game was also played in a circle, as portrayed by the circle of people in the sky that Joe Carrion witnessed in his first game vision. The northern and southern horizons were divided by an east-west midline, whether the game was played in a properly oriented tepee or outside. (Formerly, some Pawnees had society earthlodges oriented on the east-west axis from each other.) In Pawnee latitudes, the sun always travels in the south, and therefore bright colors (red, yellow, white) were associated with the south side, and dark colors (black, green, blue) with the north. The crow was associated with the north, but eagle feathers had different shades and could be attached to either side, depending on the vision mandates of the variant forms of the game.

Two opposing teams formed two halves of a circle, with the head end situated at the west marked by an altar. The number of players on each side was unimportant, and equal numbers weren't required. A leader from each group sat at the altar and served as tallymen. They were sandwiched by two assistants chosen because they possessed great luck. The contents of the game bundles were displayed on the altar. The kit held the game's tally sticks and counters, marked by the colors, feath-ers, and bird icons attached to one or the other team. The ceremonial peace pipe, a horn spoon for the food offering, a drum decorated with stars, animal and bird skins, hair ornaments worn by the participants as crow or eagle insignia, and other bundle contents were spread sym-metrically on the altar alongside the game instruments.

The Ghost Dance hand game was based on the old game, but with many variations determined by visions and the symbolism of the old bundle rituals.[10] The tallymen kept score on counting sticks and selected the player to do the guessing on their side. To put the game into play,

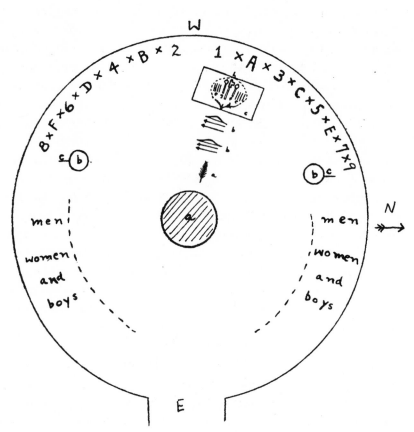

Layout of one Pawnee Ghost Dance hand game played inside a tepee. The central cir-cle marked "a" is the fireplace, and the two smaller circles marked "b" are the major drums with their accompanying drummers, "c." Tally sticks and black rattles flank the pipe laying on an eagle skin on the rectangular altar. The feather beneath the two sets of bows and arrows also belongs to the eagle. Number 1 is Emmett Pierson I, the artist of this plan and an Eagle player. White, apparently the Pawnee Ghost Dance prophet, is Number 2 and also an Eagle. The rest of the even numbers on the left are Eagles, while the odd numbers on the right are Crows. The alternating "x's" are "men." The remain-ing letters mark the positions of the following dance society altars: A—Horn Dance; B—Old War Dance; C—Young Dog Dance; D—Crazy Dog Dance; E—Roached Heads; F—Big Horses. (after Lesser, 1978)

the two guessers rose and faced each other on their side of the midline, each with one counter. The guesser of the host side put his hands behind his back (or under her skirt, if a woman)[11] to conceal the counter in one hand or the other, then brought both clenched hands forward, moving them in rhythm while his opponent guessed the counter's location. Whatever the outcome, the first guesser then hid his counter for the other to guess. The object was for one side or the other to eventually win both counters. The winner took these two counters to two players sitting next to each other on his side. They concealed the counters in one or two of their four hands, moving rhythmically. The opposing guesser came across the arena to guess the location. Certain hand gestures were used to indicate which hands might be concealing the counters. If the guesser successfully guessed the proper hands for both counters, he won them for his side. No points were scored. If he missed altogether, the concealers won two points recorded by the tally sticks. The same two concealers tried their luck again. If the guesser won only one counter, the concealers won one point, and only the successful concealer tried to fool the guesser again. This went on until the guesser won both counters, and took them to two concealers on his side to begin another round. Scoring for the game could be mathematically challenging, and also involved ritualistic hand gestures.

The hand game, whether in the old form or the new, was never ended by merely winning a game. Lesser compared it to a "rubber" in bridge. In the old game, such rubber games were played until all the wagers were exhausted. In the Ghost Dance game, the event was over when seven games had been finished, regardless of who won or lost. In the old game, based on economic gain, concealers and guessers were selected by virtue of their luck. In the new games the routine was formalized and the concealers played in order, usually clockwise from west to east and back in the traditional Pawnee ceremonial circuit.

In the old game, the visiting war party performed the preliminaries: smoking the pipe to the deities in their respective corners of the universe, placing the bets, selecting the guessers, and dancing the war dances. In the Ghost Dance hand game, the host team performed the opening dances and rituals. Special attention was placed on altar arrangements and displaying the bundles and in the detail of the pipe smoke offering.

Three or four Ghost Dance songs, borrowed at first from the Wichitas and Arapahos, were performed during the intervals of the game. The singer of the team currently winning began the dance in the west and led the large circle of dancers, side-stepping in a clockwise direction, until he or she returned to the starting point. The leader of the winning team meanwhile danced north from the center holding the gaming objects in the air. Then the losing team performed the same ritual. The intervals ended with a ritualized changing of the guessers or concealers to musical accompaniment. The war drum, carried over from the old hand game, was decorated to take on the new meaning. In games associated with particular societies of a band, the songs came from those societies. A final Ghost Dance followed the end of the games, along with society songs, speeches, an elaborate food offering, and a feast.

Trances were part of the Ghost Dance intervals of the hand game ritual in the beginning, but the practice faded as visions were no longer necessary to develop the ceremony. What was important were the intermissions for playing, dancing, and feasting with kin and tribal associates. The people had embraced ghost-dancing because it had filled a void. Not only were dancing and playing games reinforced as a group activity, but the people could also dance and play alongside the imagined dead ones doing the same thing in the other world.

The new gaming ritual did not involve material betting, although the atmosphere of gambling with fate remained. As Lesser pointed out, gambling luck was considered a quality of the divine world. Winning had always meant that the gods were on one's side, whether in war or in returning to the dead relatives. Being assured of possessing good luck was essential to surviving in a precarious world, and winning meant that unforeseen luck and ultimate benefits were available. In Ghost Dance times, luck seemed to be against the Indians. The Ghost Dance hand game doctrine promised luck in the hereafter. One still needed the luck of visions as well as to be assured that one would be saved when the great destruction came, and that one was in touch with the controlling influences of the spirit world.

In early games, men imitated animals as they played, believing that the animals also played (as we have seen in the countless animal gambler myths). When one encountered the birds while in a trance, one became associated with them. In the hand game ritual, one played as a crow or eagle to find out which was luckier. Losing, of course, was devastating. Winning was a sign of greater spiritual gain, but to lose was to sin and to believe that one could not be saved. Players, incidentally, gambled to see who would have to rise early the next day to begin the dancing and to supply and cook the food.

The Resurrection in Bundle Ceremonies and Myths

White, the Pawnee Ghost Dance prophet, had started the trend of mixing the Ghost Dance with ancient tribal ceremonies. He began simply, gradually adding paint, feathers, songs, animal symbolism, and complex rituals as he went along. He had mixed the revisionist dance with all of the ancient symbolism that could be recalled. White resurrected the old Pawnee creator Tirawahat, and the Sun, Moon, Evening and Morning Star (sometimes called Mother Born Again), and the pipe-smoking ceremonies made to them. He was supposedly responsible for reintroducing the ancient attention paid to sky coordinates and cardinal directions.

Back before things began to go so drastically wrong for the Pawnees, they had possessed a highly developed religion. The sophisticated priesthood, who may have been influenced by ancient Mexican civilizations early on, taught that all energy was derived from the stars and constellations. The chief of each village received instructions from a celestial body, whose sacred bundles he held. In the new Ghost Dance—and the subsequent game—the old mythology was mixed with Christianity, according to Lesser. Christ was the child of the Father in Heaven. He was chief of the western sky and protector of the dead who lived there. He did not usurp Evening Star and her priests, but fused with them.

The crucifixion of Jesus was reminiscent of the human sacrifice to Morning Star. The Morning Star bundle of the Skiri Pawnees involved a sacrifice of a captive maiden who died thonged to a scaffold. The cross had always been used by the Pawnees as a symbol of the star, and it was natural to conceive of the cross as such a reference to Christ. The idea of the west being the place of the dead was evident in many of the gambler myths already discussed. In the Southeast, gamblers, good and bad, "went west" at the end of the story. The sun in the myth of the

Thompson Indians of the Plateau took dead people to his home in the west to eat them.

Lesser drew much of his material on the old bundle rituals and symbolism from *Ceremonies of the Pawnee* by James Murie, an educated Pawnee. In 1910 Murie had been given a grant by the BAE to document the former religion of his tribe, much of which was "no longer viable," relying almost totally on the recall of Murie's informants. The manuscript would not be published for seven more decades, but Lesser had access to the manuscript when he researched the Ghost Dance hand game during the 1930s. Murie's work began well after the Pawnees had moved several times, finally from Nebraska to Oklahoma, where the culture no longer initiated buffalo hunts, warpaths, or, no doubt, human sacrifice. The warpath and buffalo-hunting metaphors of the original bundle rituals, which Lesser said were no longer in use, were still evident in Murie's work. Ghost Dance references were absent from *Ceremonies of the Pawnee*, but that may be because of the emphasis placed on the lost religion and the federal prohibition against practicing the new rituals. Lesser did not give great attention to how each specific bundle ceremony was transformed into a hand-game bundle ritual, although he did make some generalizations. Considered alongside George Dorsey's survey of myths in *The Pawnee*, Murie's and Lesser's works help us to piece together a mythic/ritual pattern among the Pawnees.

Murie mentioned, sparingly, the role of games and game paraphernalia in the ceremonies, but not in the enormous detail Lesser reported. The complex rituals were many days long and will not be addressed here, except where it pertains to games and gambling. The bundle ceremony of the Human Sacrifice to Morning Star had some reference to gambling.[12] Murie supplied a rambling Pawnee narrative outlining the beliefs behind the ritual. It is something of a creation myth and contained gambling stick symbolism which had to do with creation, death, and rebirth themes of the Ghost Dance. The myth, similar to the Origin of Basket Dice myth discussed earlier, is summarized as follows.

Tirawahat placed the stars into the heavens and gave each the power to watch over people. (The common stars were once people.) Morning Star had to overcome Evening Star in order to create the earth. People were placed on the earth, and each star gave a bundle to the various bands. All required a sacrifice of scalp or buffalo tongue or heart, but Morning Star required a human sacrifice from the original race, the stars. A girl was sent down from heaven via a rainstorm. From this girl came a great people who were to leave their first grass lodge. At the time of the flood there were four animals who touched the heavens. A turtle came from the north, and the animals climbed onto its back, but as the waters rose, they slipped off to the cardinal directions.

In the Sacrifice to Morning Star ceremony a man handled the counting sticks from the bundle and kept tally of the songs as they were sung. This was spoken of as gambling with the Morning Star. When all the sticks were sung over to the people's side, the people "won" and could go on with the sacrifice. The sticks were symbolic of one's life struggle as one wrested his or her life from the gods in heaven, Murie summarized. Gamblers also wrested their achievements from the unlucky powers. In the ceremony, the idea was that they were winning from the gods by singing the counting sticks over to the people's side. The set of sticks were kept in the Morning Star bundle for this purpose. No other bundle had them. Perhaps the Morning Star bundle, plus the bundles described in the following paragraphs, were the ones that were displayed on the altar of the Ghost Dance hand game, as Lesser described.

The Creation Ritual bundle belonging to the Kitkahahki Pawnee division also contained gaming implements among its buffalo and warpath objects, including a buckskin bag containing plum-seed dice and a bundle of counting sticks for the same, one miniature game wheel and stick for same, and six sticks wrapped in buffalo skin.[13] This bundle was the keeper of all games, said Murie. The ring (hoop) represented the horizon and the stations of different gods. The white bead (probably suspended in the hoop) represented Tirawahat, as well as the fireplace in the lodge where Tirawahat sat with great power. The ring and two sticks constituted a game played by old learned men who counted into the hundreds. This is how the young men learned to count.

The Pitahawirata division of the Pawnees had two villages: Pitahawirata proper and Kawarakis. The bundle from the latter is the mother from which sprang most of the other bundles.[14] It contained objects suggesting the history of cultural inventions, including a flint knife, a baby board with a Big Star icon, and a (corn) grinding stone obtained from Woman Count Coup on Enemy with Goods. A bunch of sticks for the woman's stick game and a stone wrapped in skin were also included in the bundle. The women threw the sticks on the stone used for pounding corn for other bundle ceremonies, and the count depended upon the way the sticks landed. "When a victorious war party returned and the victory dances were held, the priests allowed the women to play the stick game," said Murie. This type of stick dice, with varying symbolism, occurred elsewhere, especially among the Apaches, Navajos, and Pueblos of the Southwest.

A formal gaming myth was told on the third day of the White Beaver Ceremony of the Chawi, a southern Pawnee band.[15] The thirty-day ceremony was conducted in the spring to revive hibernating animals, particularly those living in the waters. It is a further example of how the gambler myths coincide with rejuvenation themes. Naturally, this was a song of the War Chief, for rites of spring, war, gambling, and buffalo hunting are not mutually exclusive.

When the Pawnee lived on the banks of the Platte River, all the games belonged to a woman thought to be a witch, and in order to play they had to travel to her mud lodge. The middle-aged men especially liked to play hoop and pole.[16] One man noticed that one time when a stick hit the ring, it ran off into the weeds like a woman. When it stopped and stood on end, the man saw a beautiful woman standing in its place. The other players only saw the balanced ring and considered it an omen that some of their members would be killed by enemies or die of a sickness.

Later, the ring woman materialized to the perceptive one in a dream, instructing him to make a ring out of the vulva and hide of a buffalo cow.[17] He was to wear the ring always on his arm; embodied in the ring, the woman would help fight the enemy and take their ponies. The weed that had concealed the ring during play was also a woman who taught the perceptive one to use the weed medicine to help women in labor. He later used the weed and the ring as directed and was rewarded. He became a doctor and made up songs about the ring game and women.

The witch woman in the preceding story was most likely Spider Woman, who is associated with the game of hoop and pole, closely tied to killing buffalo. In another story, Blood-clot Boy bends an ash twig into a ring and winds it with a string made of boiled buffalo hide so that it looks like a spider's web, as hoops of many different tribes do.[18] The grandmother (presumably Spider Woman) rolls the ring, and the boy shoots it with arrows and kills buffalo. Dorsey said the spiderweb ring referred to the belief that the Spider Woman controlled the buffalo and produced them from her web.

Spider Woman and buffalo appeared in quite a number of gaming and gambler myths recorded by Dorsey. None of the myths mentioned the Ghost Dance or its hand game, although Dorsey's book was published in 1906, well after the movement had been established (in 1893, or so). Perhaps this was not enough time for the gambling myths to be affected by the new gaming ritual. The purpose of the myths was most likely to store the traditional beliefs in cultural memory. Lesser said that the only part of the old culture the Pawnees could put to use was that which had been public and could be remembered. It's almost as if the gaming myths are material objects of the sacred bundles, the mythological appendices of the gaming instruments. Or perhaps the impact of the Ghost Dance hand game was not as great as Lesser purported.

The buffalo was a central figure in Joe Carrion's vision that mandated the hand game be included in the Ghost Dance. The animal played an important role in the former ceremonies and myths associated with the renewal of spring. If the myths were recited during ceremonies and games such as the hoop and pole designed to call the buffalo, then it would stand to reason that the ceremonies would merge with the Ghost Dance and hand game devised to bring the herds back to the Plains at the end of the world. In this sense, although the original bundle rituals were altered, the buffalo and associated gaming symbols were still valid, and the myths that could be recalled still provided usefulness. The myths did not have to reflect the updated Ghost Dance hand game rituals, but served as a lexicon for the old ways and a beacon for their return.

A Pitahauirat Pawnee medicine man told George Dorsey that a set of gaming sticks formed part of their sacred bundle and that the playing of the game brought the buffalo nearer to the village. It was believed that the relating of this story, which describes a successful buffalo hunt, would inform the buffalo spirits that they were talking about them and so they would come and allow the people to slaughter them.[19] In a version of the same story told by White Eagle, owner of the "left-hand"

and "skull" bundles, Tirawahat gives the game of ring and sticks to the people after he places them on earth.[20] The morning after they play their first game, they see unusual marks on the playing field. One of the young players meets a young woman on the opposite end of the field and mates with her. She gives birth to a buffalo calf. Shortly afterward, a bird leads the man to a buffalo herd belonging to the young woman and her calf. The herd challenges him to identify his wife and calf, and he does so. He tells his people the buffalo will come to them in four days. They play the game and thank Tirawahat for the game and buffalo.

Coyote comes into play in several of the buffalo motif gaming myths. In one, Coyote swings a girl from a strap tied in a tree, and when the buffalo come, she turns into a ring.[21] In another, Coyote rescues a maiden who has been abducted by the buffalo bull javelins and transforms her into a ring.[22]

The Arapaho, among others, also had a cycle of stories treating the buffalo and the hoop and pole game.[23] Spring-Boy is blown away by a terrific wind and is found by an old woman, who names him Found-in-Grass. He induces her to make him a bow and arrow set and a netted wheel. She complies. One morning, he gives his netted wheel to his grandmother and directs her to roll it toward him while envisioning a buffalo cow. The cow appears and is shot with arrows.

The Pawnees also had their gambling brothers and although these myths are laced with the buffalo, the plot elements are typical of other myths dealing with the duality theme. In this myth the older brother is associated with yellow paint, cougar quiver, black arrows, and a dark red bow, while the younger brother is more quiet and wonderful.[24] The men of the village lose their lives to the gambler living in the east and are eaten by his wife, Spider Woman. Older Brother also loses his life to the gambler because the human-eye soup fed to him drains his power. Spider Woman dances around as his head is chopped off and placed in the lodge.

Younger Brother comes to the village to rescue his brother and is warned not to eat the soup.[25] He accepts the gambler's invitation to play sticks but only after he has been asked four times on as many days. Younger Brother goes to a buffalo slaughtering place and beseeches the skeletons for game sticks. Buffalo come from all directions and stamp on the graveyard. A stick appears from the bones of the strongest bull and instructs the youth in burning its tip black. The same process brings another stick from the bones of the youngest bull. The young bull has not yet mated, so the stick made from his bones would be unsuccessful in chasing the ring. This would be the gambler's stick. A ring was produced by the same process from a cow. The ring says, "This is the way I will chase your stick." She turns into a ring, rolls and falls on the black stick. Old Bull tells Younger Brother to hang the sticks on the north side of the lodge and retrieve them after he breaks the gambler's set.

As they play, the boy loses until lives are wagered. He breaks the sticks, and Gambler sends Coyote for a new set in the lodge. Coyote hears buffalo stampeding, which causes him to fail the task despite the number of times Gambler sends him back inside. Black Bird is sent in, and when he hears the stampede, he flies on the backs of the buffalo and gets the sticks. Upon wagering the lives of Younger Brother's people, Gambler chooses the weak stick and fails to hook the hoop. Younger Brother wins with the aid of his strong bull sticks. Gambler protests, but the people defeat him with the sticks, and then throw the sticks and ring, which turn into buffalo and run away. Gambler, Spider Woman, and Coyote die.

Several versions of this myth were recorded by Dorsey.[26] In one, Gambler got his sticks from Witch Woman. He loses power because his ring is stolen by a buffalo said to have been aided by a traitor. In another version, the brothers dress alike. Younger Brother obtains the magical gaming equipment by praying to the skulls on the prairie. They become live animals—a strong young bull and a cow rolling in the dirt. The chances of success are greater in this myth because the javelin and ring represent the two sexes coming together.[27]

Not all Spider Woman stories involve the hoop and pole buffalo. In a surrealistic story, Spider Woman is the bad gambler and wins by calling storms and freezing the players.[28] She has several daughters, and her game is dice. Older and Younger Brother live in the next village, and hearing of Spider Woman, they set out to defeat her. One of Spider Woman's daughters warns the brothers that her mother is a cannibal and not to eat any of the eyes or flesh she offers. Like the Caterpillar and other insect gamblers mentioned previously, Spider Woman collects heads like trophies in her lodge. The brothers do eat her food but a root eaten previously helps them to regurgitate the power-draining effects. Accepting her invitation to play the basket game, the boys rub their bodies and faces with white clay and paint white streaks down from their eyes. From what I can make out, the game involves the people jumping like grasshoppers as if they are the dice, and they fall off a cliff to their death during the storm. When Spider Woman calls the storm, the brothers turn into larks. She wagers her daughters, but the boys decline. They continue playing the game in this manner, and despite the worsening blizzard, the boys escape like snowbirds. Then the weather switches and becomes too hot for Spider Woman. A swarm of grasshoppers lift her and fly her to the moon. The grasshoppers fly on to the sun, and that's why we see them flying around the sun in summer.[29] Such are the severe conditions of the Great Plains.

The role of Grandmother Spider is reversed in the Southwest, where she is not the destroyer, but the creator. Even so, much of the symbolism in the Pawnee gambler myths and games has analogues in the religion and myths of the Southwestern Pueblos and Navajos, where the gambler is strongly associated with the moon and sun. The Pawnees used the symbolism described in the myths to transform their warring and hunting culture to a sort of death cult in response to the devastating effects of history; the Pueblos and Navajos extracted certain symbolic elements of a violent history and stored them in the myths.

In the next chapter, we will explore how the gambler myths of the Southwest became intertwined with a history and a prehistory beginning around fifteen hundred years ago. We will also see evidence of how the Mexican cultures, particularly the Mayas and Aztecs, complete with their own gambling myths, directly influenced the religion and culture of the Southwest. A word of caution when venturing into the mires of that high-desert and mountainous region: Spider Woman's web of creation is entrapping, for the strings of myth and history, which stretch across whole continents, overlap in myriad and intractable ways.

FOUR

The Great Gambler:
A Navajo Legend in
Pre-Columbian Archaeology
of the Southwest and Mexico

*He shot into the sky. He stopped halfway and said, "For a long time my
thoughts have been at the earth's heart." Again he stopped. "Always my
thoughts will come back to the center of the earth," he said again. He
stopped the third time and said, "My thought will come back to the center
of the world, it may be for good, it may be for evil." When he stopped the
fourth time he said, "Adios."*

—Parting words of the Great Gambler
as recorded by Earl Pliny Goddard,
"The Emergence," *Navajo Texts* [1933]

It ended . . .
With his body changed to light,
A star that burns forever in the sky.
—The Flight of the *Quetzalcóatl*, anonymous Aztec poem

The Emergence of the Gambler at Chaco Canyon

Native stories of the Southwest usually begin with the land-
scape, and the Chaco region is particularly dramatic. Eighty
million years of geodynamics forged the rust and buff-colored
spires and chasms that characterize the San Juan Basin of northwest-
ern New Mexico. Shorelines ebbed and flowed; volcanoes erupted
intermittently; coal, shale, sandstone, and ash stratified in alternating
layers. Landmass tilted upward and surrendered to eroding forces; its
sediment accumulated at the bottom of the basin on the crest of muddy
floodwater, cutting deeper and wider swaths as it drained. Receding

waters carved ghostly hoodoos out of the rock on the plano and left lone bluffs sailing across seas of sagebrush. Such was the vitality of this arid cradle of gambler legends.

The Navajos say they ascended from a flooding underworld into this world through a hole in the ground.[1] They emerged in a lake on an island bounded by high cliffs and sprawling plains. Blue Body threw stones toward the four cardinal directions so that the water could drain away. While they waited for the ground to dry in order to walk to the mainland, the women erected a shelter of deerskin on four poles and beneath it played a game of three sticks, or *tsidĭ*, one of four games they brought with them from the underworld. Similar dice games have since been traditionally played on a circuit symbolizing the emergence and the shape of the world.

The people also sought to divine their fate by throwing a hand-scraper into the water. "If it floats, we will survive; sinks, we will perish," they said. The scraper floated, and the people rejoiced. But Coyote threw a stone into the water with the same provisions and, of course, the stone sunk and the people became mortal. Coyote's mischiefs caused the Navajos and Pueblos to separate over a dispute involving corn. The Pueblos adopted the lifestyle of living in stone houses while the Navajos lived in hide-and-pole housing.

First Man and First Woman then created the seven sacred mountains that formed the borders of their world and hung the sun and moon. The diurnal and nocturnal animals played *Kêsitcè*, the moccasin game they brought with them from the underworld, to determine the division between the light and dark parts of the day. Of course, Coyote, being a creature of both night and day, did his best to spoil the game by constantly trading sides. The sun rose right in the middle of a round, and so it was decided that night and day would alternate.[2]

The people then moved four times every thirteen years to escape monsters, finally coming to a place called Chaco Canyon where they witnessed the Pueblos building a gaming temple for a gambler god named Noqoìlpi.[3] Not only had Noqoìlpi systematically won all the people and their riches, but he had also stolen the turquoise earrings from the Sun. Desiring the return of his turquoise, Sun asked Talking God (Hastéyalti) to enlist a Navajo husband to retrieve them. The young hero defeated Noqoìlpi in a number of games with the help of a menagerie of supernatural animals[4] and then shot him into the sky. There, Noqoìlpi encountered a deity named *Begochídí*, the Carrier of the Moon, who outfitted him with his own race of people and a new animal called a horse, before setting him back down on the earth. Noqoìlpi established a number of villages along the Rio Grande in New Mexico before returning to Old Mexico to become God of the Mexicans.

The archaeological record tells us that Chaco Canyon, a single gully in the San Juan Basin, began attracting big-game hunters ten thousand years ago. The returning groups over the millennia sought out the local caves, which they gradually enclosed with rock for better shelter. Maize imported from the Valley of Mexico allowed them to develop a tiny garden subsistence over time, and slowly they moved into circular dugouts covered with straw and mud. Extreme temperatures, dust, wind, and estranged rainfall were the conditions under which the aboriginal people existed in the remote bone-bleached drainage. They took their time, another millennium, to learn how to turn their pithouses into apartment complexes. In their leisure they played games with decorative bone dice the size of thumbnails. It was at this glacial pace that the Chaco culture developed.

Like a new star bursting in the dark night, something in the middle of the eleventh century of the current era inspired the Chacoans to suddenly expand three modest apartment complexes into ziggurats of exaggerated proportions and to build six more over the next century.[5] To the floorplans of these "great houses" engineers added exceedingly large, round, underground chambers (great *kivas*)[6] and a multitude of roomblocks, all with consistent angles and orientations which marked solar and lunar cycles and the cardinal directions. Elaborate boulevards rolled out from the great houses toward distant cities, resources, shrines, or to nowhere in particular.

Pueblo Bonito in downtown Chaco Canyon served as the flagship great house; by the time it was completed, it contained thirty-three kivas and 530 rooms terracing up to five stories high. Its exquisite core veneer masonry was pieced together like a Moorish mosaic mural— only to be hidden by a coat of mud plaster. The contents of this great house revealed not only the greatest find of turquoise ever, but hundreds of bone and wooden gaming pieces. Eventually, 150 imitation Bonito houses could be found across the Colorado Plateau, and Chaco Canyon's cultural or economical system expanded to twenty-six thousand square miles in area.

And then, for reasons unknown, the meteoritic civilization burned out within a hundred years, and a major exodus from Chaco Canyon occurred around 1130 C.E. After 1250, the great houses essentially became ghost towns until the Navajos arrived several centuries later. They claimed the ruins as sacred property, remnants of a previous world where humans were larger than life and the buildings were built on a bet by a gambler god.

The original Chacoans vanished like rain down dusty arroyos, leaving their impressive masonry houses and most of their belongings behind. Some families followed the retreating border eastward and built new towns in the Jemez Mountains. Others continued on through the Rio Puerco Valley to the middle Rio Grande, while still others headed to the mesas and valleys near the preexisting villages of the Acomas and Zuñis in the south or the Hopis in the west. Like the fallout of Babel, the surviving Pueblos speak six different languages and belong to as many cultural groups.[7]

It would seem reasonable that the cultural memory of the Pueblos would include Chaco Canyon. But for a few isolated anecdotes, the Pueblos do not formally assign their mythologies to actual Anasazi sights, nor are they concerned with their own historical origin. The only history of significance to them is their mythical emergence from the underworld and the subsequent migration to their present locales. The premiere mythical settlement for the Keres Pueblos was a great white house called Kush Kutret, a paradise lost that had been occupied by people of Olympic virtue and fault who competed in games to settle disputes, to prove paternity, and to ceremonially shift the power from one season to another. It is conceivable that Kush Kutret is Pueblo Bonito.

Something compelled these dryland farmers, whom the Navajos call the Anasazi (ancient aliens), to erect oversized buildings and roads during an eighteen-year drought in such an exposed, out-of-the-way place. Archaeologists envision Pueblo Bonito as the seat of an empire, a ceremonial center, a food redistribution warehouse for a communistic system, a turquoise cottage industry, an astronomical observatory, a Toltec slaving outpost. The culture may have encompassed at least half of these explanations, but there is no inscribed stela, no Rosetta Stone to decode the Chaco phenomenon. What remains are the occasional sun, moon, and star images carved in rock—and a handful of legends.

* * *

Beginning more than a century ago, Chacoan archaeologists and historians of the Southwest became intrigued with Noqoìlpi, the quasi-historical, legendary, mythical gambler, and his possible connections with the Anasazi, in a vein similar to how classical scholars look to the legendary figures and events in Homer (c. 700 B.C.E.) for insights into the Mycenaean empire that ended 500 years earlier. Nineteenth-century scholars thought Agamemnon and the Trojan War to be pure fiction until Heinrich Schliemann discovered and excavated the actual sites of Mycenae and Troy beginning in 1870.[8] The Navajo Great Gambler, as he is most often referred to, was carefully preserved in numerous folktale journals and excavation reports. Some accept the anecdotes about him, though all agree that his existence would be difficult to prove. We can at least review the various accounts gathered by these and other scientists and match them against the archaeological record.

First, however, we must ask if it is reasonable to rely on Navajo accounts if they did not arrive in the Chaco Canyon area until several centuries after its abandonment. Despite the fact that the Navajos supposedly came from the Athabaskan area in Canada, their mythical place of emergence is near Huerfano Peak (*Dzil Ná'oodilii* or Turning Mountain), less than ten miles northeast of Chaco Canyon. Spaniards didn't record any sightings of the Navajos until a full century after they began exploring New Mexico themselves and, for that reason, scholars regard the early 1600s as the Navajo entry date. Archaeological surveys of Navajo settlements in and around Chaco Canyon date to the seventeenth century; most of the sites are refugee camps shared with the Pueblos during the 1680–92 revolt against the Spaniards.[9] The Navajos, though, were hunters and foragers who dragged their housing around with them and didn't put down roots until they took refuge from the Spaniards with the more house-conscious Pueblo farmers. For that reason, they may have tiptoed into the region much sooner than the records imply.

Race, language, and culture are independent variables, said Chaco archaeologist David Brugge.[10] Some Navajos don't even consider the Anasazi a foreign race.[11] They believe that pure Navajos once existed, but through time some joined with others for shelter, food, or protection while the remaining groups continued to lead a restless life. Even if the Navajos were present when the Anasazi were still viable, could they remember the events of a thousand years ago? The Navajos believe that a story can be passed down in that range of time in only twenty tellings if the tellings are from 70-year-olds to 20-year-olds.[12]

Most academic investigators agree, however, that a historical event or a real personage survives in popular memory for two or three centuries at most. Historical truths "are not concerned with personalities or events, but with forms of social and political life . . . in a word, with archetypes," said Mircea Eliade.[13] After two or three hundred years, the memory of historical events is modified in such a way that it can enter into the mold of archaic mentality which rejects what is specific and preserves what is representative. Popular memory "restores to the historical personage of modern times its meaning as imitator of the archetype and reproducer of archetype gestures." Since collective memory cannot possibly retain personality traits, an individual's personal qualities revert to archetypal qualities. The historical personage is associated with a mythical model such as a culture hero or twin, and likewise a historical event is categorized by such mythical models as a fight with a monster or a battle between enemy brothers.

Although we stated earlier that the Pueblos have no formal mythology about Chaco Canyon, the first telling of the gambler story to a white man did not come from a Navajo, but from a Jemez Pueblo governor named Hosta.[14] In 1877, Hosta led a geological surveyor, William Jackson, through Chaco Canyon.[15] Intrigued by the relative isolation and panoramic view of the great-house ruins on the canyon's north mesa, Jackson asked Hosta for an explanation. At first Hosta merely shrugged his shoulders, but a few days later he told Jackson a story about one man called El Capitan or El Jugador (the gambler) who "was above them all, not only in position but in strength and influence." Jackson was certain the explanation "was gotten up for the occasion" because "he [Hosta] did not wish to confess his ignorance." We will return to Hosta, for it is likely that gambler myths, culture hero cycles, and other relevant tales were liberally exchanged between the Jemez and the Navajos and stirred into one giant cauldron.

A frequent anomaly of the Navajo Great Gambler is that the story changes venue from one teller to the next, an important consideration for us since the great houses all have distinctive archaeology relative to the legend. Hosta had specified Pueblo Alto as being the home of the gambler, and this was echoed by a Navajo medicine man named Old Torlino.[16] From Alto, the richest "house" in the region, the "chief" could keep an eye on his own people, who lived below in the canyon's great houses. Confusingly, however, Torlino had told Washington Matthews that the gambler conducted his business at Kĭntyél, the home of the gambler in his 1889 version, which Matthews believed to be Chetro Ketl next door to Pueblo Bonito, although the ruin was not to gain scientific fame until the 1920s and 1930s.[17] It was never again cited as the setting for the gambler legend, except within a ceremonial chant called the Prostitution Way, which we will examine in the next chapter.

As the eighteenth century passed into the nineteenth, Navajo and American attention became riveted on Pueblo Bonito, the site of intensive archaeological and economic activity. And for awhile, Pueblo Bonito was the focal point of the Navajo legend. Richard Wetherill, a trader and amateur archaeologist, and George Pepper, an archaeologist, excavated the great house under the auspices of the Hyde Exploring Expedition for the American Natural History Museum in the summer of 1896. Wetherill and Pepper almost randomly chose the richest section of Pueblo Bonito to excavate. The dig produced fifty thousand pieces of turquoise, ten thousand pieces of pottery, five thousand stone implements, a thousand bone and wooden objects, countless items imported from Mexico, ninety-eight skeletons, and hundreds of wooden and bone gaming sticks and dice chips.[18] The rich find no doubt verified and enhanced the gambler story in the eyes of the Navajos who helped exhume it.

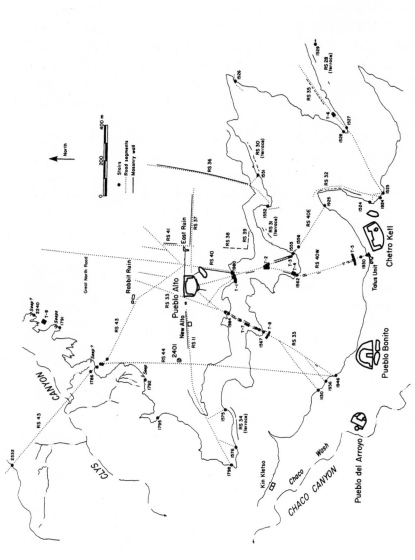

Pueblo Alto, Pueblo Bonito, and Chetro Ketl, the ruins of the prehistoric Anasazi (900–1130 C.E.) of Chaco Canyon in New Mexico, are the principal settings for the Navajo Great Gambler legend. Ancient roads linked Pueblo Alto, presumably the Gambler's House, to the Chaco communities in the canyon as well as within the greater Anasazi system. (Courtesy National Park Service)

Pueblo Bonito became a social and economic hub for hundreds of Navajos during the Wetherill tenure in Chaco Canyon (1896–1911). Wetherill employed the Navajos at fifty cents a week in the excavations and later leased sheep to them on shares. They pawned their own jewelry for canned goods, coffee, and supplies at the nearby Wetherill store. He organized one of the first Navajo blanket factories in the Southwest and shipped the weavings to New York and other cities in the East. Wetherill ironically sponsored a nine-day *yéibichai*, or Night Chant, to counteract Navajo contact with the dead while excavating the ruins.[19] Two hundred Navajos gathered on the last day of the ceremony for a variety of gambling games, rooster pulls, and horse and foot races. Perhaps they had in mind the major mission of the hero in the gambler legend: to win back the turquoise or shell jewelry for the deity through gambling.

Brugge points out that external economics and politics may have "doomed [Wetherill's] ambitions from the start, but for a few years Chaco again had its Great Gambler—an analogy that I do not doubt was made more than once by Navajo orators at local gatherings."[20] As if foreshadowed by the legend, Wetherill was murdered by a Navajo in 1910 for one of several unproven reasons: a cattle grazing dispute, self-defense against his alleged abuse, mistaken identity, or governmental conspiracy. Thus, Richard Wetherill became a legend in his own rite.

Navajo medicine men told Marietta Wetherill, Richard's wife, stories about the fat buffalo hunters who came from the north and east to gamble with the Anasazi at Pueblo Bonito.[21] They called them the Blue Cross people because of the design decorating their moccasins. These hunters were so successful at gambling that the Anasazi in their desperation traded off their wives and children to pay off their gambling debts. Although Marietta Wetherill does not mention the gambler in her own oral history, of all the myths, legends, and anecdotes told about Chaco Canyon, this may be closest to the truth.

Not surprisingly, Pueblo Bonito was the principle setting for gambling in a myth reported by Lulu Wade Wetherill, although it doesn't specify the home of *Noel-pee-ie*, the Winner.[22] Lulu (Louise) was the wife of John Wetherill, who helped his brother Richard establish the trading post at Pueblo Bonito before opening his own store at Kayenta, Arizona.

Lulu's version had been handed down through many generations of the Ushinnie (also spelled Ashiihnii) or Salt Clan (now extinct) and told to her by several of the oldest and most influential medicine men. In the story, the people of Chaco are controlled by a Pueblo-born gambler with a narcotic called blue gum.[23] After he wins the Chaco people, he steals the Sun's wife, a virgin imprisoned in a dark room in Pueblo Bonito. The world turns into eternal winter until she is restored. The story has strong Puebloan overtones and is reflective of the agrarian lifestyle of the Anasazi, who tracked the sun's movements with solstice markers built into their architecture.

Neil Judd, archaeologist for the Smithsonian Institution, resumed excavation of Pueblo Bonito in 1921, and though his work produced much scientific data toward understanding the ancient people, the dig itself did not visually compare to the Wetherill/Pepper dig. Judd personally discovered a necklace containing twenty-five-hundred turquoise beads, but little else of impact on the native employees and the gambler legend, except perhaps the sixteen bone dice and three game counters he also found.

In 1927, Judd skeptically recorded a version of the gambler legend from Hosteen Beyal, "described as one of the oldest Navajos on the eastern part of the reservation [about 95], totally blind, but possessed of an unusually keen memory."[24] In this version, the gambler's house is Pueblo Alto, although the people lived in Pueblo Bonito. The hero is born to a grossly ridiculed old woman who lives somewhere near "Shorty Widow's" store, eleven miles north of the canyon. He becomes a good hunter, and at age four he learns of the gambler (Noqoìlpi) and wants to kill him. His mother discourages this since he and Noqoìlpi are brothers, their father an undisclosed supernatural. But the boy learns the gambling games in secret and then wagers twelve women from as many clans against twelve of the gambler's slaves in a game and wins. By doubling the stakes during twelve more games, he eventually wins back all the people. After being defeated, Noqoìlpi rises like a bird and disappears into the sky. The people are released, and they scatter to the four directions.

A contemporary of Beyal's, the "gentle, kindly Padilla," upon hearing this rendition volunteered another story, passed to him by his uncle Manuelito, a famous Navajo chief. The story followed Hosteen Beyal's version except that the Navajos, Mescalero-Apaches, Utes, and Laguna Pueblos play against Noqoìlpi and strip him of his possessions.

Pueblo Alto: Actual Gaming Palace?

The spectacular finds unearthed at Pueblo Bonito may have enhanced its role in the gambler story, yet as archaeological research played out through the 1970s, speculation on the gambler's address shifted back to Pueblo Alto. Despite the early testimonies, Tom Windes, a principal archaeologist with the National Park Service (NPS) in Chaco Canyon, half-romantically speculated that Pueblo Alto, and not Pueblo Bonito, was the gambler's headquarters.[25] In a report on Pueblo Alto's excavation (1975–1979), he based his assumptions on previous publications of the myth and personal investigations and conversations with Navajos and other archaeologists.

Many local Navajos referred to Pueblo Alto as "*niyiilbiihi bighan*," or "home of the one that wins (you) by gambling" and they considered it the paramount village of the Anasazi. Several of the Navajos who

Some versions of the Navajo Great Gambler legend predicted the avalanche of Threatening Rock that finally crushed a quarter of Pueblo Bonito in 1941. (Photo by Patty Gabriel)

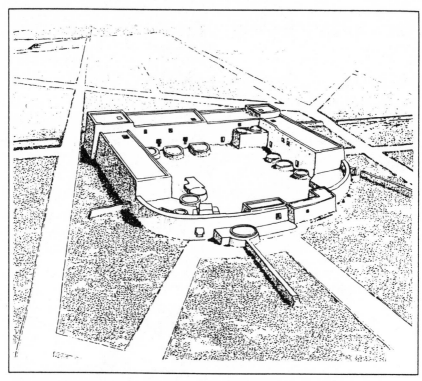

Artist's rendition of the Great Gambler's casino, Pueblo Alto. Legend says sentries in watchtowers along the road were able to alert the gambler of approaching marks. (Gabriel, 1991)

worked with Windes informed him that the Great Gambler gambled at Pueblo Alto but lived in nearby houses. Some stories suggest that he died in exile "where the cranes stand up," a place marked by a crane petroglyph on the south side of the De-Na-Zin Wash, about thirty kilometers northwest of Pueblo Alto. The large seeps located just west of Pueblo Alto in Cly's Canyon are referred to as Great Gambler's Spring.

It is surprising that Pueblo Alto became the primary site for the tale despite the impressive architecture and archaeological work at Pueblo Bonito and Chetro Ketl, said Windes. Pueblo Alto clearly dominates the canyon from its lofty position, but desert mounds reclaimed the great house, making it look insignificant compared to the majesty of the other more intact houses. Its ruined condition may have suggested greater age and thus importance to the Navajos, but there are literally hundreds of such mounds in the Four Corners region. Its physical appearance alone would not inspire such notoriety.

Once excavated with techniques far more sophisticated than had ever been used in the canyon, Pueblo Alto revealed some mysterious characteristics that could be explained by a gambler legend.[26] For one thing, only a hundred people lived in the great house at a time, as opposed to the originally estimated thousand or so. The great house was unusual in that it had no obligatory great kiva, dance floor, or small-house neighborhood surrounding it. Remote sensing techniques exposed a couple hundred miles of ancient roads (with a potential of 1,500 miles) linking as many as seventy outlying communities to the canyon. Pueblo Alto sat at the intersection of five of these roads connecting it to Pueblo Bonito and Chetro Ketl at the floor of the canyon, as well as to other outlying communities.

Archaeologists first thought that Chaco Canyon was the adminis-trative or political hub of an empire that thrived on a redistribution sys-tem. It seemed plausible that the roads would aid in transporting goods, connecting communities, and moving great numbers of people. One road stretching 50.5 kilometers due north from Pueblo Alto was not heavily traveled, and the unique shrines and structures along it suggest ceremonial use. But Windes noted that the roads may have served Pueblo Alto's economy and politics. As Old Torlino told George Pep-per, the "chief" stationed men in rude watchtowers along the peaks to signal the approach of fresh marks. Indeed, there is an interconnected network of shrines spaced at intervals along the canyon mesa tops in view of Pueblo Alto. It began to dawn on researchers that some group or individual was not redistributing the goods, but hoarding them and storing them at the various great houses. An extensive exchange net-work centered in Chaco Canyon with ramifications of wealth and power for a few is not dissimilar from that of a gambler who wins pos-sessions and control of others, Windes said. He added, "Despite the skepticism . . . there remain certain aspects of the [gambler] story that hint at prehistoric origins."

Pueblo Alto possessed other unusual characteristics, such as large rooms that were never lived in and smaller rooms that opened onto roads as if they were storage facilities for pedestrian offerings. The centrally located plaza or open commons area was not used for dancing as it is at currently occupied pueblos. This plaza was periodically resurfaced with clay rather than compacted by constant and rhythmical side-stepping feet.

In the context of the gambler legend, Pueblo Alto is an Anasazi-style Olympiad. Aileen O'Bryan's gambler version claimed several of the games were played inside the "gambler's house" (although it doesn't specify Pueblo Alto), including the first game ("seven sticks"); the third game ("that of the stick the shape of the rainbow"); and the fifth game ("the guessing game").[27] A number of the games described in the gambler legend are outdoor activities, such as pushing timber posts over end or throwing balls across lines, which may have been played on the clay plaza. A second plaza was located outside the building at the juncture of several roads, which may have served as race tracks.

In Gretchen Chapin's version of the Navajo legend, published several decades prior to the realized vastness of the roads, the gambler challenged opponents on tracks in Chaco Canyon.[28] In this version the Great Gambler has four race tracks: one up canyon, one down canyon, one to the north, and one through the gap to the south. Both the Animal People and the Holy People lose a race with Gambler. When Gambler finds out that the Holy People want to bet again, he suggests a game to take place on the north track.

Pueblo Alto's roads, with their cardinal alignments, may have had ceremonial significance in relationship to gaming. In the Maya *Popol Vuh*, the twins come to a crossroads on their journey to the underworld to play ball with the Lords of the Dead.[29] The four roads correspond with the lowland Maya color-directional scheme. The twins chose the Black Road, or the Road to *Xibalba* (underworld), which could either represent the sun's path as it sinks in the west or a black cleft in the Milky Way in conjunction with Venus. The game's rubber ball either symbolizes the sun or Venus. The idea is that the roads, the cardinal directions, the celestial events, and the Maya calendar all intertwine with the ball game and its mythology.

Certain facts make Pueblo Alto suspect as the gaming headquarters for the gambler. Relatively few gaming pieces, such as dice, were found in the area that was excavated.[30] Its lack of a great kiva and such items as copper bells, pyrite mirrors, and cloisonné jewelry means that it was probably not influenced by Mexico, the gambler origin in some stories and destination in most of the others. Furthermore, Pueblo Alto has no burials. Pueblo Bonito features all of these elements, which, as we shall see, speculatively points to an actual gambler, his official occupation, and the period in which he arrived in the canyon.

Pueblo Bonito and the Merchant of Tula

The twin Sierra Madre ranges bordering the Mexican Plateau ushered many a traveler to the perforated line of mountain ranges that cut through New Mexico. The landforms created a natural corridor connecting the Valley of Mexico to the Greater Southwest. The very route that gave the Spaniard entree into Pueblo country would have given the ancient trader the same access. Today highways and railways follow these royal roads.

Wildcat archaeologists have proposed that architectural plans for the Anasazi pithouses and later apartment complexes were traded up from Mesoamerica, possibly through the Hohokam, living in the low-lying regions of present day southern Arizona, and the Mogollon in the mountain areas of east central Arizona and southwestern New Mexico. All three cultures rose out of the gradual deceleration of nomadism as they found ways to cultivate the dry environment.

Chacoan scholars have pointed to the macaws, copper bells, roads, and certain architectural features such as kivas in Chaco Canyon as proof of an early and intermittent network between the Anasazi and Mexico.[31] Communities may have traded items through intermediary cultures or directly via an itinerant trader. The high cultures of Teotihuacán, Tula, and Maya are popularly thought to be the sources of this exchange system, but a myriad of smaller cultures most likely influenced Mexico's northern frontier directly or indirectly. One such group were the *Chalchihuites*, a more or less homogenous culture living in a broad area between the Mexican states of Jalisco, western Zacatecas, and northern Durango. Chalchihuites is taken from the Nahuatl word *chalchihuitl*, for green stone, jade, or turquoise.

Archaeologists J. Charles Kelly and Ellen Abbott Kelley introduced the controversial *pochteca* as the import/export mogul of Chaco.[32] The idea was based on the Aztec itinerant traders who probably postdated Chaco Anasazi, but the Aztecs built their society on what they knew of Toltecs families, possibly the innovators of the long-distance trading business. The Toltecs likely also influenced the Chalchihuites traders.

The Aztecs arranged their trades into something like guilds, which formed the economic base of society.[33] Each guild had its own district of the city appropriated to it, its own chief, tutelar deity, and festivals; the pochteca were one such guild. The Aztec merchant made his journeys to the remotest borders of Anahuac, and to the countries beyond, carrying with him merchandise of jewelry, slaves, and other valuable commodities. When he returned home, he reported to the monarch, who addressed him as "uncle." The pochteca's wealth and stature provided him with the essential advantages of hereditary aristocracy, including high-status burials.

Pepper and Wetherill uncovered such an elite burial at Pueblo Bonito, which archaeologist Jonathan Reyman believed to be of a pochteca.[34] A pochteca was usually buried with the symbols of his transactions and insignia, such as lip and nose plugs, earrings, shell trumpets, decorated canes, and the items he typically imported and exported. The mortuary suite at Pueblo Bonito, specifically Rooms 28, 33, 53, 56 (which interconnect) and nearby Room 38, contained such riches.[35]

Reyman contends that the twelve dismantled skeletons in Room 33 were sacrificed to attend the two intact skeletons, numbers 13 and 14, entombed beneath the floor planks. Skeleton 14 is the presumed pochteca, our possible Great Gambler. The riches accompanying these two men to their afterlife have never been seen north of the Mexican

---

Pueblo Bonito in Chaco Canyon—Mexican imports and local riches, a plethora of gaming pieces, and elite burials were found in the mortuary suite of rooms 28, 32, 33, 53, 56, and possibly 38. Skeleton 14, our potential gambler, was buried beneath Room 33. The large circles, like the one marked "A," are great kivas, supposedly another Mexican design element. Note the general "D" shape of the ruins and the long wall that nearly dissects the ruin in half. One artist believes it corresponds to a petroglyph depicting the bow and arrow. (Courtesy National Park Service)

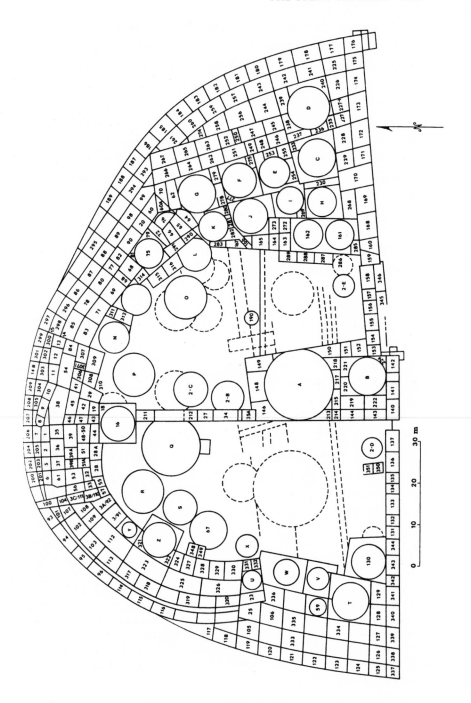

border. Skeleton 13 was accompanied by ten turquoise pendants and 5,890 beads, and Skeleton 14 with 698 pendants and 9,000 turquoise beads. A nearby cylindrical basket inlaid with turquoise contained more than 2,300 turquoise beads and pendants, and 3,317 shell beads and pendants. The wooden planks above the two bodies and the layers of yellow sand and wood ashes beneath the skeletons at the bottom of the burial pit suggest that the grave was specially prepared as one for pochteca personnel. Despite his station, Skeleton 14 died a violent death, as if he had fallen or was assassinated. His upper jaw was broken, his cranium crushed, and he received two holes and a gash in the frontal bone.

Germane to Reymen's pochteca theory are the more than three hundred "ceremonial" sticks stacked in the corner of Room 32.[36] The pochteca merchants were usually buried with similar canes that marked their status as members of their particular guild and rank. Wherever the

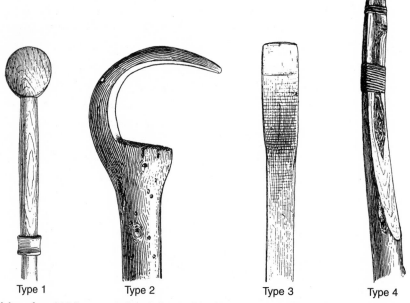

Type 1   Type 2   Type 3   Type 4

More than 300 "ceremonial sticks" were found in a mortuary suite at Pueblo Bonito in Chaco Canyon. One archaeologist said the Type 4 sticks may have been used in a Zuñi-style field hockey. But another archaeologist said they all belong to itinerant traders from Mexico who carried such symbols of power. Perhaps the sticks served both purposes. (Pepper, 1920)

freight-train camped, the canes were collected, bundled together, and placed at the head of the encampment to represent *Yacatecuhtli*, their patron of trade.[37] Silver and gold-headed canes remain the symbols of office among Pueblo governors today. Pepper, however, thought that a fourth of the canes were similar to the gaming sticks the Zuñi used in a ceremonial shinny game played to control the weather. For example, the victorious south clan brought rain, while wind responded to the winnings of the north clan.[38]

The great kivas, according to Kelley and Kelley, also represent contact by the Chalchihuites trader, and their appearance in Anasazi archaeology coincides with leaps in population and culture.[39] The most significant in terms of the gambler legend coincides with Chaco Canyon's classic period (1040–1120 C.E.) when the Anasazi began building their monolithic sandstone cities oriented toward the sun. These traders modeled the great kivas after the underground chambers in their Mexican villages and used them for the same purposes.[40] In Jalisco, for instance, employees sat in them and painted cloisonné ceramics on order for major local ceremonies, some that included human sacrifice. Kelley and Kelley said it is through the Chalchihuites that the kivas incorporated the *sipapu*, represented by an opening in the floor at the north end of the kiva. The sipapu is a Mesoamerican concept of the central place where the gods lived, or through which they emerged and departed. One deity associated with the sipapu is *Quetzalcóatl*, they said. The sipapu symbolizes the original place of emergence from the netherworld for both the Pueblos and Navajos. To the homesick Mexican traders, it may have served as a threshold to the past. Interestingly, the

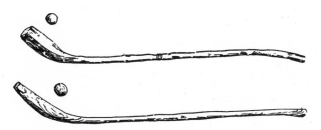

Compare the shinny sticks of the California Mono Indians to those shown in the figure to the left. (Culin, 1907)

Keresan Pueblo word for underworld, *shipap*, sounds like the Nahuatl word *Xibalba*, also meaning underworld, where the twins play ball with the rulers of death. We'll compare Maya gambling myths to those of the Southwest peoples in the next chapter.[41]

The Sun-Moon-Star-Hand Writing on the Wall

One of the ideas that genuinely came to the Southwest from Meso-america was the propensity to build city-temples on a cardinally aligned grid with special attention paid to solstices, equinoxes, and other celestial patterns. The Anasazi had most likely tracked the sun and moon for many centuries, as is evidenced by solar markers in and around Chaco Canyon and throughout the Southwest. They worked the choreography of the sun and moon into the buildings at the beginning of the Classical Period, about the same time they began building the strange Pueblo Alto and formalizing the great roads. This conjunction of events spotlights 1050 C.E.[42]

Recall that when the Great Gambler is defeated, he is shot into the sky to be with the sun or the moon, before being resurrected as the God of the Mexicans. The image of Noqoìlpi being catapulted to the white god Begochídí, Carrier of the Moon, near his adversary the dawning Sun, may have been an allusion to a real astronomical event.

On July 4, 1054 C.E. (Julian Calendar) the Sung Dynasty in China documented the violent explosion of the Guest Star in the Sung-Shih. This was the Crab Nebula in Taurus, the result of a supernova that occurred five thousand light years away. It was visible for twenty-three days during daylight, 653 days during the night, and shined six times brighter than Venus.

In the early 1950s, British astronomer Fred Hoyle said the Crab Nebula came into association with the waning crescent moon on July 5, 1054, just before sunrise.[43] He challenged scientists to search for petroglyphic recordings of the event by ancient Southwestern sky watchers. In 1972, a good specimen was discovered in Chaco Canyon by a University of New Mexico archaeological survey team.[44]

The prehistoric rock art in question is in a secluded alcove in the canyon's west wall. It is less than a half-mile from the mesa-top Peñasco

Blanco, one of Chaco's three original great houses, which took on astronomical orientations around 1050 C.E. Pecked into the top of a twenty-foot sandstone wall is a large sun symbol—a dot within two concentric circles. Painted on the rock ceiling above the petroglyph and slightly to the right is a reddish-brown crescent moon, star, and handprint. You can almost envision the scene: a dawning sun beneath the starburst and moon. The horns of the moon indicate it is waxing rather than waning, but astronomers consider the reversed moon an accident of recording and the optical illusion presented by the location of the pictograph.

Suppose the felling of the cruel ruler at his gambling house more or less corresponded with the celestial event. The drama in the skies coupled with the passion play on the ground just might inspire a sudden change in building code. When the Crab Nebula became visible just before dawn in the eastern sky near the waning moon and the summer solstice, it would have pronounced the murder official and the place

Some archaeoastronomers believe this sun-moon-star-hand pictograph in Chaco Canyon depicts the Crab Nebula, which was visible at dawn on July 5, 1054, in conjunction with the crescent moon. Others say this was a sun-watching station and Venus–crescent moon shrine. (Photo by the author)

sacred. Some of the pyramid cities in Mesoamerica were oriented toward similar astronomical events.[45] "Unusual celestial events tend to be noticed and recorded if they seem to correspond with an earthly event of great importance," said archaeoastronomers John Brandt and Ray Williamson.[46] Take, for example, the 1066 C.E. record of Halley's comet on the Bayeux Tapestry or Thucydides's frequent mention of solar and lunar eclipses in his Peloponnesian War.

What stumps astronomers is the life-sized handprint east of the crescent. Handprints are common near pictographs in the canyon and in Southwestern Rock Art, and most researchers agree that they indicate a sacred site.[47] What we may have here is not the crude lab notes of an Anasazi astronomer, but a sun-watching station and a sky altar. The dot-within-concentric-circles pictograph often marks a place where Pueblo sunwatchers consistently watch the course of the sun as it rises along the horizons, each day moving a little further south toward winter, or a little further north toward summer. Another measurement of time for the Pueblos is the regular reappearance of the new moon. The moon and sun appearing together is considered to be a good omen.

Brandt and Williamson agreed that the pictograph near Peñasco Blanco is a sun-watching station, particularly because the location offers such a good view of the eastern horizon. But as to whether or not the star picture in Chaco is really Venus, they said, "It is entirely possible that the more recent practice of associating the crescent moon [with] the morning or evening star is the remnant of a tradition which began with the supernova appearance." Although the morning star was absent from the sky when the supernova appeared, the two appearances may have become confused with one another through time. But there is no reason to believe that the Anasazi would not record such an unusual event as the supernova/moon conjunction, particularly if it occurred near a socially significant event in the life of a pueblo.

Chaco archaeologist Florence Hawley Ellis believed the so-called supernova star is actually the Morning Star or Venus, which is frequently portrayed with moon/sun combinations. For instance, the Zuñis have a pillar sculpted with the face of the sun, the sacred hand, the morning star, and the new moon, just like the unit at Chaco. A Hopi *kachina* (spirit) associated with the winter solstice carries a crescent moon and

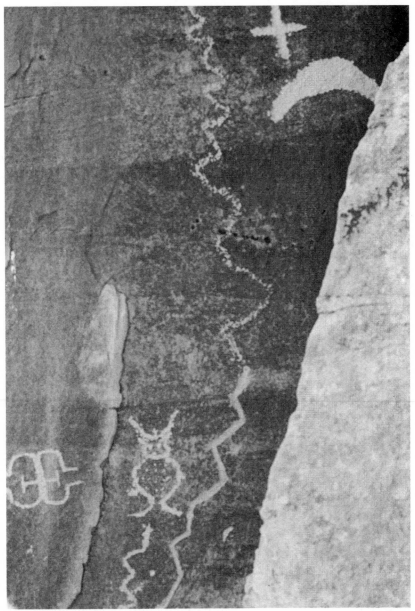

Morning star–crescent moon petroglyphs, like this one at the Village of the Great Kivas near Zuñi, are prevalent among Pueblos. At Zuñi, Venus symbolizes the Twin War Gods who are the patrons of games, and the moon symbolizes hunting prowess. (Photo by the author)

the Big Star or Morning Star on his mask. Morning Star was watched because it followed Moon so closely, but prayers were also made to Orion and the Pleiades. Ceremonial paraphernalia and chambers were also littered with these icons.

Assuming Ellis was correct, that the pictograph near Peñasco Blanco is a depiction of a Venus-Moon conjunction as opposed to the Crab Nebula, it would still be associated with Pueblo gambling symbolism. The Morning and Evening Stars represent the Twin War Gods, the off-spring of the sun, whom among the Hopis and Zuñis are considered patrons of gaming. In the Rio Grande Valley on the eastern edge of Pueblo country, the Morning and Evening Stars were associated with a society of clowns known as *Koshare*, who are also sons of the sun and appear in a number of Pueblo gambler myths examined in the next chapter. In Mexico, Venus represents the dual aspect of Quetzalcóatl; it also may have been imported from Mexico.

There are nonetheless problems with the pochteca trail theory. Not the first to examine the Mexican connection by any means, Kelley, Kelley, and Reyman triggered an onslaught of point-counterpoint papers between the "Mexicanists," who believe the Chaco culture was stimu-lated by foreigners, and the "antagonists," who argue for independent development.[48] Modern arguments favor a series of exchange systems between the Anasazi and Mexico which would include the cultures of Casas Grandes in northern Mexico as the go-between traders. This makes it less likely that our Gambler God was a pochteca-like merchant from Mexico.

One other point to consider. The pochteca society liked to gamble at ballgames and dice.[49] The Anasazi played dice but did not have ball-courts, and the Hohokam, their counterpart in Arizona, played ball but did not shoot craps.

Ancient Ball Courts in Mesoamerica and Hohokam

It is said that Mesoamerica[50] was one long, continuous culture, despite the many political groups that gave it form. The same can be said for their recreational activities. Pre-Classic Mexicans invented a game played with a rubber ball later called *ullamaliztli* which thrived for twenty-five-hundred years. One source said the earliest evidence of ballplaying in Mexico dates back to 1000 B.C.E.—a terra-cotta padded ball player found at Xochipala in the Mexican state of Guerrero.[51] Most scholars agree that the Olmecs, a fishing and trading culture, invented the game, which began to appear in the Central Plateau when the social religious organization became more complex—around 1200 B.C.E.—and when their influence spread into wide areas of Mesoamerica. Their figurines imply that games were played during religious celebrations.[52] They probably played on a flat field until they built their second capital at La Venta (700 B.C.E.) on an island in western Tabasco near the Gulf of Mexico.[53] The La Venta court is so far the oldest ever found. As many as six hundred courts have been discovered throughout Mexico.

Surviving hieroglyphic codices testify to the symbolic play of the gods in the court, *teotlachtli*, the divine court of the gods.[54] Players personified the celestial deities by battling and balancing the opposing forces of nature. The object of one version of the game was to keep the hard rubber ball, symbolizing the sun or Venus, in motion by bouncing it on heavily padded hips. The games legendarily ended with the ritual decapitation of one of the players. The utmost sacrifice on behalf of the hero made to the presiding gods ensured the continuance of fertile life for the whole. A large mural at Teotihuacán (powerful between 100–650 C.E.) depicts the playing of several different versions of the game and alludes to the sacrifice of losers. Late Classic Maya art (500-900 C.E.) depicts mythological ballgame scenes on funerary vases and plates.

About two hundred ball courts have turned up in 163 sites among the prehistoric Hohokam, a Pima word meaning "that which perished." The Hohokam regional center, an area encompassing a hundred thousand square miles, was centered in the low-lying desert regions near Phoenix and Tucson where wood is not suitable for tree-ring dating. Archaeologists trace the beginning of the Hohokam to 300 B.C.E. but disagree over whether the native archaic population developed into pottery-making, non-nomadic farmers, or Mesoamerican migrant workers displaced the locals with a full-blown, early version of the Hohokam culture. Most agree that the Hohokam were influenced by Mexico sometime between 750 and 900 C.E. They built

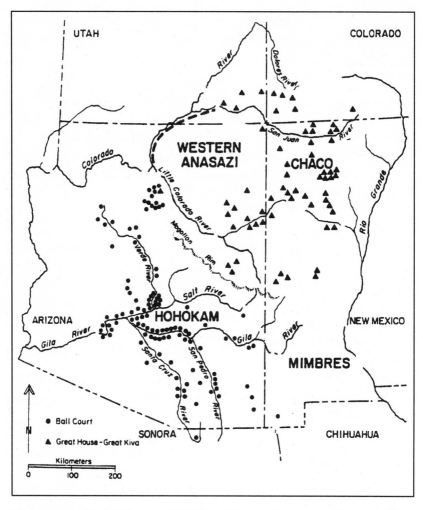

Map compares the distribution of Hohokam ball courts to Anasazi great houses/great kivas. Both are said to be the result of Mexican influence, yet the cultures and games of the Hohokam and Anasazi are so diverse. (Courtesy David E. Doyel and Stephen Lekson, *Anasazi Regional Organization and the Chaco System*, Maxwell Museum Paper No. 5, Albuquerque, N.M., 1992)

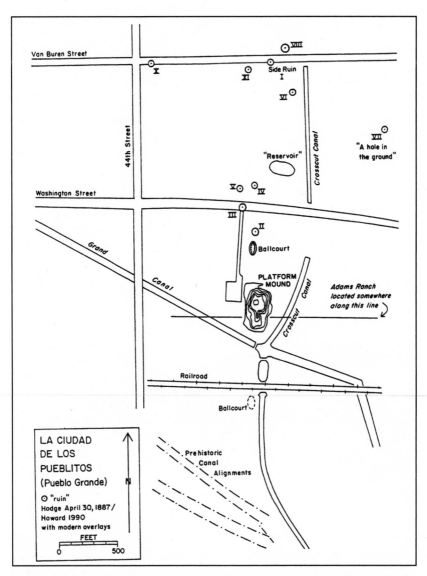

Diagram of the Pueblo Grande complex in Phoenix, Arizona, shows the spatial relationship between the ball court and the platform mound. (La Ciudad de los Pueblitos, reconstruction of Hemenway Expedition map by Jerry Howard, 1990; Archival Report Vol. 1, courtesy Pueblo Grande Archival Collection, City of Phoenix)

ball courts amidst their Mesoamericanesque platform-temple mounds, all meticulously aligned on north-south or east-west grids.

The Hohokam started building the courts in the Colonial Period (775– 975 C.E.), and by the Sedentary Period (975–1150 C.E.), courts were present in nearly every village and hamlet associated, even peripherally, with the culture. Whether the courts were based on Mesoamerican styles or developed independently is still unknown, although considering that the Hohokam may have themselves come from Mexico, one can safely guess that some form of the Mesoamerican ball game was played in the Hohokam courts. The ball courts—long, oblong craters with high crescent sides and end units the length of football fields—do not look like Mexican ball courts, which had thick, sloping side walls of stone, with walls at one or both ends to give the court an overall I or T shape. But archaeologists there say the court evolved from a flat playing field with no walls. The game in Mexico was a cross between no-hands soccer and basketball, except that the hoops were attached to the sides of the stone court on the center line. Hohokam

Hohokam ball courts, like this one at Pueblo Grande near the airport in Phoenix, may have been developed from Mesoamerican prototypes. (Photo by the author)

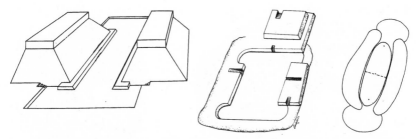

The availability of building materials may explain the architectural differences between the Mesoamerican ball courts (left) and Hohokam ball courts (right). Casas Grandes in Mexico (center) was the intermediary trading community, yet ball courts have not been found among the Anasazi, who also traded with Casas Grandes.

courts had no hoops, but their genesis was likely Mexican, according to Hohokam archaeologist Emil Haury.[55] It was only one of many elements in a constellation of attributes that identifies the Hohokam as a northern outlier of a high cultural nucleus in Mexico. Ball games have been played as far north as Sinaloa and Casas Grandes in Chihuahua, within 300 miles of southern Arizona, the intermediary trade center.

The games likely expressed basic elements of the Hohokam cosmology and world view, said ball court scholar David Wilcox.[56] They integrated public life within and between the settlements like a sports stadium, church, flea market, district court, and town hall rolled into one.[57] The presence of ball courts reflects an overriding binding force, undoubtedly religious, though the competitive aspect of the games was determined by the politics of the group. There is no full consensus on what actually transpired in the courts, but most scholars agree they "provided for face-to-face interaction between populations which resulted in greater distribution of goods, services, and presumably, marriage partners."[58] Among the Anasazi, this sort of integration was replaced by kivas and roads, which Hohokam sites lack. The Anasazi probably borrowed their canal engineering technology from the Hohokam, who built seven hundred miles of canals to divert the waters of the Gila and Salt rivers to their fields; yet the Anasazi never embraced the ball court.

In relation to the ball court, Haury discovered something else the Hohokam had that was absent in the Anasazi culture—stone rings. The purpose of these basalt doughnuts or pulleys has long been the subject

Stone and lava rings like these have been found in Hohokam sites and among more recent tribes across North America. Similar rings and bowls were found among the Mound Builders. (Culin, 1907)

of speculation.[59] The plain rings were from early periods, and the pulley types were from later periods, some dating from 300 B.C.E. to 100 B.C.E. I once handled a couple of smooth, heavy specimens with flat sides, belonging to the Pueblo Grande Museum in Phoenix. The curator told me their purpose is obscure and controversial; they could have been used for shelling corn or for a game similar to chunkgé played by the prehistoric Mound Builders of the Eastern Woodlands discussed in Chapter 2.[60] Like the Hohokam, the Mound Builder cultures were apparently influenced by Mesoamerican cultures, particularly the Olmecs. This raises two questions: Did the Olmecs also play with stone rings? Why did the Anasazi, supposedly also influenced by Mesoamerica concurrent with the Hohokam, never play with stone rings?[61]

The Anasazi may have been in part derived from the Mogollon culture, an older tradition of settled agriculturalists who flourished between 100 B.C.E. and 1400 C.E. Quick learners, these mountain people may have been the first of the three major cultures in the Southwest to build permanent housing and to produce ceramics. They may have introduced the bow and arrow to the Southwest, being more skilled at hunting than their farming neighbors. Since their villages lay between Mexico and Anasazi domain, they were the most likely transmitters of Mesoamerican architecture, especially the pithouses and kivas. But the Mogollon did not have ball courts, either. Bone dice, however, have been found in Mogollon sites.

The Pima and the Tohono O'odham, descendants of the Hohokam, did not play ball in deep dirt courts, but they played dice games similar to those of the Pueblos and Navajos, yet dice were virtually nonexistent among the Hohokam.[62] Haury found an exception at Snaketown—a couple of shell disks that may have been used as dice.[63] Bone and stick dice were found in many of the great houses and small houses in Chaco Canyon and in the Four Corners region where New Mexico, Colorado, Utah, and Arizona join. The earliest bone die was found in a Folsom site (in northeastern New Mexico) dating to 10,000 B.C.E.,[64] and a few

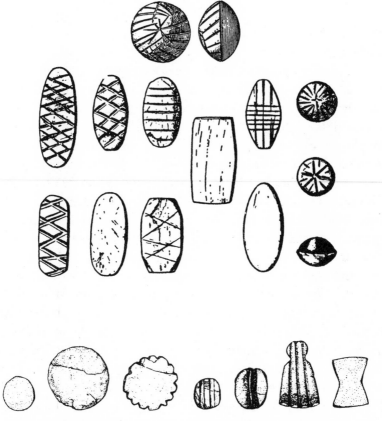

Assortment of bone gaming pieces from Pueblo Bonito (Anasazi, top), and shell gaming pieces from Snaketown (Hohokam, bottom). (Judd, 1954; Haury, 1976)

gaming pieces were found at the Fresnal Shelter near Alamogordo, New Mexico, dating anywhere between 1 and 1600 C.E.[65] The heaviest users were the earlier Anasazi known as Basket Maker III (500–700 C.E.), particularly of Colorado.[66]

* * *

The presence of a gambler figure of Mexican origin in Chaco Canyon's prehistory is speculative at best. Further examination of the Great Gambler in the Navajo ceremonial chants shows that gambling mythology was imposed onto the surrealistic Anasazi setting in Chaco Canyon, with a sprinkling of certain themes from a more recent history. Mexico, however, is not entirely ruled out as an influence on the gambler legend/myth.

Enemy Way

What scholars understand now but overlooked a century ago is that Anasazi ruins are backdrops for the Navajo healing rituals called chantways, which incorporate the gambler among many other mythic figures and stories. The ruins have less to do with history or prehistory and more to do with the healing power of the stories attached to them.

For the basically nonagrarian nomadic Navajos, chantway narratives were recited during ceremonials conducted to bring sick people back into harmony with the universe. Their illnesses, mental or physical, were caused by upsetting the precarious harmony, either intentionally by ghosts or witches or unintentionally by persons breaking a religious taboo or unwittingly coming into contact with snakes, bears, lightning, or death. For instance, the Night Way or Night Chant, more commonly referred to as the *yéibichai*, is a major nine-day winter ceremony involving Talking God; it is performed to cure patients of nervousness or insanity. The Great Gambler forms part of the Navajo ceremonial chants called the Prostitution Way, to be discussed in fuller detail in the next chapter. Both of these address excessiveness in gambling, which would upset the balance of nature as well as personal well-being.

Pueblo Alto, Pueblo Bonito, and Aztec Ruin or Pueblo Pintado are all mentioned in Clyde Kluckhohn's version of Prostitution Way, which encompasses the Great Gambler. The gambler's house in Washington Matthews's version, Kin Teel (Kíntyél) or Chetro Ketl, is associated with the Navajo origin stories told in their ceremonials Excess Way, Water Way, Bead Way, and Shooting Star Way. If Kin Teel is not Chetro Ketl as Matthews thought, but Pueblo Pintado, it is known to be the starting point for the Bead Way and may have served as a setting for Pueblo battles mentioned in Beauty Way, Mountaintop Way, and Enemy Way. Various mythical gambling episodes are included in most of these chantways.[67]

Enemy Way, or *Entah*, was formerly given as a purification rite for warriors who had been contaminated by contact with the enemy. Later, it was given for sickness caused by contact with whites or other non-Navajos. Chaco ruins were considered to be places where ghosts of the dead Anasazi still lingered. These sacred places were so powerful and dangerous that entering them without discretion, spiritual reverence, or medicinal license was considered taboo. Navajos escaping the Spaniards and other enemies hid in the ruins under the protection of the superstition. By way of proof, the term "Casa Fuerte Navajo," or Navajo stronghouse, was mentioned in the historical records of the Spaniards to signify a ruin or group of ruins in Chaco Canyon where the Navajos took refuge, sometimes with the Pueblos.[68] It is my belief that the battles held at the ruins, or the protective shelter they provided, later accentuated their power in the chantways—and this is why they became settings for archetypal battles between the superdeity and the gambler. If so, the Navajo legend as a healing rite is still a response to, if not an expression of, an historical event.

The Navajos say the four sacred mountains were the posts of a great *hogan* (house) inside which all the tribes once lived together. They fought and traded with one another, but the world outside the four mountains mattered little to them. A day came when the hogan blanket was drawn back, and the winds from the four corners of the world blew inside. The people of the gambler had returned.[69] History, in other words, repeats itself.

The allusion to Mexico at the end of a number of versions of the Navajo Great Gambler[70] may be a commentary on the harsh treatment by the waves of invaders from the south. The Spaniards were the first to blow in through the hogan door via Mexico, followed by colonists from the newly independent Mexico of 1821. To be fair, the ending of the story may also refer to invaders from the east. When General Kearny marched into New Mexico in 1846, his first order of business was to protect the new Pueblo and Mexican citizens from the raiding Navajos (as well as from Comanches, Apaches, Kiowas, and Southern Utes). The tension came to a head when in 1864 Kit Carson rounded up the Navajos and marched them—on what is now known as the Long Walk—to a reservation at Fort Sumner, New Mexico. The Navajos lost at least a third of their population during the ordeal, which finally ended with the 1868 treaty outlining the present Navajo reservation, today the largest in the country.

A couple of variations of the Navajo gambler legend do tie in the white man (although the Spaniards belong to the Caucasian race, they were viewed as a different race from the Americans). In the Navajo version recorded by Gretchen Chapin, for instance, the gambler uttered a white man's word when he was shot into the sky: "And the Navajo believe that the white people began with Gambler in the new home that he was shot away to."[71] Ration, a Navajo, said that the tribes who inhabited Chaco Canyon were mixed, but One-Who-Wins-You might have been an ancient Anglo man born on a mountainous island, perhaps off the coast of California.[72] His launch into the sky is prophetic of modern rocketry. He tells the people they will play with round objects—baseballs, volleyballs, basketballs, and golfballs—as reminders of him. There are many white man's games that "remind us of the gambler wizard who became a loser." The gambler says the lightning and wind will be his power when he returns and he will travel on the rainbow. Today we travel in vehicles on highways with yellow and white stripes and the people use lightning in their houses to run their televisions and radios, or the "Wind that Talks."

These versions reported by Chapin and Tom Ration prove that the gambler archetype is transformed to embody the current dominating party. One size fits all. But the white man was not introduced into the gambler mythology as the villain until the 1940s, nearly a century after the American takeover of the New Mexican province. The prevailing theme is the allusion to the Spanish Conquest, not Manifest Destiny.

I find it incredible that Washington Matthews was able to obtain the unabridged gambler legend in the 1880s after all the Navajos had been through with the Spaniards and the American government in the previous four decades, not to mention the past four centuries.[73] The Navajos did not take their religion underground, but laid it out like silver and turquoise jewelry on a trader's blanket. The reason for the openness is articulated by the young champion after he shoots the Gambler into the sky:

> "Those whom you despise," he warned them, "may in fact be favored by the gods. While they may appear weak and of no account today, tomorrow you might discover that they possess more power than they seem to have at the moment."[74]

Thus, it repeats the general sentiment expressed by the myths across North America. The tantalizing turn in plot at the end of the gambler story represents the historical encounter with Mexico. Yet rather than being a reference to history, Mexico itself is a metaphor for reversal of fortune and personal transformation. To understand this is to understand some of the other tales told by the Pueblos concerning Mexico.

Jemez Pueblo and Montezuma

Although some elements of the Navajo Great Gambler are similar to the gambler myths told by their linguistic kin in Canada and the Pacific Northwest, it is generally understood that the Navajos borrowed much of their religion and mythology from the Pueblos. The Pueblo culture hero, who is associated with the mythical and archaeological First Houses, gambles with the people before heading toward Mexico. This aspect of the gambler myth may have been passed on to the Navajos from the Jemez Pueblos.[75] Jemez was the home of Hosta, recall, the first Southwestern native to mention the gambler in connection with Chaco Canyon.

Jemez Pueblo, settled in the red mesas near the Jemez Mountains, is the closest pueblo to Chaco Canyon and the traditional portal to Navajo country. The relationship between Pueblos and Navajos was always dubious, characterized by mutual raiding, enslaving, and trading. Navajo raiders and Spaniards nearly depopulated the Jemez in the latter part of the sixteenth century. During the seventeenth century, ironically, some Jemez people became known as the *ma-ii deeshgiizhnii diné e* clan of the Navajo. Yet many Spanish, Mexican, and American military campaigns on the Navajos were launched from Jemez, whose members knew all the hiding places in Chaco Canyon.[76]

The endings to some of the Navajo gambler legends involve Jemez Pueblo. In a story Neil Judd obtained from an old Navajo of Kin-yai near Crownpoint, New Mexico, Noqoìlpi's wife was actually from Jemez. The woman conspired to beat her husband in gambling, and following his downfall, returned in triumph to Jemez. In the version recorded by Chapin, the people scattered in the four directions: some east to Jemez, some to the Zuñi in the south, some west to Hopi, and some north to Utah and Colorado. According to Goddard, some went off to investigate the area of the Jemez Pueblo.

Hosta, however, was a peculiar fellow. When he led the American military to the edge of Chaco Canyon in the summer of 1849, just a few months after the war with Mexico had ended, he didn't mention the gambler. Instead, with the confidence of a Christian with four aces, he told First Lieutenant Simpson that Montezuma had built those ruins. That's right, Montezuma.

Although Jemez, not to mention the other occupied pueblos, did not compare in scale to the Anasazi ruins, Hosta tried to emphasize that the more modern villages were also built, if not by Montezuma, then by his example. Hosta said their underground ceremonial kivas, intrinsic to all pueblo and Anasazi architecture, were "churches of Montezuma." In the spring, Hosta's people went there to chant to Montezuma to send them rain, and in the fall they sang to him to obtain any good thing they wanted.[77]

This was what Simpson wanted to hear, for it supplemented his theory that the Aztecs and Anasazi were one people.[78] Popular legend says the abandonment of Chaco Canyon (1130–1250) coincides with the beginning of the Aztec's hundred-year wanderings in the desert. According to their own legends, the Aztecs (or Mexicas) journeyed to central Mexico from the north. They were called *Chichimecas*, barbarians, because they dressed in skins of animals they killed with darts. Their point of origin was called *Aztlan*, "Place of Whiteness," which modern Mexican and Spanish scholars locate in the lake-side region of Yuriria-Cuitzeo, in El Bajío. There are several versions of the "Messianic journey" related in chronicles and codices, but all agree that Aztlan was an island occupied by a temple-pyramid in the center. In the year "*ce-tecpatl*," "one flint," or 1116 C.E., the people were ordered by divine mandate to find the symbol that would ordain the center of the universe, where they would start their military rule. During the migrations, they encountered many tests and adventures later symbolized in their rituals and ceremonial ball game. When they reached the Valley of Mexico, they tempered their warlike nature (but were still battle-conscious) and conquered and merged in identity with the Toltec culture. At the end of this lengthy journey, 1325 C.E., in the year *ome-calli*, "two house," the Mexicas discovered the sign they had been looking for: an eagle resting on a nopal cactus devouring a serpent. There they founded the city of México-Tenochtitlán on a lake.[79] The emergence and migration stories parallel those of the Navajos and Pueblos.

Montezuma—or rather, Moctezuma II—did not take the throne until 1502 and was killed during the Spanish Conquest in 1521, far too late to spawn the Anasazi or Pueblo cultures. Whether the Aztecs are related to the Pueblos is not only controversial, it is also not the point here. The upshot is that the Pueblos, along with tribes in Arizona and northern Mexico, have a storehouse of tales dealing with Montezuma, which in turn are melded with the Pueblo culture hero whose prowess includes farming, hunting, magic, jugglery, and gambling.

Ellis recognized the strong parallel between Mesoamerican and Pueblo mythology, which could have been borne on something as simple as a kernel of maize imported from Central Mexico.[80] "We cannot imagine seed and technique for growing corn having been transmitted [to the Southwest] without instructions as to the gods and rituals believed necessary for success," she wrote. Corn grew to be the central symbol of Pueblo religion and power, and the gambler in his persona as Pueblo culture hero is the purveyor of that symbol. In their gambling myths, the conflict has more to do with fertility than politics.

The mythological and religious aspects of the gambling myths of the American Southwest and Mexico have been studied to a great extent, and therefore, provide much insight into those myths of other Indian nations. For this reason, it is useful to explore this region further. In the following chapter we will examine the Montezuma tales and Maya gambling mythology in the context of the Southwestern gambler myths.

FIVE

Birth, Death, and Resurrection:
Gambling Messiahs in Post-Conquest Mexico and the Southwest

He was tall
and he had a handsome face
but he always wore spruce greens around his head, over his eyes.
He dressed in the finest buckskins
his moccasins were perfectly sewn.
He had strings of sky blue turquoise
strings of red coral in his ears.
In all ways, the Gambler was good to look at.
> — Leslie Marmon Silko, "Up North," *Storyteller* [1981]

Ollama ollama huehue Xolotl
nahuallachco ollama Xolotl
He playeth ball, old Xolotl playeth ball
in the ball court of the sorcerer.
> —Song of the Atamalcualiztli Celebration,
> translated by Fray Bernardino de Sahagún

The Gaming Halls of Montezuma

Mythological characters, especially the ones swapped between Mexico and the American Southwest, tend to bleed into one another. They are not sharply distinguishable according to Anglo-European conventions. A handy term for this is "prehuman flux," which refers to the malleable world of mythical times where all living beings are bound to no particular shape or attributes and are even inclined to switch roles with one another.[1] Gladys Reichard, an authority on Navajo religion, calls it the theory of multiple selves.[2] This applies to the gamblers who, in the Mexico-Southwest corridor, include legendary emperors of the Aztecs and Toltecs, Spanish soldiers and religious figures, Pueblo culture heroes, the divine twins, Venus and Sun personified by their many acolytes, and, of course, the good gambler and the bad.

We have seen in gambling mythology across the nation that the detent of power can suddenly flip because of excessiveness, greed, and avarice. In the Southwest, the very act of gambling transforms players into their opposite polarities. When dealing with kings, heroes, and gods, the stakes are high and the transformation takes place on the cosmic level, but the drama is intended to teach personal ethics.

The Navajo Great Gambler wins all the people and property, but when he is defeated by a divine hero, we know that he resurrects as the God of the Mexicans. He is no longer a villain, but a progenitor of a new race of people and culture; his Second Coming is much anticipated. Likewise, the mythical Montezuma figure in northern New Mexico is attributed with the same Christlike qualities. We are tempted to assign the specifics to historical influence and the mistaken identities to cultural illiteracy, but for those who were there, it may have been more like history imitating myth.

Interaction with the real Aztec ruler was well documented by Spanish priests and officers; after Montezuma's death, he became something of a legend to them. When the Spanish began exploring New Mexico, they imported Montezuma stories, no doubt altered and exaggerated, along with other saints, saviors, and Mexican gods. For Navajo and Pueblo storytellers, the exotic stories would have been like milling a new breed of maize in with the old corn.

For one thing, the Pueblos would have learned that Montezuma (Moctezuma Xocoyoctzin the Second)[3] was an archetypal gambler. When he took the throne in Anahuac, the Valley of Mexico, in 1502, the inaugural games, sacrifices, and religious ceremonies lasted several days. Even captured enemy spies infiltrating the celebration were given a good seat at the ball game held in the court adjacent to the double temple shared by *Huitzilopochtli* (god of war) and *Tlaloc* (god of farmers).

Montezuma added a recreational flair to the ball game during his reign in order "to animate the people and divert them." Lords and Principals challenged each other's teams, giving rise to the professional athlete and to gambling by the general population.[4] Most of the Aztec rulers could not help but take the game seriously. The lord of México-Tenochtitlán competed against the lord of Xochimilco just to test his skills, but the contest turned into a deadly duel when the Tenochtitlán ruler strangled the other to avoid the shame of losing to him.[5] While one ruler bet his

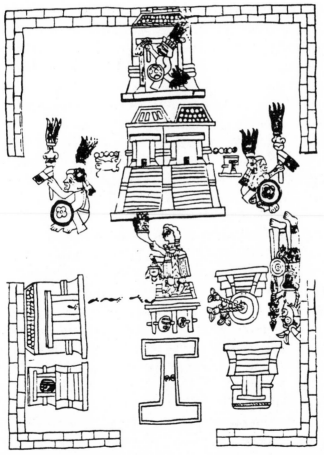

When Moctezuma II was coronated on the steps of the Great Temple at Tenochtitlán, ball games were played in the adjacent double-T court in his honor. (Sahagún, in Diaz, 1918)

garden against the market of the other, the general populace staked gold and feathers, cotton or *ixtle* blankets, or corncobs, depending on their personal finances. Sometimes men who had no possessions risked their own freedom, becoming slaves on the defeat of their team.[6]

The career gamblers in Montezuma's time "made a thousand cere-monies and superstitious deeds and invented prognostications and idol-atries," wrote Diego Durán. At nightfall they placed a ball on a clean plate, hung the leather loincloth and the gloves (worn in play) on a pole, and crouched before them in worship. During the incantations to the ball, they "invoked the aid of the water and springs, the ravines, the trees, the wild animals and serpents, the sun, the moon and the stars, the clouds, the rains and at last all created things, and to the gods which they had invented for each thing."[7]

Montezuma's court also had a passion for a dice game called *patolli*, and he apparently looked on as they played.[8] Rulers wagered avidly on the game, but patolli was not class exclusive—all were "covetous game-sters." The gamblers went from one gaming house to another with the game mat carried under their arms and the dice and stone counters tied in a cloth and nestled in a basket, like little gods. A player would set the basket in a place of adoration and begin a private ceremony of homage. He waved incense over it and sacrificed an offering of food in front of it, whispering loving words all the while to a dice god named *Macuilxochitl* (Five Roses or Flowers), whose name was invoked every time a player threw the dice from his hand.[9] So zealous were the play-ers that they would not only gamble themselves into slavery, but stake themselves as human sacrifices.[10]

Montezuma didn't spend all his time gambling. He waged many wars, thereby expanding the economic base and supply of prisoners for the sac-rificial altar and game court. Counterbalancing his statesmanship, according to Spanish chroniclers, were his intolerable arrogance, his political indiscretions, and his lavish expenditures and grievous taxes. His oppression of the people led to insurrection and resistance, causing such hostility in the latter years of his reign that the forces of one half of the empire were constantly suppressing the commotions of the other.[11]

All of this changed on the day of One Reed—Quetzalcóatl's birth-day—in 1519. Hernán Cortés, a blonde-bearded man, landed in Mex-

Aztec elite played a dice game called *patolli*, as depicted in the *Florentine Codex, Book 8.*

ico from Spain on the heels of a decade of ominous floods, fires, comets, and fantastic lights in the sky. Such omens supported that he was the returning deity, Quetzalcóatl, yet another ingredient in the South-western gambler soup. This hand-me-down god, in existence since at least 300 C.E., is known by a multitude of names: the Plumed Serpent, Lord of the Land of the Dead, Ehecatl the God of Wind, Venus the Lord of Dawn, and Precious Twin. As the morning star, he is the twin brother to Xólotl, the evening star. In another aspect, he is creator of the Fifth Sun and the human race, and god of sacrifices. Historical rulers and heroes often took the god's name as a title so that mortal legends merged with mythology. By the time he had been adopted by the Aztecs, he had been confused with an immortalized king, Topiltzin Quetzalcóatl, from the late tenth–early eleventh-century Tula, who was credited with many fabled feats. This king, said to have been tall in stature, with white skin, long hair, and a flowing beard, incurred the wrath of one of the principal gods and was exiled. Before he sailed for the mythical land of Tlapallan in his wizard skiff made of serpents' skins, he vowed to return with his descendants.

Montezuma was first a priest and did not want to offend the return-ing deity embodied in Cortés, but he was also skeptical and a little afraid. He sent Cortés a hundred slaves bearing gold and silver along with his regrets that, with all due respect, he was not welcome in the city. Cortés examined the rich gifts, particularly the Spanish helmet brimming with grains of gold and the two circular plates as large as car-riage wheels (probably calendars), one a golden sun and the other a sil-ver moon. Cortés was impressed by the wealth, but not threatened by Montezuma's message. Had he noticed the checkered patolli cloths among the lesser gifts, he might have better understood his adversary.

Cortés and his army, now including the native Tlaxcalans who trained for battle by competing in public games, entered the white stucco neigh-borhoods and causeways of México-Tenochtitlán on November 8, 1519, with nothing less than awe. After being received in flamboyant style, Cortés dogged Montezuma for a week, touring the temples, schools, mar-ket, and vaults. Everywhere he turned he saw a mixture of religious devo-tion and blasphemy, the amazing architecture stained by blood, the hearts smoldering on braziers amid a rapture of flowers. He looked into the jaws of the Quetzalcóatl statue and saw its dismembered victims. Cortés was never able to reconcile the dichotomous nature of the Aztecs, but frankly, that wasn't his job. And the man who would be the returning god was looking mortal to Montezuma. Despite opening the Great Temple to his guest, Montezuma was criticized for his religious beliefs and was besieged by the Spaniards to plant a cross on top of the pyramid.

Sometime during their "visit," Montezuma took the Spaniards to a ball game. A priest from the Templo Mayor consecrated the field with certain ceremonies and "sorceries" before the game could begin. For men whose country was in the throes of the Spanish Inquisition, the opening ceremonies must have seemed liked heathenism. But Cortés was so impressed with the game that in 1528 he presented an exhibi-tion team to the emperor Charles V in Spain.[12]

During the five-months Cortés kept Montezuma in captivity, they competed in *totoloque*, another dice game played with small, smooth pellets of gold. The Spaniards didn't know that totoloque was similar to most North American Indian dice games, but they did notice its similarity to *tables*. Like any two-sided lot, one side of the gold pellet was marked, so that the winner was determined by the number of dice that fell a certain side up. In five strokes players gained or lost whatever pieces of gold or jewels they had staked. The Spanish soldier keeping score for Cortés always marked one point more than he had gained. When Montezuma saw it, he commented on the cheating, making even Cortés laugh.[13] Cortés gave the jewels he won to the servants of Montezuma, and when the ruler won, he divided them among the soldiers on guard, in addition to giving them daily presents of gold and cloth. "He had, in truth, a most munificent spirit," wrote Bernal Diaz del Castillo, a soldier in attendance. "His enemies accused him of avarice. But if he were avaricious, it could have been only that he might have the more to give away."

Cortés was not really interested in dice. As they played, he persuaded Montezuma to relinquish his country's treasures and his hereditary rights to him. It took three days to melt down all of the gold, amounting to 162,000 *pesos de oro*—equal to 6.3 million dollars by Prescott's estimate in 1843 alone! The soldiers gambled for each other's take with cards they made out of drum parchment. Thus, Montezuma's treasure changed hands many times in a manner of days.[14]

Six months after the arrival of Cortés, the natives rioted in the capital. Montezuma was killed on the double steps of the great temple overlooking the ballcourt. The fighting went on for four days, during which time half the Spaniards, encumbered by their heavy winnings of gold, and thousands of Tlaxcalans lost their lives. Cortés retreated, and after a year of preparation, he marched on Tenochtitlán with two hundred thousand Tlaxcalan allies. The siege lasted eighty days, during which time thirty thousand warriors and nearly a quarter million Aztecs died from smallpox or warfare.

As his first order of business under the new government, Cortés outlawed gambling—especially with golden dice.[15]

Spain was now firmly ensconced in the New World. Spanish Conquistadors began pushing up the Rio Grande in New Mexico some twenty years later in search of the rumored Seven Golden Cities of Cíbola. They carried with them the stories of the Aztec monarch they defeated. Imagine their disappointment when they found only the Pueblos living relatively peacefully by their various rivers.

Reverse side of a Spanish playing card, Mexico, 1583, of a clown kicking a billet. Five-inch-long billets are still used in racing among Mexican and Southwestern tribes. (Culin, 1907)

Waxing Montezuma

Spanish Conquistadors launched at least five explorations into New Mexico between 1536 and 1591. Coronado had counted a hundred adobe communities on the northern frontier, which he dubbed "pueblos" (Spanish for village), but the count diminished to nineteen in the coming centuries.[16] Juan de Oñate established the first capital at the Tewa-speaking San Juan Pueblo north of the present capital of Santa Fe in 1598. Under Spanish colonial rule, a number of colonists settled along the river and built missions that infiltrated the Pueblos. The new regime often treated the Indians harshly, forcing them to work for colonizers and to convert to the Cross. In 1680, the Pueblos collaborated in a rebellion, driving the newcomers temporarily back to Mexico.

The first mention of Montezuma in New Mexico was in 1680 during the Pueblo Revolt.[17] Several Tewa-speaking Pueblo prisoners testified that they had participated in the uprising under the mandate from an Indian who lived in the north, "from which region Montezuma came."[18] They said Montezuma was a lieutenant of a pan-Pueblo prophet and progenitor named *Poseyemu*.[19][20] In 1680 the two icons were regarded as separate figures, but as politics wore on, the figures converged.[21] The center of the Spanish government in the Southwest was at the heart of the Tewa world, in what was to become Santa Fe. Tewa Pueblos received the full force of the Roman Catholic missionary and Spanish military effort and most likely became the geographical crossroads between the Pueblo demagogue and the Aztec ruler.

In 1692, the Spaniards regained control of New Mexico. In 1706 the Spanish and the Pueblos formed a working alliance that lasted until Mexico won its independence from Spain in 1821. The new rule in the province was less harsh, but the Pueblos continued to lose much of their land, and it was then that the Montezuma tales really began to flourish. The Spanish conquerors may have imported the Montezuma myth, but the Pueblos adapted it in response to the conquest and their forced conversion to Catholicism.

Adolf Bandelier, a scholar of the Southwest, said that in 1846 the powers in Mexico City, on the cusp of war with the United States, wrote and circulated an unpublished document called "History of Montezuma." The history introduced the legends that fused the Pueblo culture hero and Montezuma in order to gain Pueblo support and to integrate the American Southwest into the Mexican culture. Bandelier said this "campaign document" was conceived to strengthen the claims of Mexico upon New Mexico in the eyes of the Pueblos and to refute anything that would favor the United States.[22]

The Montezuma legends were deeply entrenched in the Pueblo belief system by the time of General Kearny's arrival in 1846, but they did not accomplish the Mexicans' objective. Not only did the legends fail to support Mexico's claim to the northern province, but they also encouraged the Indians to see the Americans as their deliverers from Mexico.[23]

The Pueblos used the stories to their own advantage. Bandelier said the mythical Montezuma figure was trotted out for angry governors, gullible military reconnoiters, and nosy tourists for the express purpose of screening their "own sacred traditions from pryers into secrets which the Indian considers as his own and no one else's." The storyteller could discriminate between the modern imaginary figure and historic god, while he might repeat the Montezuma tale to "an unsophisticated listener, fresh from the outside world, with the greatest apparent sincerity." Bandelier's theory would explain why Hosta, the governor of Jemez Pueblo, had told Lt. Simpson that Montezuma had built the Chaco ruins and the Rio Grande Pueblos and established the kiva rituals. Hosta had reason to screen his religion from outsiders. The pueblo had had their share of Franciscan monks on their doorstep, many of whom they murdered.[24]

The mythical Montezuma, as it was developed by the 1800s, is born at the Tewa-speaking Pecos Pueblo, and his mission is to work for the prosperity of the Indian people. He overcomes Catholic and Spanish forces and is regarded as a born-again savior of the people, an inventor of the Pueblo religion, and a hunter and a farmer with the power to bring rain. He is the mythical leader of a group that migrates south and founds a great city on a lake, hence the fusion of Montezuma with the Aztec migration myths relayed in the previous chapter. After his journey through Mexico, he returns to his people. Some Pueblos associated Montezuma with a sacred fire cult symbolizing purification, redemption, and release from oppression. Priests at Pecos were charged with keeping the fires burning and keeping alive the giant snake that represented Quetzalcóatl.

The large complex known as Pecos (from *pekush* or *peco*), twenty-five miles east of Santa Fe, was established around 1450 C.E. In 1540, Pecos representatives led part of Coronado's expedition in search of the mythical Gran Quivera to divert them away from the pueblo. In the 1620s, Franciscan friars built the first mission at Pecos, deemed to be the most powerful of all the pueblos, and tried to convert the Indians to Catholicism (hence the battle between Montezuma and the Christian God). The Pecos people burnt the mission during the Pueblo uprising; Comanche and Apache raids, disease, migration, and political/religious divisiveness diminished the population in the 1700s. In 1838, survivors moved to Jemez where they shared the same language stock, and where their heritage is still acknowledged and celebrated by the Jemez people. It is via this route that the Montezuma/Poseyemu tale traveled to the Navajos and merged with the gambler legend.

Like Montezuma, Poseyemu is born to a mistreated Pecos virgin and is fathered by the Sun. He represents fertility, provides for the general well-being of the Pueblos, and—like Jesus—successfully mediates between heaven and earth.[25] He is a hunter, agriculturalist, war leader, and the instrument of social integration. In post-Conquest days, Poseyemu also facilitates the preservation of religion. During his stay in some villages he institutes new dances and rituals. In other villages, he orders the dances and rituals to be held underground, and in effect invents the kiva religion. In still other villages he opposes the alien religion in direct competition. He also founds Mexico City. Poseyemu, too, performs miracles, is put to death by jealous men, and promises to return. In one myth Poseyemu vies for the rule of the Pecos Pueblo. The people rise up and drive him from the village. They capture him, bound him with gold and silver, and cast him into a lake. An eagle feather falls to him; he touches it, rises with it, and lives again.

The born-again phenomenon may be tied into the resurrection of Venus (Quetzalcóatl) and might represent real diffusion from Mexico. In one of Quetzalcóatl's many personas as the exiled king, he manifests himself as the planet Venus. He sacrifices himself and sinks in the west as the Evening Star and resurrects as the Morning Star. In a Maya story, the deity's twin brother, Xólotl, the god with a dog's head, guides the Sun through the underworld.[26] Xólotl transforms into Quetzalcóatl in order for the Sun to be reborn in the east. Xólotl is represented as a fire falling from the heavens, or the lightning that pierces the earth and opens a natural stairway to the underworld. At Jemez Pueblo, Poseyemu is also associated with the Morning Star.

Richard Parmentier, author of "The Mythological Triangle: Poseyemu, Montezuma, and Jesus in the Pueblos,"[27] said that Poseyemu became a mascot for Pueblo religious nationalism during the 1680 revolt, while Montezuma served the Pueblo political purpose after 1680 and through 1848, when Hosta helped the military flush the Navajos from the Anasazi ruins. Montezuma is the buffer between the familiar Poseyemu and the alien Jesus. All three share universal elements as redeemer, miracle worker, and mediator with the One Above the Clouds. Anthropologist Alfonso Ortiz, a native of San Juan Pueblo, has said that the ubiquitous Montezuma tales hint that the Pueblos "grappled, after the coming of the Spaniards, with the prospect of being thrust forever into the ebb and flow of history."[28]

I submit that the story of the Navajo Great Gambler, when told outside of its religious context, is a Montezuma tale in disguise designed to grapple with the ebb and flow of power and fortune and to warn against hostile religious takeover. The battle may be archetypal, however, as demonstrated by the following Keres Pueblo tale.[29] The Kachina society chief becomes angry with the Moki society chief for imitating their dance and asks him to stop, but the Moki chief says they will paint and dance as they please. They hold a moccasin game to decide the issue, wagering one society against the other. Spider Woman directs one of the Moki men in successfully defeating the Kachina men, and he becomes the leader of that group. The Kachina chief concedes to the Moki the privilege of dancing and painting with Kachina paint.[30]

Just to add one more muddy layer to this scheme, the Keresan-speaking Pueblos further fused Poseyemu with the Spanish saint Santiago (St. James the Greater). The fusion represents another effort on the part of the Pueblos to assimilate aspects of both belief systems.[31] Recall that the Navajo Great Gambler was given the horse as well as the Mexican people. Well, at some of the Pueblos, Santiago takes the form of an equestrian impersonation during solemn processions on Santiago's feast day, Christmas, and other Catholic feast days.

In these processions, a man dresses up like a rider, wearing a horse costume around his waist. The head, neck, mane, and tail are made from real horse hide and horsehair. The fact that this little horse has no legs is disguised by a sheet which falls almost to the ground all around the horse's body, although the moccasins of the impersonator can be seen. The horse has a bridle and reins, but no saddle, and is fastened to the rider's waist so that his hands are free to carry a quirt and hold the reins. Gifts of tobacco or candy are offered, especially chocolate "because [Poseyemu] came from Mexico."

The impersonation might be seen as an editorial comment on the Spanish invasion, but the ceremony is serious. Poseyemu is said to be the father of horses and cows, which are considered sacred among the Pueblos. The implication is that the little saint of horses is still associated, if indirectly, with the mythical Mexican ruler because, as one informant told anthropologist Leslie White, Poseyemu was Montezuma's Indian name. Games played by Poseyemu were also played during certain Catholic rituals such as the Feast of the Dead, All Saint's Day on November 1, and Easter. Since these games are played during celebrations dealing with death, the implication is that the games themselves helped to facilitate immediate needs of agricultural regeneration and, more broadly, the renewal of the old ways as in the Pawnee Ghost Dance hand game.

The Pueblo Messiah as Gambler

The following Keres Pueblo myth collected by self-made ethnologist Matilda Coxe Stevenson between 1887 and 1890, marries all three

Native drawing of Santiago as seen in horse impersonations in Catholic ceremonies at the Pueblos. Santiago is fused with the Pueblo culture hero as well as with the Gambler, and the mythical Montezuma. (White, 1932)

figures: Montezuma, Poseyemu, and the Navajo Great Gambler.[32][33] This Poseyemu was also born to a Pecos virgin; she had become pregnant by eating two piñon nuts given to her by the sun. The child is unwanted, and grows up as an orphan. Nobody pays attention to him, so he sits in the kivas and quietly absorbs the priest's duties. He attains a reputation for his gambling genius in a dice game and as a deer caller.

Poseyemu visits Zia Pueblo soon after their move from the mythical Kush Kutret, the great white house (which I believe to be Pueblo Bonito at Chaco Canyon), near the place of emergence. The holy leader wants Poseyemu's bracelet, which had been given to him by his mother. He stakes his great house and people of the north for the bracelet in a dice game called *wash'kasi*, played on the same principle as Montezuma's patolli.[34] In the second game, six stick dice are tossed from a bowl, playing for the chief's house in the west. The next game, consisting of finding a pebble hidden within one of four reeds, is played for the priest's house in the south. The final game, of finding the stone hidden in one of four mounds of sand, is played for the house in the east. The first three games are then repeated in the same order for the priest's house in the zenith, the nadir, and finally for all the people. Poseyemu wins, but unlike the Navajo gambler, he is benevolent and returns the houses and people he has won. Poseyemu continues his tour of all the pueblos before going into Mexico. In Chihuahua, Mexico, he

```
O  O  O  O  O  O  O  O  O  O
O                          O
O                          O
O                          O
O        ┌─────┐           O
O        │     │           O
O        └─────┘           O
O                          O
O                          O
O  O  O  O  O  O  O  O  O  O
```

Dice-game diagram legendarily played by the culture hero at Zia Pueblo. (Stevenson, 1894)

marries the chief's daughter,[35] and is soon murdered out of jealousy. But, of course, he resurrects, promising to return.

The core and, likely, older portion of the Zia myth is that Poseyemu teaches the people how to hunt game using certain rituals and chants, along with the help of the divine twins. When he calls the deer, they come to him on the roads of the four cardinal directions. Now we are paring down to the truer purpose of the myth.

The Zuñi Poseyemu gambles with the Sun to permit men to emerge from the underworld. This may correspond to a professional gambler at Acoma Pueblo named *Gaupot* who invented the dice game called *Bishi-i*; a Bishi-i society devoted to the game existed there.[36] "He was the greatest of gamblers, and lost everything. He played against the sun and was beaten, and lost his eyes and became blind."

Poseyemu is probably based on an older deity named Sun Youth, who may be a purer character and who also gambles. But the following Keres-speaking gambler myth is typical of the gruesome myths told across the country. Sun Youth's job is to liberate the Storm Clouds locked up at Reed-Leaf-Town under the watch of the gambler's goose.[37] Dead bodies hang from the ceiling of the house, and blood drips into the cornmeal the gambler serves to his guests who have come to bet against him. Spider Woman gives Sun Youth medicine and instructions for defeating Gambler. Nearing Gambler's house, he squirts a narcotic on the gambler's guard goose four times, once for each direction, and the goose falls asleep. Sun Youth wisely forgoes Gambler's dinner and gets down to gambling. Gambler tosses the gambling sticks and loses his clothing and the Storm Clouds he keeps in four rooms. He then challenges Sun Youth to guessing games, and the youth correctly guesses the contents of a receptacle as the Pleiades and the symbols on the east wall as the Orion constellation.[38] Victorious, Sun Youth tears the eyes out of the gambler and throws them into the sky, where they are transformed into stars. With lightning and flint, he liberates the Storm Clouds, and it begins to rain. Released by Sun Youth, Gambler starts a fire and burns the earth while going east.

Purification by fire is an element in a number of Southwestern gambling myths. In a Keres myth, for example, *Pais-Chun-Ni-Moot* the Firebrand Boy defeats *Kai-na-ni* the Gambler at reed-dice in order to release

The hero must guess that this figure on Gambler's wall in the Navajo myth is *Ash'ke chili*, the Guard of Water Jars or the Zuñi God of Dew (see note 38). (O'Bryan, 1956)

the people Gambler has imprisoned in a mountain cave in the west.[39] Pai-Chun-Ni-Moot is the son of *Kochin-ni-na-ko*, or Yellow Woman, who is the daughter of the secular leader of Kush Kutret. Sun, the boy's father, teaches him to play dice. The youth slips past Gambler's guard crane by blinding him with his brilliance. Gambler wagers his house and loses, then wagers his eyes and loses them, too. Angry, Gambler throws the stick dice into the side of the mountain and causes it to erupt into a lake of molten rock, forcing the people to escape to the next world.[40] The dice in the story are named and described: *Tso-yot*, white with black band around middle; *Kai-shi*, black with white band; *Nai-ya*, white, with black spots; *Pai-shi*, black with white spots. Nai-ya means earth. Are fire, air, and water represented in the other dice names?

The Zuñi fire god is called *Shulawitsi*, or Firebrand Youth, and is associated with the winter solstice. He is similar to the Hopi *Maasaw*, god of the underworld, fire, and the sun.[41] In an amusing Hopi myth, Maasaw, out of curiosity, sneaks up on a group playing *sosotukwpi* in a kiva and is frightened by the players.[42] Sosotukwpi is a guessing game that frequently figures in Hopi myths; older people recall that it was often played through the night. In an unrelated legend, everyone in the village of Pivanhokyapi, including the chief's wife, became so addicted to the game that the chief arranged for the destruction of the village through fire to purify the dissolute community.[43]

Sun Youth is a dubious character among the Pueblos. He is "strictly the fertilizing and sexual power of the Sun molded into anthropomorphic shape, a force, when pursued as far as it will go, that ends in the phallic grossness of the clown societies," said Hamilton Tyler in *Pueblo Gods and Myths*.[44] Sun is the presiding god of the seasons, and Sun Youth is his deputy as the original patron of the clown society (Koshare) and ravisher of Corn Maidens. He is most often seen surrounded by myriads of butterflies, playing his seductive flute from which the butterflies emerge as objectified musical notes. As we shall see, butterflies are an important symbol in the Navajo gambler chantways.

Like Sun Youth, Poseyemu is associated with the cult of clowns, which portrays controversial subjects in skits performed during ceremonies. According to anthropologist Elsie Clews Parsons, the cult was opposed: "On the traditional migration southward, at least Cochiti society chiefs, jealous of the Clowns, criticized them for performing 'miracles' and doing 'whatever came into their heads.'"[45]

Among some Pueblos, Poseyemu carries a negative value. At Laguna Pueblo, Poseyemu is "a despised little boy, a miracle worker or nothing more than a juggler [of the dual forces] and deceiver who has finally to be killed," said Parsons. In one myth he deceives the people, and in the end his mother has to send Masewi (the elder twin brother) to drown him in the ocean.[46] Poseyemu leaves, traveling in a clockwise fashion from the northeast, south into Mexico, against Masewi's counterclockwise movements. From then on the priests have bad fortune: The sky dries up, the plants die, and the people are struck with famine. Only when Poseyemu is found and killed is the fortune reversed.

Parmentier said the story of the Pueblo culture hero is about the reversal of fortune. The divine mediator transforms poverty into plenty, childlessness into parenthood, small game into large game, anonymity into identity. The "final resolution is an affirmation of the female principle over the male principle, an affirmation strong enough to balance the male and female forces."[47]

One of the feats the culture hero accomplishes is the ability to unite the conflicting halves of himself. This process is often projected into stories about the divine twins. Sun Youth is sometimes the father of the War Twins (by Yellow Woman), who expressed his dual nature as companion to and mocker of the Sun.[48] Sun Youth portrays half of the Sun's twofold power, that of fertility, while the War Twins (frequently sons of the Sun) represent an elaboration of the power of war. The twins, by extension, represent the disparities in the single characters of Poseyemu, Montezuma, Sun Youth, and Noqoìlpi the Gambler.

Dueling Gamblers

"Those curious children" the divine twins: "always contending, they are original patrons of play, and their games are the games now played by men," wrote Culin.[49] They live in the east and in the west, rule night and day, winter and summer, and represent the two halves of Venus as the morning and evening stars. We have seen their pervasiveness in gambler myths across the country. The Pueblos have their share of gambling twins, which may have been yet another export of Mexico.

Opposing players at Zuñi, particularly the Bow priests who were members of the esoteric society of war shamans, represented the Twins War Gods in game festivals held in their honor.[50] The members of the Bow society corresponded to the sacred precincts of North, South, East, West, Upper, Lower, and Middle regions, and we can extrapolate that the districts were integrated by the games. The theme of duality continues in the use of four sets of four cane arrows in the stick-dice game, shó'liwe. Each set was tied together and ribbed with red or black paint to symbolize the quadrants, each with a numerical value.[51] The nature of the game was essentially a sacred tribal process of divination. The game was played to forecast war or peace, prosperity or adversity, and was accompanied by gambling. At other times it was played for the determination of peace and war, of the directions or precautions to be taken in defensive or offensive operations or preparations. In that case, there were necessarily four participants, each with his own canes. A shrine for the game existed in the uppermost room of the pueblo (now fallen), where the players gathered to divine at night or during terrific sand storms.[52]

Mythical pairs of siblings present a different kind of dualism in the Pueblo system of duality. They are rarely adversaries but fight on the same team. The characteristics of the twins are not opposite, but complementary. Despite the fact that they are twins, they are referred to as older and younger brother; the older is the extrovert who often fails, while the wiser, younger one succeeds. (In most of the myths explored in earlier chapters, youth prevails over age. The young hero is always victorious over the old gambler, with the counsel, of course, of an old sage or deity.) Rather than represent good versus evil, the twins unify the feminine and masculine principles. As the miraculous offspring of the Sun, their adventures are the origin of war and hunting, the outward bound aspect of the masculine principle. Representing their feminine nature is their virgin mother (usually Yellow Woman or Corn), who appears also as their sister and their wife, is constantly spoken of as their grandmother, and is the Moon and the Earth, the Spider Woman. Ortiz said the Pueblos devoted endless myth cycles to bringing the Sun and Earth back together, which is achieved through their conception and further achieved through test-theme sequences.[53] The twins are sent by their mother or grandmother to meet their father, grandfather, or higher authority, but they must prove their parentage in gambling and guessing contests.

The following Keresan myth parallels a previous myth about the singular Sun Youth versus the gambler.[54] This story takes on the flavor of Rumpelstiltskin, and the father is not the Sun but a bird called Cliff-Dweller.[55] Cliff-Dweller abducts Yellow Woman (Corn), the daughter of a chief at Acoma Pueblo, by rolling a water-jar support ring (from hoop and pole game) toward her. He imprisons her in a room at his cliffhouse and orders her to grind all the corn by the time he returns, or he will kill her.[56] Spider Woman hears her crying and magically transforms the corn into four baskets of meal.[57] This is repeated the next day, but Cliff-Dweller decides to kill her anyway.

He lowers Yellow Woman down the cliff in a spider web (representing a gaming shield), and when she runs toward Mt. Taylor (west of Albuquerque), he knocks her down with the ring. The twin heroes emerge from her dead body. White Crow raises them, gives them bows and arrows after they have rapidly grown, and sends them to their grandfather, a gambler chief who lives at Acoma Pueblo. When the boys arrive, they are mistaken for Navajos, despite their attempts to reveal their true identity. The chief takes them into the next room to gamble with four gaming sticks for clothes. The boys win, and the chief realizes they have magical gaming powers. They tell him their identity, and he weeps at finding his long-lost grandsons.

In another version, Yellow Woman kills her abductor, but she gives birth to the twins after being clubbed by the kachinas (spirits).[58] After four days she sends her sons to her father, the Acoma chief, known as Remembering Prayer Sticks. On their arrival from the south, they spot the chief's house marked by three ladders with parrots perched on each one. (The parrots hint at a tie-in with Mexico.) The chief challenges them to a guessing contest, and the boys stake their hearts. The boys must guess the contents of the bag: the Dipper on the north wall, the Pleiades on the west wall, Orion's Belt on the east wall, the Scorpion on the south. The boys win and are accepted, thereby again reconciling Heaven and Earth.[59] In other myths, Yellow Woman, as the daughter of Remembering Prayer Sticks, gets caught in battles between Winter (her jealous husband) and Summer (her lover), which represent the formal transference of power from one season to the next.

The twins are not always male. Consider *Iyatiku*, the Earth or Corn Mother, who is interchangeable with Yellow Woman as the mother of the gambler twins. She is the inventor of all the games[60] and is frequently referred to as the mother, sister, or boss of Poseyemu and Montezuma.[61] Iyatiku also has a twin sister; one sister is always the mother of the people (Indians) while the other is the mother of the aliens, usually whites or Navajos.[62] They compete in guessing games, races, or wrestling matches to determine, among other outcomes, whose people would live and whose would be destroyed. The sisters are models for the religious and secular leaders of the pueblos. In the following Keres story, which describes the destruction of an island and the beginning of gaming, some of the elements are again reminiscent of the gambling episodes involving Sun Youth or the twins and represent the wish to exert power over the seasons.

Iyatiku goes home to Shipap (the underworld) because she is annoyed by her sister, this time referred to as *Istoakoa* (Reed Woman), for bathing in the big water.[63] The rains recede in her wake. Fearful that her sister will die of famine, Iyatiku sends a runner to bring her home. When the sister returns, so do the rains. The runner then reports to Iyatiku that along the way he has been challenged by the *Kopot* brothers to a race.[64] She consents and gives him a trick *towaka* (a kicking stick made of two-inch wood or bone) to exchange for the one the Kopot brothers use.

The runner meets with the brothers and bets an eye for an eye over a race around the world where the water and the land meet, during which time he makes the exchange after getting past the guard turkey. With the ill-fated towaka, the Kopot brothers fall into a hole (sipapu?) in the roof of a house while the island runner has kicked his stick out of sight. He wins and claims an eye from each of them, which he throws into the sky, where they remain in the tail of the constellation of the Scorpion. The angry Kopot brothers throw the bad stick into the side of the mountain, and out of the resulting hole comes the big water animal, *Wa-wa-keh*, vomiting streams of water. Kush Kutret is flooded. The people escape to the top of the mountain and throw heated stones into the Wa-wa-keh. The water subsides, but the people turn to stone and the crows pick out their eyes.[65]

The following Maricopa/Pima myth demonstrates how twins participate in the apocalyptical creation, destruction, and regeneration of the world.[66] In the beginning, the twins—*Kokmat* (middle earth or mud), who the Pima call Earth Doctor, and his brother, *Kokmat hairk*— are born in a whirlwind. Earth Doctor turns his brother into a spider and sends him to stretch his web outward from the center of the earth in the four directions.[67] Upon the web he shapes the earth, and he pushes the sky back with his hand, creating five stars. The twins manufacture a race of people, but the spider brother's people are misshapen. This causes a feud between the twins, which results in more constellations; eventually, a flood wipes the slate clean.

A new set of twins are born to Sun and Moon: Coyote Man (*Hatelowish epash*) and Fox Man (*Quokosh epash*), who copy everything the first twins did with the same results. A flood wipes out the humans, and Earth Doctor creates a third generation, which multiplies so rapidly that they eat each other. It is decided to burn the earth and store the ashes in a vessel for a fourth generation, then flood the earth clean again.

While playing hide and seek in the Milky Way, Coyote spots the vessel carrying the human seed and chases after it. Earth Doctor joins the race, and it turns into a contest between the two. During the fourth race, the two continuously kick the vessel in front of them, but neither reaches it.[68] Fox intervenes, proposing that they draw lots for the vessel. He makes four sticks, one for each brother, and paints them half white and half red while no one is looking. He asks Earth Doctor to choose one for himself and his brother, but Earth Doctor strikes them on a stone, turning the process into a dice game. If they fall all white, the count would be one, and if they fall all red, the count would be two, but if they fall mixed, the count would be nothing. Coyote and Fox quibble and cheat, but their sticks can only fall mixed. During the distraction, Earth Doctor sends the red-haired woodpecker to plant the seed from the vessel into the burned ashes of trees throughout the world. The new people play the games invented by the primordial twins to create the world.

Whereas the Zuñi, Keresan, and Pima/Maricopa twins must integrate the heavens and earth through gambling, the Maya twins must unite the sky-earth with the underworld via the ball games described in the Popol Vuh, the Dawn of Life, preserved by a Quiché Maya nobleman after Spanish colonization in 1527.[69] The poetic narration is a five-part origin legend illustrating the rising and setting dates of Venus and other astronomical events. The story would have been used by a "daykeeper" to divine the future in much the same way priests referred to the Chinese I Ching, Book of Changes.

The Popol Vuh, involving several sets of heroic twins, takes place in alternating above-ground and below-ground episodes, which are what the Quiché call "sowing and dawning movements" prefiguring the present-day movements of the sun, moon, planets, and stars.[70] The polar activities of setting and dawning are synonymous with sowing and reaping and sacrifice and fertility. Once again we may consider these dualities in general as complementary rather than opposed, interpenetrating rather than mutually exclusive.

The sowing and dawning occurs at the Genesis of the Maya scheme. The gods of the primordial sea (including the Plumed Serpent) and the gods of the primordial sky conceive of the emergence of earth from the sea with the growth of plants and people on its surface. The sprouting of seeds sown in the earth is their dawning. The sowing of the sun, moon, and stars is followed by a difficult passage through the underworld and by their own dawning. Human beings are sown in the womb and emerge into the light at birth. At death, their bodies are sown in the earth, and their dawning follows when their souls become the stars.

The gaming sequences in the *Popol Vuh* are complex and numerous. For a taste, we will review the first ball-game sequence between two sets of twins in a court on the eastern edge of the earth's surface: The noise disturbs One and Seven Death (another set of twins) in Xibalba, the underworld, and they challenge the upperworld twins to a game downstairs. Accepting the dare, One and Seven Hunahpu, a set of twins, traverse perilous terrain before arriving at the Xibalba ball court on the western edge. They must spend a night in the Dark House and are warned to keep the two cigars lit all night. They fail the test, and instead of playing ball, their hosts sacrifice them and bury them at the Place of Ball Game Sacrifice. But One Hunahpu's severed head is hung in a Calabash tree. The tree, for the first time, bears fruit the size and shape of a human head. One Hunahpu's skull spits into the hand of Blood Woman, the maiden daughter of a Xibalban lord named Blood Gatherer, thereby impregnating her with the hero twins and regenerating himself. These twins grow up to avenge their father's death.

Retold from a calendrical point of view, anthropologist Dennis Tedlock said Venus rose as the morning star on a day named Hunahpu, corresponding to the ballplaying of One and Seven Hunahpu in the east. After being out of sight in Xibalba, Venus reappears as the evening star on a day named Death, when One Hunahpu's head is placed in a tree in the west. Venus will be reborn as the morning star in further scenes.

Esther Pasztory, author of "The Historical and Religious Significance of the Middle Classic Ball Game," suggested that the ball-game sequences in the *Popol Vuh* symbolized the death and rebirth of the sun.[71] The Sun and his brother, Venus, are sacrificed during the game by the night deities of death, so that night falls. Together, they defeat the power of darkness in the underworld, and Sun, reborn, once again rises the following morning. By extension, the game may have been played during the equinox as, through white magic, the descending sun immediately ascends, being reborn from the underworld. The stars must die for the sun to feed and light up the earth.

The themes of fertility (water, plants, sowing) and sacrifice (beheading and removal of the heart) were interrelated and associated with the ball game among the Aztecs. The *Codex Borbonicus* shows a gruesome ceremony involving the brother and sister in the construction of a ball court.[72] The picture shows a beheading to the left of a ball court where a ball is volleyed through two suspended stone rings (representing the division between night and day). Under the righthand ring there is an image of water flowing from a dark opening. To the left of the opening is an emerging skull. According to the codex, *Huitzilopochtli*, the Aztec god of war, made the actual hole in the court as shown in the pictograph and addressed the people, "So, Mexicans, this is already done and the well that is made is full of water; sow now and plant willows." In the very ball court, he seized his sister, *Coyolxauhqui*, killed her, beheaded her, and tore out her heart. These themes of fertility and sacrifice echo in the Navajo gambling chantways.

The Navajo Gambler and His Facsimile

On the surface, it would appear that the Navajo Great Gambler is exempt from this duality scheme. A closer look reveals that every god in the myth has a counterpart who reflects and expresses the complexity of the other. When these characters appear in other mythic contexts they adopt the persona of their counterpart. Heroes and tricksters, therefore, are not wholly good or wholly evil.

Both the bad gambler and the hero gambler are sons of the Sun and in some versions are considered twins.[73] The Sun teaches his first son gambling games and magic and gives him some exquisite jewelry to stake at games with the people. But because this gambler goes overboard in his obsessions, the Sun sends another son to retrieve his jewelry through gambling.[74] The second son is a twin and, in versions where the duality isn't mentioned, he masquerades as the gambler. This may be viewed as good versus evil, but not by Western standards.

What is actually being said is that the dual aspects of the Sun, which has the power to both destroy and procreate, must be kept in balance. Evil is not destroyed but transformed. Rare is the death of the bad gambler in Navajo circles.

Matthews's version encompasses three sets of counterparts: Sun and Begochídí; Talking God (*Hastséyalti*) and House or Growling God (*Hastséhogan*); and Noqoìlpi the Great Gambler and the young husband. The pairs are ranked vertically with Sun naturally at the zenith, the gamblers at the nadir on earth, and Talking God and Growling God as the mediators between the two. The dual forces allow for interchangeability between the "twins." Furthermore, each of these beings radiates certain Sun-like qualities, and it is through this commonality that each can reflect the traits of any one of the others.

The pivotal character is Begochídí, who transforms Noqoìlpi from that of a tyrannical gambler to a returning prophet on horseback named *Nakai Digini*, or God of the Mexicans. Begochídí's transformative power has precedence in a story where First Man ascends to him in heaven, promising to return in two days.[75] Upon returning, he reports on the decree of eternal punishment in hell or happiness in heaven for the people, thereby drawing parallels between the Navajo underworld/sky-world and the Christian hell/heaven.

Matthews erroneously assumes that Begochídí, the Carrier of the Moon, is synonymous with the God of the Americans. That is an easy mistake to make. His hair is shiny, and little rays of light sparkle from him. In some stories he creates, destroys, and restores the underworlds.[76] Begochídí invents horses, and Navajos who want horses sing songs to him.[77] In one story, the twins go to "their father" Begochídí, who gives them horses, identifying him with the Sun, who is blond and lives high overhead and creates the sky, the stars, the earth, and some of its people.[78]

But Begochídí is actually a mischief maker—his name literally means "One Who Grabs Breasts."[79] He can move invisibly as rainbow, wind, sand, or water, enabling him to sneak up behind women and grab their breasts, shouting, "be'go be'go" (hence his name). He grabs men's testicles while they hunt and similarly molests couples during intercourse.[80] He takes pity on people who have fallen on hard times, especially for angering the gods and even when they create their own misfortune.[81] This is why he recasts Noqoìlpi and gives him horses.

In Matthews's version, Talking God, sent by Sun to recruit the hero, is himself an aspect of the Sun. Matthews claimed that Talking God is the god of dawn, the eastern horizon, and horses, while House God is the god of evening.[82] Talking God can easily be confused in the minds of Western recorders as the sun, but Matthews makes a razor-fine distinction between the light god and the sun god; morning light always precedes the sunrise.[83]

The young champion also has a dual nature and can be associated with many different branches of the mythological tree, especially the twins. In one version, he is linked with Monster Slayer, chief of the earth and the more aggressive of the twin war gods.[84] Like the Pueblo culture hero Poseyemu, the young champion is analogous to the Pueblo Sun Youth. Paul Zolbrod, author of Diné bahane': The Navajo Creation Story, said this young husband is a pale prototype of the culture hero who "begins the civilizing process by fighting greater-than-human reality configurations." In other words, he is a wise man who can balance reality with spirituality. By mediating between the people and the sources of power, he becomes awe-inspiring himself. But the young husband in this version is a weak example, said Zolbrod. "Largely of the trickster, nonwarrior variety of culture hero, the young husband here is seen as a direct extension of the will of the supernaturals and exercises no purpose of his own choosing." His only claim to being a trickster hero is his willingness to cheat in order to win.[85]

Cheating can be viewed as a strategic method of increasing one's chances and is not negative, but rather anticipated and funny. This is contrary to the Western stance that cheating robs the action of the play character and spoils the game, said Huizinga.[86] Many mythological heroes win by trickery or help from without. Huizinga noted that he had failed to discover a direct connection between the hero who attains his objective by fraud and cunning, and the divine figure who is at once benefactor and deceiver of man. But this connection indeed exists in the Messiah trickster gambler.

The young husband is actually an outline of a Navajo character named Rainboy or Downy Home Man of the chantways from which the

Great Gambler proper was abstracted. By examining a few chants, one soon detects many of the story elements that were thought to be exclusive to the isolated gambler stories. In the context of the lengthy chantways, it is not the bad gambler who undergoes personal transformation, but the hero himself. He is the divine child in exile.

Excess Way

In the Navajo chantway narrations, the hero is transformed from a self-willed and irresponsible youth to one who undertakes and fulfills serious ceremonial obligations for his people.[87] In a constellation of chantways, the youth is exiled for indolence, lack of direction, negativity, or excessive gambling and is forced into solitary wanderings—during which time he learns about sacred gambling. Obsessive gambling provokes punishment and sometimes death. Through sacred gambling, the hero undergoes a metamorphosis, but he does so through trickery and witchcraft.

Once the young hero embarks on his own adventure in the different chants, he plays games with children, submits to a suitor test, and witnesses his people and the Holy people in various gambling ceremonies.[88] He continues to learn that excessive gambling leads to unfortunate results. In Enemy Way, for instance, he contends with others who are indulging in games and observes women arguing over stick dice. In the telling of these stories the narrator sometimes stops to explain how such games lead to quarreling. Some gambling is sanctioned, especially when the hero must bet against his skills in life-threatening consequences.

The Great Gambler proper is embodied in a Navajo ceremonial chant called Prostitution Way.[89] Prostitution Way is the subject of Clyde Kluckhohn's quintessential gambler myth in *Navajo Witchcraft*. Everything—the original intent of the myth and the archetypal conflict—comes together in this body of work.

The young hero is sexually rejected from Jemez Pueblo; that is, no woman there wants to sleep with him. After many years of travel to more than fifty-seven authentic ruins in and around Chaco Canyon, he is taken by Talking God to Cone Towards Water Man, who teaches him chants and plant uses for love magic. He uses his love magic on two "non-sunlight-struck maidens" who live underground in the kivas.[90] Their father identifies him by matching his feet to the footprints leading away from his daughters' cell and calls him son-in-law. As payment for his wives, the hero kills twelve antelope by drawing them to him with sunbeams. On succeeding days he kills up to fifty antelope and eventually gains six wives. "That's the reason we call this story Prostitution Way," said Kluckhohn's informant.

The boy leaves the wives and earns his new name, Downy Home Man, when he covers himself with feathers to keep warm at night. Wishing to seduce two more non-sunlight-struck maidens, he boasts that he can beat Earth Winner (the gambler) at House On Top (Pueblo Alto), for which he is ridiculed. He shifts into birds, butterflies, and a corn beetle to successfully con the women into becoming his housewives while he travels to other pueblos.

Offsetting Earth Winner is a gambler named White Butterfly who steals Downy Home Man's wives in his absence. Tracking the women toward Chaco Canyon, the hero runs into a big meeting of the gods, who are discussing the girls living in the kiva of Kin Teel.[91] Everyone, including Earth Winner, is trying to release them. He competes with White Butterfly for the girls and wins every game through trickery and help of the supernaturals.[92] White Butterfly finally admits defeat and asks to be killed, and in some versions he offers the rebounding ax.[93] When Downy Home Man smashes White Butterfly's head with the ax, all the colors of the rainbow come out of it—this is why the world is full of butterflies. Downy Home man releases some of the girls but keeps some as wives.[94]

The above story is a battle of the seasons, for here again we return to the Pueblo trickster Sun Youth who is associated with butterflies and fertility. Trickery/witchcraft, clown-like pornography, and fertility continue to be linked in the gambler mythology. In a related Keresan myth, Sun Youth uses a butterfly to entice Yellow Woman, Blue Woman, and Red Woman into taking their clothes off.[95] The myth is played out at Zuñi in a winter solstice ceremony which reenacts Sun Youth's seduction of the eight Corn Maidens (six represent the corn of the colors of the six directions; the seventh and eighth represent sweet corn and squash). They are personified as plump virgins who are coveted by other men, and their dance is as erratic as the flight of butterflies. The transformation of one season into the next is seen as a death, and in winter, the crops and the sun die. Sun Youth, as a god of the season, must also die, and after a contest he is dismembered by his eight evil sisters (who are the opposite of the Corn Maidens). The eldest sister blows Sun Youth's flute, and out come the butterflies of the directional colors. The fourth butterfly is multicolored and represents Sun Youth himself. He lures the sisters into removing their clothes, etc.[96]

The fertility aspect of the Navajo gambler story has been overlooked by interpreters. Since the Navajo culture is significantly less agrarian than its Pueblo models, it could be that the fertility of crops is replaced by hunting and animal husbandry. Nevertheless, the Navajos are just as interested in keeping the world in harmony. A gambler who wins too much is the same as having a world with too much daylight or darkness or too much summer or winter.[97]

Witchcraft plays a role in maintaining the balance of power,[98] and to this end, the Prostitution Way serves several purposes. The chants and plant usages the boy hero finds on his journey are referred to as Frenzy Witchcraft, a type of witchcraft for "love magic," or for success in trading and gambling. Second, Prostitution Way is a ceremonial chant used to cure a victim of Frenzy Witchcraft. Third, Prostitution Way describes a form of divination using *datura*.

In the appendix of *Navajo Witchcraft*, Kluckhohn published voluminous notes on this sort of witchcraft in the context of gaming. In one passage, a Navajo informant described the use of a plant called Cone Towards Water (assumed to be datura), which was mind or laughing medicine.[99] Players put the plant in their mouths and rubbed it on hoops, stick dice, or race horses, and the possessions they wagered. As the medicine took effect, players often pushed each other "like bucks getting at the ewes." Then, lethargy set in, which produced the reversed effect of losing the game. "The way to get cured is to get the fellow who knows how and he spits in your mouth and you get back to life," said Kluckhohn's informant who never touched the plant or "you go crazy." It will also work on women as an aphrodisiac.

Here's one informant's recipe for the use of datura in gambling:

For winning the games, if you use all the turquoise and the Game Way songs and prayers and it doesn't work, then use these Frenzy Witchcraft plants. Take a little piece of deer from a deer that has been shot a few days ago. Just a small piece of meat or fat. Put the meat with these plants on four sides of a firepit and put some in the middle too. Sing the Frenzy Witchcraft song. If this doesn't work, go into the sweathouse and sing the Frenzy Witchcraft song and take a very little of these plants yourself. You must put spruce needles on the floor of the sweathouse. You can also get deer this way in the sweathouse with these plants. Pray to Talking God to see just one deer, no matter how poor.[100]

The use of trickery to restore homeostasis is sanctioned in the myths, but there is good witchcraft and bad. In one myth, the gambler bewitches his opponent by shooting magical objects into his body four times during a race.[101] When the bewitched man staggers, the gambler passes him. His cursing at the end of the stories is evidence of witchcraft. So, too, is the red paint he uses to paint his face and the back of his head so that the enemy cannot tell if he is coming or going; red is the dominant color of sorcery. Furthermore, gambling witches often put their left hand or foot forward in games. Getting his or her opponents to participate in the cannibalism of the victims is a typical ruse exercised by the witch gamblers in myths across the continent.[102]

Gaming paraphernalia can sometimes have a witchcraft connotation. Hoops and rings play a large part in ceremonies that emphasize exorcism. They symbolize swift travel and are closely identified with wind, stars, hail, buffalo, and snakes; they also are employed on the first day of the Night Chant.[103] Talking God carries the ring of yucca leaves on his back and cures diseases during the Night Chant ceremony.[104]

Gaming itself "is not regarded as a bad activity, it can lead to the sort of excess that prudent individuals would do well to avoid," said Zolbrod.[105] Although gamblers are frequently associated with witchcraft and evilness, in many of the stories, songs, ceremonies, and games we've looked at in this book, never once was there a sense that gambling was morally wrong. If games were discontinued, such as the hoop and pole by Navajos, it was not because they were taboo, as some thought, but because making the equipment and finding a suitable course to play them on became inconvenient.[106] Furthermore, not all

Navajos gamble or have the means to gamble. One Navajo said he never learned to play stick dice because he never had anything to bet. If gambling were considered wrong, then it wouldn't be allowed at the intermission during the long ceremonials when the singer and his helpers are idle.

The sense that gambling was bad was superimposed on the culture by whites, said Janet Cliff, author of an article titled "Navajo Games." Some influential Navajos opposed gambling on the grounds that it wasted money and time, and this more than anything led to the decline of some of the traditional games. Bureau of Indian Affairs regulations prevented gambling and the selling of dice or cards by traders on the reservation, but government stockmen and Navajo police looked the other way when wagering took place at the Squaw Dances. Gambling was no more common among the Navajos than among the rough whites who surrounded the reservation. Nevertheless, good Navajo names in the 1920s included: The Hoop-Poler, Son of the Late Hoop-Poler, Slim Gambler, Stick Bounder, Woman Playing Cards, and Woman Who Flips Her Cards.[107]

Chantways and origin myths testify that gambling is an acceptable, even sacred, activity. The women who sat down after the emergence to a match of stick dice were not considered lazy or irresponsible. The leisure activity implies well-being, since it does not satisfy immediate biologically based survival needs, said Cliff. People who play games are "civilized," for it is less threatening when an enemy knows the game you are playing. Huizinga might agree that the play-element is a civilizing function in the growth of a culture, but once a society reaches a certain point, games become less important. Above all, the myths caution that gamblers must guard against excessive gambling, or one will not only lose their shirt but their families, and even their body parts.

* * *

In Navajo sports today, the goal is not so much to win as simply not to lose. One's status as an athlete is based on effort and ability; the competition is, therefore, with one's self. Although players do not want to lose, they do not want to appear better than their opponents and must shun publicity to avoid the accusation of practicing witchcraft.[108]

The young husband in gambler mythology is also unsung. To play with honor is a civic and sacred duty. In India, this religious responsibility in play would be called *dharma*, as displayed in the gambler myth embodied in the *Mahābhārata*. In that work, *Yudhiṣṭhira* is not unlike the Navajo champion who must gamble with his cousin at dice to determine who will be universal monarch. The ancient texts of Eastern and Western civilization explored in the next chapter will affirm the valiant gambler and sacred gaming, with all of their properties of transformation, as global archetypes. As we have seen in the Southwest, indeed the Western Hemisphere, they accommodate the complexity of almost any context, profane or profound.

SIX

Sacred Lots in the Old World

The superior man casts
the positions of the stars
and makes clear the seasons and times.
　　　　　　—"Ko: the Sun Below, the Marsh Above,"
　　　　　　Hexagram 49, *I Ching* (Reifler, 1974)

The Ancients bequeathed us the rules of the game.
There is no evil in it, nor blows.
. . . If we gamble, the heavenly gate will be nearer;
It is proper for us to engage in the game.
　　　　　　—*Mahābhārata, The Book of the Assembly Hall*[1]

Achilles's Astragalus

Although early explorers expressed disapproval of the indigenous population for its gambling obsessions and associated heathen practices, games of hazard were rampant in the New World. Lotteries were critical to funding the colonization of America, the Revolutionary War, and even such universities as Harvard and Princeton. Southerners wagered slaves, plantations, and fortunes at horse racing, cribbage, cards, dominoes, and a shell game called thimblerig. New Englanders were split. Some aligned with the British economist Sir William Petty, who called gambling a "tax upon unfortunate self-conceited fools." Others quoted the casting of lots in the Bible as sanction for their backroom betting. Indeed, classical and religious works are permeated with such examples of sacred gaming.

Old World divination was different from the Native American application of gaming. The native ritual was performed to bring down tyranny, to revitalize life, or to bring back the rains and the buffalo—to reverse fortune. Conversely, classical/religious lots were cast, in ever-evolving methods, to invoke decisions by the Supreme authorities that often culminated in the reversal of fortune. Both systems experimented with the laws of chance, which they viewed as sacred, and both had the potential of producing a psychological frenzy with disastrous results.

Biblical reliance on lots had a practical side. In Isaiah (34:17) dice were cast in order to determine the land allotments given to each family to pass on from one generation to the next. The process gives rise to the word *lot*, which actually has a Middle English origin. In Dutch it encompasses a sense of destiny—that which is sent or allotted. Translators of the Bible may have substituted the familiar word for the more obscure biblical terms *Urim* and *Thummim*.[2]

What the Urim and Thummim were and how they were used remains lost to antiquity. Scholars speculate that they were the names of two divining stones employed by priests in an unknown fashion as a channel for the will of God—one stating the affirmative and the other the negative. In Exodus (28:30), for example, God tells Moses that whenever Aaron comes into His presence in holy places, he must carry the Urim and Thummim in his breastpiece (*ephod*) engraved with the names of the tribes of Israel. In so doing, God would always remember His people, and Aaron could determine His will for Israel.

To determine whether Saul's son, Jonathan, is guilty of eating honey against orders, Saul petitions God to speak through the divining lots. "If the guilt is Jonathan's or mine, answer by Urim; but if it belongs to your people of Israel, answer by Thummim." The stones indicate Jonathan and Saul, and the people are cleared. Then Saul says, "Decide between my son Jonathan and me," and Jonathan is implicated.

Lots are cast or drawn to decide which of the Levites would bring the wood offering into the house of God (Nehemiah 10:34); to choose one out of every ten to live in Jerusalem (Nehemiah 11:1); to choose goats for sacrifice (Leviticus 16:10); to determine the duties of Aaron's heirs (I Chronicles 24:5); to cast blame on Jonah for a storm (Jonah 1:7); to assign duties to Zechariah according to the custom of priesthood (Luke 1:9); and to choose Matthias to take over the ministry which Jesus had assigned to Judas. The drawing of lots has stayed with us to the present in the form of draft lotteries and government fundraising schemes, minus the ritual.

The lot motif predates the Bible in Homer's *Iliad*.[3] The characters occasionally play dice for diversion, but they cast lots to make important decisions. Through this form of divination, the Olympic gods make their will known. In Book Seven, for example, the gods are called upon through the lots to determine who will fight Hector.[4] Nine candidates throw their marked lots into Agamemnon's helmet, and the people lift their hands in prayer to Father Jove that the lot fall on Ajax. Nestor shakes the helmet, and the lot of Ajax falls from it. The revealing of the chosen lot is performed with dramatic ritual as the herald carries the lot around to all nine contenders, each rejecting it until it is placed in the hand of the man who has scratched his mark on it. Hephaistos then pours wine for the gods.

The relationship among oracle, chance, and judgment in these instances is clear. "Is not the sacred balance in which Zeus, in the *Iliad*, weighs men's chances of death, much the same" as the Urim and Thummim give voice to the Christian God? asked Huizinga. The scales of justice are the emblem of uncertain chance. One of the devices on the shield of Achilles, as described in Book Eighteen, represents a legal proceeding with judges sitting within the sacred circle. At the center of the circle are two talents of gold for him who pronounces the most righteous judgement. These are commonly interpreted as objects of litigation, but Huizinga believes they are a stake or prize better suited to a game of lots than to a judicial session. The word *talenta* originally meant scales, and the weighing of scales was the same as oracle by lot. Themis (Right or Divine Justices) and Diké (Human Justice) sit with Zeus in Olympus. On Greek coins, Diké sometimes turns into Tyche, the Goddess of Uncertain Fate (Fortuna). The Hebrew word *thorah* (right, justice, law) has affinities with a root that means casting lots, shooting, and the pronouncement of an oracle; *urim* might come from the same root, Huizinga said.[5]

The Greek passion for dice games is demonstrated by Achilles's squire, Patroclus, who kills the son of Amphidamas in a "childish quarrel over dice," which was apparently invented by Palamedes to relieve the boredom of soldiers during the Trojan Wars. The Lydians of a wealthy kingdom in Asia Minor claimed the invention of games, according to Greek historian Herodotus (484–425 B.C.E.). But he added, "The plan adopted against famine [c. 1500 B.C.E.] was to engage in games on one day so entirely as not to feel any craving for food, and the next day to eat and abstain from games. In this way they passed eighteen years." The Lydians played such games as dice, knucklebones, hucklebones, and ball, but not tables (i.e., backgammon), "the invention of which they do not claim as theirs."[6]

The roll of the dice that produced a one count was called the *dog* by Greeks and Romans or sometimes, less frequently, the *vulture*. The best of all throws with four bones was called the *venus*, when "all the sides uppermost were different." In the *Lives of the Caesars*, Roman historian Suetonius (c. 69–141 C.E.) mentioned the passion for gaming. In the *Life of Augustus* he said, "When the dice were thrown whoever turned up the dog or the six, put a denarius [coin] in the pool for each one of the dice, and the whole was taken by anyone who threw the venus."[7] The scoring may have been alluded to in the very first verse of Book One of the *Iliad*, in which Achilles's wrath sent many a brave hero to Hades as carrion for dogs and vultures.[8]

In Book Twenty-three, *vertebra* is the word used for dice, probably referring to the game of hucklebones, Patroclus's downfall.[9] F. N. David, a mathematician and philosopher, asserted that in classic literature, the word astragalus was often interchanged with knucklebone, hucklebone, talus, and die.[10] In fact, whenever the word *dice* was used, the astragalus was intended, and in Greek, *astragolos* means vertebra.[11] The astragalus in the deer or antelope is a bone in the heel lying above the talus, "which, in strict anatomical sense, is the heel-bone," he said. Large numbers of decorated astragali have been found in prehistoric sites all around the globe, and to say they are dice in prehistory is conjecture—

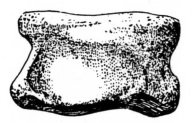 

Bison (left) and deer astragali. (Culin, 1907)

but we know the Babylonians, Egyptians, Greeks, and Romans of the pre-Christian era played with astragali in dice games. A number of Greek vases depict Achilles and Ajax playing a sort of backgammon with astragalus dice. In light of the fact that the Trojans played dice and also cast lots to determine the will of the gods (who were always intervening in the battles and races) Achilles's heel—his mortal vulnerability—carries a new meaning.[12]

Greeks and Romans customarily used four astragali in temples for gaining insight into one's circumstances from the gods.[13] The forecasters entered the temple, stated their wishes, and cast the astragali provided for them on the sacred table. Reference tablets inscribed into the dice table spelled out the meaning of each count. Even numbers meant an auspicious event represented by the venus-throw, while the odd number was for the dogs. Roman poet Propertius (c. 50–15 B.C.E.) lamented, "When I was seeking [the fortune of] Venus with favorable *tali* the damned dogs always leapt out." Suetonius said Tiberius, before becoming Emperor, sought his fortune by throwing golden tali into the fountain of Aponus.[14]

Since the binary nature of "odds and evens" does not give the gods much scope for self-expression, the Greeks also employed a more sophisticated method. The possibilities using five astragali were as follows: the throw of Savior Zeus (15), the throw of Good Cronos (18), the throw of Poseidon (22), and the throw of child-eating Cronos (24). For example, this is the fortune of the zeus-throw:

> One, two threes, two fours,
> The deed which thou meditates, go do it boldly.
> Put thy hand to it. The gods have given these favorable omens.
> Shrink not from it in thy mind, for no evil shall befall thee.[15]

One Egyptian tomb-painting (c. 3500 B.C.E.) depicts a nobleman in his after-life playing a game using an astragalus to move his hounds and jackals along the squares of a board. This not only lends a sense of antiquity to both the game and the symbolism of the dog but suggests a connection between the game and death or the after-life.[16] Although game playing was highly developed in Egypt—as evidenced by the tomb-painting—gaming may have arrived with Ptolemy from Greece around

300 B.C.E., as evidenced by a cubical limestone die engraved with the sacred symbols of Osiris, Horus, Isis, Nebat, Hathor, or Horhudet on subsequent sides.

Tibetan Buddhists used dice in a more elaborate way to predict the next stage of reincarnation as late as 1893. The priest threw the six-sided die (with letters instead of pips on each side) onto a large rebirth chart of fifty-six squares, each corresponding to a possible future life. The prediction was based on whichever square a particular letter landed. The letter Y had something to do with a ghostly existence and necessitated the performance of many expensive rites to counteract the undesirable fate. (It is frequently the letter that unhappy recipients of the fortune tried to rub off the die.) Laymen carried pocket divination manuals for interpretation.[17]

A game board is little more than a three-dimensional abacus, and when it is used the focus of play becomes a race between the counters as opposed to the count of the dice throws. Greek mathematicians in as early as 500–400 B.C.E. carried out their calculations with colored pebbles. The conjunction of colored pebbles and astragali in prehistoric sites and of the pebbles and astragali in early board games is suggestive, but not provable. That gambling was developed from game-playing is at least a possibility. David suggested that gambling was a further idealization of the board game, where the random element was retained and the board dispensed with. "It is, however, equally likely that gaming developed from the wager and the wager from the drawing of lots, the interrogation of the oracles, and so on, which have their roots deep in religious ritual."[18]

While poets, priests, and the elite mused over the sacred luck of the draw in Greece, Tibet, Egypt and elsewhere, Greek mathematicians and philosophers were beginning to intuit the randomness of events and fumble toward a theory of probability. Roman writer and statesman Cicero (106–43 B.C.E.), in *De Divinatione*, Book I, through his character Quintus asked, "When the four dice produces the venus-throw you may talk of accident: but suppose you made a hundred casts and the venus-throw appeared a hundred times; could you call that accidental?" In Book II, he answered his query with another, "How then can an event be anticipated and predicted which occurs fortuitously and as a result of blind chance and of the spinning of Fortune's wheel?"[19]

Fortune, it seems, was commonly seen not as a random event but a *fait accompli*, a thing done. As Homer illustrated in Book Twenty-four of the *Iliad*, it did no good to grieve a friend's death when it was his destiny: "The immortals know no care, yet the lot they spin for man is full of sorrow." But Cicero was leery of the casting of lots: "As a matter of fact the whole system of peering into the future by means of lots was the invention of tricksters who were only interested in their own financial welfare or in fostering superstition and folly."

Superstition and folly aside, Romans bet future wages, homes, wives, and children at the gaming tables, prompting legislators to establish antigambling laws. Through the ages other governments tried to legislate gaming. The Scottish parliament banned golf in the fifteenth century because it distracted too much from archery practice. Sixteenth-century town council statutes in Europe limited marble games to fields beyond village limits and authorized the use of a cat-o-nine-tails (whip) on boys who "refused to be warned off" from playing beneath fish stands. Sir William Petty (1623–87) argued that the Sovereign should guard "gamblers, lunatics, and idiots" from their own worst instincts. Throughout the Dark Ages the Church vigorously and unsuccessfully fulminated against gaming as a vice or because it was too closely woven to the gods of the pagan religions the Church wished to exorcise.

In the seventeenth century, at the celebrated prompting of Chevalier de Méré, Blaise Pascal and Pierre Fermat worked out, through the mail, the mathematical probability of the fall of the dice. Pascal believed, "It is the heart that experiences God, and not the reason." Yet the scientific and intellectual advancements of Pascal's time gave rise to *The Age of Reason*, in which Thomas Paine summed up a new course of thinking: "My own mind is my own church." This reflected the general scientific approach Paine's colleagues took to social and political issues, slouching toward a belief in the mechanical clockwork order of the universe. The theory of probability promoted a new confidence in gamblers, almost as if reason could override chance, of particular interest to insurance underwriters. Insurance is "an ingenious modern game of chance in which the player is permitted to enjoy the comfortable conviction that he is beating the man who keeps the table," wrote American author

Ambrose Bierce (1842–1914). Spirituality and gambling thus became forever separated in Western thought.

Dice Games in India and the New World Order

In the Old World, the casting of lots might have produced a favorable venus-throw, determined bravery or guilt, divided the land, and decided holy wars. In India the roll of the dice represented a concept known as *mahayuga,* or "great time," in a game played by the gods of creation, destruction, and regeneration. India's complex and ancient mythologies define a connection between divinity and gambling that is nearer to the Native American symbolism.

Players in India were fond of a game called *panchika,* a precursor to *pachisi.* The game was played with five, six, or seven cowry shells on a dissected, cross-shaped circuit embroidered into cloth.[20] The word "pachisi" means "five and twenty," the ultimate count one can receive when all five cowry shells fall mouth up. Panchika may have also been referred to as *ayanaya,* meaning "luck and unluck" in San-skrit. So popular was the game that fanatics carried their silken game cloths around in their turbans. The elite played the game in a marble courtyard on which live "draught" men, dressed in green, red, yellow, or black, walked the circuit and hustled one another off the squares.

Edward B. Tylor presented the following Sanskrit cryptic description of the game:

> In a house where there were many, there is left but one, and where there was none and many come, at last there was none. Thus Kâla and Kâli, casting day and night for their pair of dice, play with human beings for pieces on the board of the world.[21]

The riddle parallels a verse in Book Thirteen of the *Mahābhārata,* which says the world was conceived as a dice board upon which *Shiva* played dice with his queen, *Shakti.*[22] India's mythologies are based on a number of traditions, religions, and books, all as interwoven as those of the Americas, especially in the Southwest and Mexico. The deities are constantly mirroring the qualities of their counterparts while interchanging roles with others. One way of expressing this fluctuating duality is to switch genders.

Shiva is the god of destruction and is one-third of the Hindu triad completed by *Brahma*, god of creation, and *Vishnu*, god of preservation. The three are the principle interacting forces of the universe. Shiva also plays all three divine roles of destroyer, creator, and protector. It is his job to periodically destroy the universe, which he does with a frenzied dance; but like the beat of a drum, his dance is rhythmical, controlled, and inevitable.[23]

In some Hindu texts the universe springs forth from Shiva's sexual union with Shakti. Shakti is often described as the half of Shiva that represents the feminine principle and the reproductive organs. Her pure, raw energy is transmuted to creative power, but without Shiva's control it can be unpredictably disruptive, as it is when she takes on the form of Kali, the daughter of the mountain king. With Kali, luck is ambivalent:

> As good fortune, the goddess bestows wealth on men's homes in times of prosperity. In times of disaster she appears as misfortune for their annihilation.[24]

Kali can also be portrayed as male. In the *Mahābhārata*, the exiled hero comes across a story about Kali, here called the god of misfortune. Kali becomes so enraged over his lover's plans to marry King Nala that he enters the king's feet when, before a ceremony, the king fails to wash after urinating. Being possessed by Kali, King Nala loses his stakes of raw and refined gold, wagons, horses, and clothes. He is crazed by the thrill of the dice, and none of his friends are able to restrain his mindless gambling.[25]

Either force, Shiva or Shakti, is by itself annihilative, but together—whether in union as man and wife, or as male and female halves of the self (anima and animus)—the forces keep each other in balance, and the continuance of life is ensured. The goddess as consort symbolizes unity in duality; the polarities of existence represented in male and female deities are united through marriage or sexual embrace. In the dice game, Kali and Kala play tug of war with yin and yang as they take turns clearing the board of each others' counters, as depicted in Tylor's riddle. When day and night are the dice and the world is a board, a win means the destruction of the worlds.

Kala is a Sanskrit word meaning time and death. The Kali *yuga* refers to that period when the universe collapses into itself to become pure potential, after which all phenomena reemerge. The *Puranas*, a source of Hindu mythology (300–1000 C.E.), conceive of the cosmology as divided into four cosmic ages or yugas of unequal duration, *kal*culated by the roll of the dice.[26] The names of the yugas are borrowed from the names of the throws in the game of dice. *Krita* yuga means the "perfect age" in dice-play, the throw that turns up the side with four pips in a winning hand.[27] This Golden or Primordial Age lasts four thousand divine years and mythologically speaks of the perfect man who leads an exemplary, archetypal existence. Next the *Treta* yuga, symbolized by three pips on the die, marks the beginning of a regression. In this Silver Age, lasting three thousand divine years, humans realize only three-quarters of their spiritual existence (dharma), and suffering and death now become their lot. In the *Dvapara* yuga, symbolized by two pips, only half the dharma survives on earth while evils and vices increase. Known as the Copper Age, it lasts two thousand divine years. The Kali yuga, or Iron Age, is designated by one pip, the losing throw, and is the evil age in which only a quarter of the dharma survives.[28] Through a play on words, this stage fuses the goddess of misfortune with time, death, and black or darkness.

When Tylor's riddle refers to using night and day as dice, it is referring to the night and day of Brahma, the Supreme Creator. One day and night (another 12,000 years) of Brahma is said to comprise a thousand units of the four-age cycle; that is, the cosmos is destroyed and recreated a thousand times in just one day of Brahma, but there is a major destruction at the end of Brahma's life, or one hundred years of Brahma. Brahma is reborn through the navel of Vishnu. According to this system, the date is now the Kali yuga (which began in 3102 B.C.E.) of Brahma's fifty-first year.

Icelandic mythology also employs the dice boardgame metaphor to express creation and recreation.[29] Loki, the trickster-shapeshifter in the *Edda*, is put away in a cave for killing Balder, god of light and beauty, with a mistletoe dart. According to prophecy, when the end of the world comes in the *Ragnarok*, the twilight of the gods, Loki will break his chains and lead evil monsters and giants against the army of Odin, the one-eyed ruling god and lawgiver, who will be devoured by the wolf. The earth will be destroyed by fire, and the entire universe will sink back into the sea. This final destruction will be followed by a rebirth in a kind of Elysian or Golden Age. The Æsir (gods) who survive will recall past events and Odin's runes.[30] They will find the golden tables on which they had played dice in the previous world and, according to Huizinga, will cast the world's fate by throwing dice.[31] As we have seen, many of the Native American gambling myths describe similar endings and renewals of the cosmos through dice games and other games.

The *Sar Bachan*, a nineteenth-century esoteric text of India, provides the definitive interpretation of the riddle of Kali and Kala as it relates to the playing elements of pachisi and the mythological comparison of time to the dice role.[32] The four groups of variant-colored markers of pachisi represent the four classes of life: human and mammal, insect, bird, and vegetation. In this case, Kali and Kala are substituted by *Brahm* [sic] (the creative/destructive power of the phenomenal world) and *Maya* (the deity of delusion), which are collectively referred to as *Kal*, the negative power. These forces play the game with the hand of *karma* (the laws of cause and effect) and the dice of the three *gunas* (energies): daylight or activity, darkness or inertia, and twilight or harmony.

In this metaphorical game, whatever actions are performed by each piece, which is referred to as the soul, determine which of the four classes it rotates or reincarnates into, and in this way the soul remains a pawn in this game through the yugas. At the end of the Kali yuga, the worlds are perpetually destroyed and recreated. Finally, after millions of chances on the dice board, a soul evolves to a point where it meets a *sat guru* (true master), who shows it how to beat the game once and for all. In the Native gambler myths, the culture hero seeks the wisdom of the Holy People in order to beat the gambler and thereby restore harmony. But in the system mentioned here, the objective is to return the soul to its true abode in *Sach Khand*, the Imperishable Region, where the creation and destruction of the worlds are no longer at issue.

Before the soul pawn of pachisi evolves to the lofty stage where it can exit the game, it must also undergo certain purification, not unlike the test-theme myths of the Native American culture hero. Just as the Navajos believed that compulsive gambling would upset the universal applecart, it certainly seemed to concern the authors of the *Rig Veda* (1500 to 1200 B.C.E.). In verse X.34.13, the speaker is a gambler who hears the voice of God within him asking him not to play with dice, but still he persists in doing so:

> Do not play with dice; cultivate they cornfields,
>   delight in the gain, thinking highly of it.
> There are thy cattle, gambler, there is thy wife,
>   So has the noble Sāvitrī himself told me.[33]

But author Jeanine Miller believed that the act of compulsive gambling was actually in harmony with Cosmic Order.[34] Certain forces at work around him compel him to gamble; he will gamble until he has reached the depths of degradation and is left with nothing but his ten empty fingers, which he will fling at Sāvitrī, the Solar Deity, as he confesses his utter destitution. Because this confession touches an innermost chord of truth within himself, he is released from his compulsion and restored to sanity, the gods being held to "cosmic harmony, the truth, the right, or righteousness, the ritual or rite that expresses Order," Miller wrote.

Participating in these tests in Buddhism and Hinduism would be proper according to dharma, the ethical act of conformity to religious law, custom, and duty. In fact, another name for Hinduism is *Sanatana* (eternal) *Dharma*, which refers to one's lot or caste in life and respect for the rules of conduct in their station. In the *Mahābhārata*, in which one of the deities is even named Dharma, the principle characters must gamble to establish cosmic order. Moreover, the match is played as if the ending has been predetermined, and as such, it is a ceremonial ritual, a duty, and even a performance.

The Great King Gambler of India

The *Mahābhārata* (the great king) is India's *Iliad* and *Odyssey* combined. Originally written in Sanskrit, it has all the elements of a Greek poem:

battle, mythology, divine interference, decision by lots, duty, personal struggle, transcendency of ego, sojourn. It is a manual in epic form, a set of rules by which to live, and a blueprint for the shape of space and time. The divine date is the transitional period between the Dvāpara and the Kali yuga.[35] The story is set in the kingdom of Kurukeṣtra in northern India, the ancestral realm of the Bharata clan.[36] Two branches of the Bharatas compete for the throne, culminating in a gambling scene that sends one set of cousins into exile for thirteen years.

In this Hindu-style Old Testament, the dharma of the fathers is visited upon the sons. Like all creation myths, the Genesis of the *Mahābhārata*, appropriately titled "The Book of the Beginning," describes the complex "descent of the generations" and funnels through all the deformities, curses, illegitimacies, and deaths to a successor and a pretender to the throne. True to mythological genealogy, the human reproductive system is intermixed with that of the deities. These in particular have committed indiscretions in heaven and are reborn into the physical world for rehabilitation.[37] At last, through a symmetrical comedy of errors, the genes and godstuff have been sifted down to the rightful family boss: Yudhiṣthira. As the progeny of the deity Dharma, Yudhiṣthira is the embodiment of righteous duty—which is to say he is the reluctant hero, not unlike the nameless Navajo young husband.

But cousin Duryodhana, the antagonist, is keen for the throne himself. He exiles Yudhiṣthira and his four brothers, known collectively as the Pandavas. During their sojourn, they come across a tournament in which a king is raffling off the hand of his daughter, Draupudī. Arjuna (the hero in the famous *Bhagavad Gita*) wins her as a wife for all five brothers. She will become the pivotal wager in the later gaming sequence between the rivaling cousins. The Pandavas set up a kingdom of their own called Indraprastha, which borders on their original homeland where Duryodhana nurtures his jealousy. Enter the *Book of the Assembly Hall*, where the plot turns on a bet.

A demon named Maya (illusion) builds a great assembly hall for Yudhiṣthira and his brothers, which is the *mandala* or center of the mundane, materialistic world.[38] In Hindu thought, the shape of space is two pyramids joined at the base; the bottom pyramid points upside down toward the earth's surface, where the Bharata hall presumably sits. The four corners of the joined bases of the pyramids represent the four points on the compass. Each compass point is represented by an ethereal hall and guardian. Brahma, grandfather of the worlds who, alone, constantly creates the worlds with his divine "wizardry," sits at the zenith "on the roof beam of heaven," and his hall "blazes as if to light up the sun."[39] Yudhiṣṭhira's assembly hall is modeled mythologically as the celestial archetype, and he is told that Brahma's "rare hall is in all the world what yours is among men."[40] Imperatively, just as a consecration was performed by the great king of the gods, Yudhiṣṭhira must perform the Royal Consecration, a series of Vedic rituals that establish him as the universal monarch. These rituals involve elaborate gift giving, a martial arts challenge, a horse sacrifice—and a gambling game of dice.[41]

The Mahābhārata doesn't come out and say that the gaming sequence is part of the Royal Consecration of the hall. Instead, the ritual is cloaked in a challenge from the jealous cousin Duryodhana. Yudhiṣṭhira, the epitome of virtue, accepts, saying "Once challenged, I cannot refuse." Of course he can't refuse, argued Mahābhārata translator J. van Buitenen. The gambling match is ordained, diṣṭa. According to the Vedic texts, dicing was the final step of the consecration, or rājasūya, following the installation of a new king. The game aligns the newly consecrated ruler of the mundane world not only in space, but in time as well.[42]

Duryodhana himself hints at the long-standing tradition and its effects, as if his own lust for an empire had nothing to do with it. "The Ancients bequeathed us the rules of the game. There is no evil in it, nor blows. . . . If we gamble, the heavenly gate will be nearer; it is proper for us to engage in the game."[43] Now Duryodhana's character is in question. He is "born on earth from a portion of Kali; creature of discord, hated by all men, who caused the massacre, who fanned the great feud into a blaze that was to put an end to all the beings."[44] The bad Bharata cousin is compelled to reverse the great king's fortune, but scholars debate whether Duryodhana is actually an antagonist or just fulfilling his dharmic duty. Just as the Navajo Great Gambler is a mirror image or twin of the young husband and descendants of the sun, both Bharata cousins are descendants of the supposed author of the Mahābhārata, Krishna Dvaipāyana, who started the parallel lines that ultimately led to the feud.

Hearing of Duryodhana's proposed dice match, his father, Dhṛtarāṣṭra, decrees that yet another gaming hall be built "of a thousand pillars with beryls and gold . . . a cry-length deep and a cry-length wide!" The hall "shone with the assembled kings as heaven shines with the lordly gathering of the Gods—with all these *Veda*-wise champions, like suns incarnate" to sit in "golden stadium seats."[45]

Dhṛtarāṣṭra sends for Yudhiṣṭhira and declares, "We shall have there a family dicing game." Since no gameboard is mentioned, the "family" game is a simple throw of the dice, and each round is over in one play. The match is between two parties who each pay in a stake. The loser adds to his stake at the end of the round while the winner's stake stays the same. The texts imply some strategy does go into the play, because Duryodhana is allowed to bring in a pinch hitter, Śakuni, who is an expert at dice. Yudhiṣṭhira poses the question to Śakuni, "Why do you praise dicing? For no one praises as proud a gambler's trickery . . .", to which Śakuni replies, "He who follows the numbers and spies the deceptions and is tireless in moving the dice about and is cunning enough to see through a gambit is a gambler who manages a game." Yudhiṣṭhira retorts with, "To game with gamblers who play tricks is an evil, but victory in battle according to the Law is a good game and superior to it . . . for even without the gambler's trickery, gaming is not honored."[46] Alas, strategy would not help Yudhiṣṭhira, as he observes, "Fate takes away our reason as glare blinds the eye. Man bound as with nooses obeys the Placer's sway."[47] Recall that in Native gambling, cheating is not only acceptable, it is sacred. Trickery, though not dharmically correct, may have been sanctioned since it fulfills the seemingly predetermined outcome of the game. With the wagers staked, "Śakuni grasped the dice, he who knew the facts of dice. And 'Won!' cried Śakuni at Yudhiṣṭhira." His competitor responds, "You have won the play from me by confusing me with a trick!" But the trick is not apparent. In fact, Yudhiṣṭhira is not to learn the secrets of dice until the end of a long exile, and the tale does not explain what those secrets are.[48]

The game continues another nine rounds before an intermission, as if by design of the ritual. Yudhiṣṭhira forfeits most of his possessions during the first half. Returning to the game, in the eleventh play he loses untold millions; in the twelfth, his cattle; in the thirteenth, his land;

in the fourteenth, the sons of Draupudī by all five brothers; then the brothers, one per round. In the nineteenth play he loses himself, and in the twentieth, he loses the most precious of all, Draupudī, the woman whom Arjuna had won in the tournament.

The audience protests but doesn't stop the play. Draupudī is dragged out, subjected to indignities, and disrobed. But every time a skirt is removed, another appears in its place. She poses the ultimate riddle: Had Yudhiṣṭhira staked and lost her before or after he staked himself? If he lost himself first, then she was not his to stake. The question is argued and found inconclusive; therefore, the game is declared a total wash. Yudhiṣṭhira and company are set free.

Not so fast. The ultimate question of royal inheritance must be decided. Yudhiṣṭhira is challenged to one more round. This time the losers will go into exile in the forest for twelve years and live in disguise among people for the thirteenth year. Still under ritual obligation, Yudhiṣṭhira cannot refuse this offer and, predictably, loses.

After thirteen years in exile, described in *The Book of the Forest*—which is a cross between Odysseus's return home after the Trojan War, and Siddhartha's wanderings—the Pandavas reclaim their patrimony. War with their cousins is unavoidable. Both branches of the Bharatas raise armies and form alliances. The war rages for eighteen days, with the Pandavas the victors. Yudhiṣṭhira reestablishes his dominion as the universal monarch with a Horse Sacrifice. At the end, accompanied by his brothers and their wife, he embarks on a final journey and returns to heaven.

As an archaic match between two opposing halves of an ordained political structure, the dice game itself is similar to the war-game rituals of the Plains Indians—particularly the Pawnee hand game. Countless Native American myths describe the deposing of a gambler dictator through gambling. Similarly, in ancient India, when claims of rivals within one ruling lineage were indeed as insolubly complex as in the *Mahābhārata*, the only answer was to decide by lot. The gaming hall is a play-sphere much like a court of law in which the contest or *agon* is an arbitration between contending parties. The hall is rooted in the simple magical circle, *dyūtamandalam*, within which the game is played, the rules followed, and the players not allowed to leave until they have fulfilled their obligations. In the Sanskrit word *dyūtam*, fighting and dicing merge.[49] "Whether the Divine Will manifests itself in the outcome of a trial of strength, or in the issue of armed combat, or in the fall of sticks and stones, it is all one to the archaic mind," wrote Huizinga. Fate, Chance, and Will are fused.

The Bharata dicing match has been compared to the potlatch practices of the Pacific Northwest tribes (discussed in Chapter 1).[50] The potlatch, according to the common definition, was the ceremony of heaping lavish gifts upon a rival group during a feast and calling for the guests to "one-up" their hosts with more gifts. Similar customs have been found in Greek, Roman, Old Germanic, and Chinese cultures. In the Arabia of pre-Islamic times, it was called "to rival in glory by cutting the feet of camels." The game is played not to win wealth and power, but to establish status. There's an element of trial and sacrifice and solemnity to the ritual. Huizinga asked, however, that the term potlatch be defined as "the most highly developed and explicit form of a fundamental human need," which he called playing for honor and glory. There is a gift-giving ritual in the Royal Consecration of the hall, but the dicing match is noble play, right play, dharmic play, play to determine the heir to the throne or, in this case, to fulfill dharmic law.

The heroes of the Native American gambling myths, some of whom have been exiled for excessive gambling, undergo ordeal by fire, water, and games, and must commune with the spirits before they can defeat the gambler. The forest exile of Yudhiṣṭhira is similar. Ultimately, he comes across a water spirit who forbids him and his companions to drink from a pool unless they can answer the spirit's questions. In the ensuing contest of riddles, nearly the whole system of Hindu ethics is expounded. Riddles are a prevalent test-theme in Native American gambling myths as well. The riddle itself is also a sacred and dangerous thing, and one wins not by logical reasoning but by intuition and divine intervention. Now it is apparent that Yudhiṣṭhira had to lose the dice match in order to hone his spirituality in the forest before he could take the throne. Van Buitenen entertained the notion that the king apparent intentionally lost as part of the dharmic ritual.

Huizinga said the struggle to win is holy. But once winning is animated by clear conceptions of right and wrong, the struggle rises into the sphere of law; and once seen in the light of divine power, it rises into the sphere of faith. "In all this, however, the primary thing is play, which is the seed of that ideal growth."[51]

While Biblical and Greek oracles cast lots to *determine* the will of the Divine, Native gamblers cast lots to *regulate* Nature. The *Mahābhārata* strikes the middle ground in that Divine Will and Nature are one and the same—the judgement of the dice eventually leads to the restoration of, or victory over, Cosmic Order, whichever the case may be. Ultimately, the player sitting across the table is yourself.

Dice Diffusion

Analogies between Hindu and Native American gambling symbolism bring up a final and controversial argument—cultural diffusion. Edward Tylor is usually accepted as the scholar who first noticed that geographically and culturally diverse groups played remarkably similar games.[52] As a nineteenth-century diffusionist, he said games provide evidence for intercultural contact. Of all the wonderful turns of the human mind in the course of culture, he said, scarce any is more striking than this history of lots and dice. While it may be possible that dice was invented more than once, the odds are slim that a Greek and an Arab and a Burmese and an Aztec "were separately seized by the same happy thought, and said, 'Go to, let us cast lots,' and count them to play at draughts by."[53]

The most ironic example of gaming diffusion, according to Tylor, is the Hindu game of *pachisi*, based on the backgammon of the Middle East and after which the Aztec game of *patolli* and similar board games of the greater Southwest were surely patterned.[54] Tylor was certain that the game was not imported into Mexico by the Conquistadors, but by crews of disabled Asian junks washed up not too far from Tenochtitlán.[55] The Spaniards, in their awkward descriptions of patolli, noted its resemblance to their own dice game of *tables*, but they did not recognize it as backgammon or pachisi, which later spread to the West commercially as Parcheesi©.[56]

A Hindu who used cowry shells or an Arab who used palm sticks might have been more familiar with the two-faced bean dice in patolli. "While the dice-game is common to the Eastern and Western worlds,

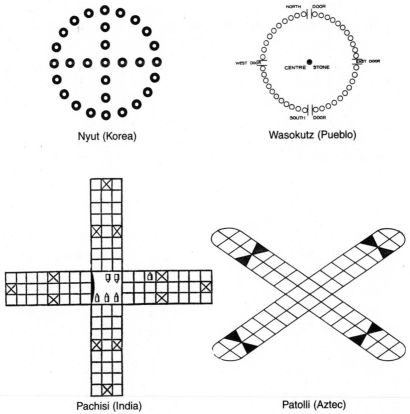

Nyut (Korea)

Wasokutz (Pueblo)

Pachisi (India)

Patolli (Aztec)

Compare the four-quartered circuits of dice boards played around the globe. (after Tylor, 1896; Culin, 1907; Tylor, 1878; Erasmus, 1950)

so that an Icelander could easily play backgammon with a Japanese on an ancient Roman board, the lot-game which seems to have preceded it spread east rather than west," Tylor said. When the dice-and-board games spread into Europe, the cubical dice went with them, but for the games that spread east through Asia and eventually into Mexico (or so he thought), binary lots replaced the cubical.

Two-sided dice games were played on most continents, even where cube dice were known.[57] In China the players threw coins, in Asia they threw flat tamarind seeds, and in the Middle East they threw four palm-stick slips. Other materials included wood, bone, or shell, with the opposing sides distinguished by color or decoration. Culin's games

A diagram of *tab*, which may have been the predecessor of backgammon in the Middle East. (Tylor, 1896)

catalogue listed the various nonboard two-sided dice games of more than 130 tribes ranging from Alaska to the Yucatán.

Except in an Eskimo dice game, played solely for the ivory figures thrown in the air,[58] most of the Native American dice games required some method of tracking the dice throws with counting sticks and involved varying degrees of mathematical complexity.[59] Tribes of the greater Southwest[60] were the only ones in the Western Hemisphere to keep track of their dice throws by moving their stick pieces (called men, dogs, or later, horses) around a ring of pebbles sectioned into four groups. The four gaps in the ring aligned with the cardinal directions.[61] To Culin, Tylor, and many others, this four-quartered dice-board strongly resembled, at least in concept, the cross-shaped playing circuits among

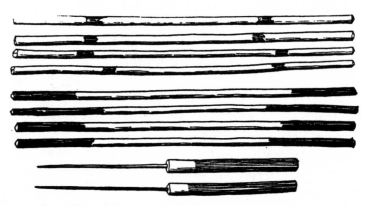

Counting sticks, such as these of the Oklahoma Kiowas, were a prelude to playing boards. Both serve the purpose of keeping track of the markers. (Culin, 1907)

the Hindu and Aztecs. The playing rules and objectives were also nearly the same.

Tylor theorized that patolli spread from Mexico northward "among the wilder tribes, where it remained in vogue." As proof, Tylor cites a game among the Tarahumaras, recorded by Father Joseph Ochs, a Jesuit missionary in the mid-1700s.[62] They played with slips of reed or wood that were distinguished by different numbers of strokes cut into each

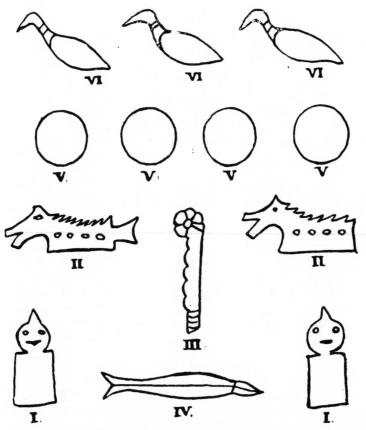

The game of "bowl and counters" described in Longfellow's *Hiawatha* was a complex dice game played by the Chippewas of Michigan. The gaming pieces are: *ininewug* or men (I); *gitshee kenabik* or great serpents (II); *pugamágun* or war club (III); *keego* or fish (IV); *ozawábíks* or circular brass pieces (V); *sheshebwug* or ducks (VI). (Schoolcraft, 1978 [1848])

one, and thrown like the "notorious game of hazard." Ochs erroneously called the game patolli, as did many chroniclers of other North American tribes. Since no gameboard existed in association with this game, it was probably not patolli, but *totoloque*, the game Montezuma and Cortez played to kill time, which in turn sounds like a game called *totolopsi* by the Hopi of Oraibi, Arizona. Totolopsi is, in fact, played like patolli, although the gameboard is not always sectioned into a four-quartered diagram.[63]

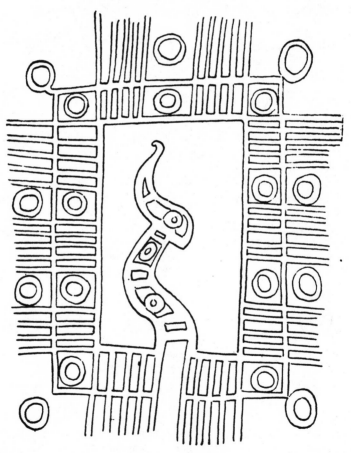

Hopi (Oraibi, Ariz.) playing board for the stick-dice game played similarly to patolli. (Culin, 1907)

Had Tylor been writing in the 1920s, when the "age-area doctrine" became fashionable in American ethnology, as opposed to the 1870s, he might have considered that the simpler but more widely spread Southwestern game could have been older than the complex Mexican form.[64] Culin, who benefited from a global perspective, was ahead of his time in that he believed the oldest form of the game did originate in the Southwest and changed progressively along lines north, northeast, east, and southward into Mexico.[65] He never ventured comment on why the Hindu and Aztec games were so similar.[66]

Pachisi and patolli share five or six features: flat dice, scoreboard, crossshape, several men, killing opponents, and penalty or safety stations.

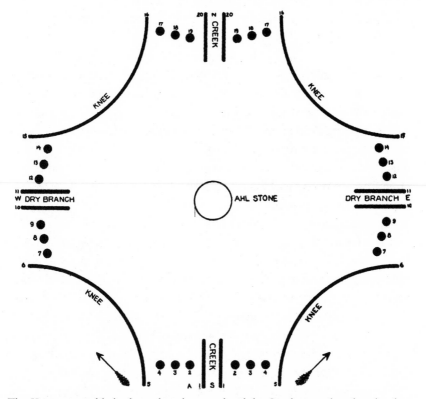

The Kiowas were likely the only tribe outside of the Southwest who played a dice board game similar to patolli and pachisi, and it appears to have been the most sophisticated. In pachisi and patolli, the free spaces are safety zones, but in the Kiowa game, the spaces, representing creeks and dry branches, are penalty zones. (Culin, 1907)

Tylor said the mathematical probability of two games invented separately agreeing by chance in so many quite specific features is very low. However, John P. Erasmus, in his article "Patolli, Pachisi, and the Limitation of Possibilities," objected to the use of probability mathematics to prove that the two games were homologous, or from the same origin. If a group of isolated natives were given a set of dice, their games would certainly not develop at the same rate or in exactly the same manner as patolli or pachisi. "We could only say that *if* elaboration took place it would be faced with the same limitations as in those games. We could not even predict with any assurance that any elaboration would ever take place at all," he wrote. Parker Brothers was never able to patent the core game of Monopoly© (except for the name and art design), because besides the print medium, it is just another version of the ancient games. The players kill each other in financial hostile takeovers.

The argument of dice diffusion can be extended to gaming mythology. Boas studied the phenomena of shared traits in mythology by breaking down story elements or mythological symbols that could develop independently—in much the same way Tylor broke down the play elements of pachisi and patolli. "Boas was not interested in attempts to link up strange practices in widely separated portions of the earth," said Erasmus.[67] Nor was he interested in working out the odds of one mythic plot originating in two places. Boas's objective was to scientifically eliminate the possibilities in order to isolate culturally pristine areas.

When a significant number of similarities leapt up in two or more separate places in the same combination, he assumed a genetic connection. But he was also careful to point out that one story point might logically follow another and might not be inherited at all. The ideas could have been broadcasted from one place to another by foot or word of mouth. Such concepts as sacred numbers, revival of the dead, and the power to escape unseen are not necessarily the result of cultural or historical transmission,[68] but of the physiological limits in the sounds we can make and the restriction of images and symbols we use to communicate.[69]

The argument of games and gambling mythology diffusion can never be resolved. It is like a gameboard without beginning or end, but with an intrinsic urge to return home—as all circular arguments tend to do. Gambling mythology, as we have seen, is as basic to human development as is chanting to spirits and chipping out sun glyphs on cliffs; few societies on this globe have ever lived in such isolation that an interesting diversion or two did not waft their way, ignoring all regional jurisdictions. There must be something about the human psyche that makes us want to tempt fate and rattle the bones. Old Iagoo, in Henry Wadsworth Longfellow's *The Song of Hiawatha*, stated it best when he said:

> Many games of skill and hazard
> Have I seen in different nations,
> Have I played in different countries . . .
> Though you think yourself so skillful
> I can beat you, Pau-Puk-Keewis,
> I can even give you lessons
> In your game of Bowl and Counters!

Myths of the Eternal Return

*The new casino starts out promising . . . as revenue falling out
of the sky.*

—Louise Erdich, "A Little Vision,"
The Bingo Palace [1994]

I defer to Laguna/Sioux author Paula Gunn Allen for the
final word on reversal of fortune. In her book *The Sacred
Hoop*, she tells a version of the gambling myth from the
feminine point of view.[1] The story, told to her by her great-grand-
mother from Laguna Pueblo, is a plea for staying in harmony with the
cosmos.

A drought came to Kush Kutret (the first house) when Iyatiku (Corn
or Earth Mother) lived there among the people. She gave them a gambling game to keep their minds off the lack of food. But the men
became obsessed and began to gamble everything away. When the
women scolded the men, they pouted in their kivas. These underground chambers were the men's domain; the women didn't go there
except for ceremony, so the men were able to continue gambling.
Famine crept over the village as the men neglected their religious duties
and lost their possessions.

Iyatiku left Kush Kutret in anger and returned to Shipap (the underworld), where she still lives and watches the people. The angry lake
spirits meanwhile flooded and destroyed the village, forcing the people
to evacuate their homes and relocate without the Corn Mother. But she
had left them with her power, her *Irriaku* (corn fetish), and told them
it was her heart she was leaving. She charged them to always share the
fruits of her body with one another, for they are all related. She told
them that they must ever remain at peace in their hearts and their rela-
tionships. The rains come only to peaceful people.

"I remember Iyatiku, Earth Woman, Corn Woman, who guides and counsels the people to peace and who welcomes us home when we cast off this coil of flesh as huskers cast off the leaves that wrap the corn," writes Allen. "I remember Iyatiku's sister, Sun Woman, who held metals and cattle, pigs and sheep, highways and engines and so many things in her bundle, who went away to the east saying that one day she would return."

Appendix I
A Summary of More Recent Indian Gaming Politics

Most tribes that now operate gambling establishments did so as a response to President Ronald Reagan's urging Native Americans to strive for economic self-sufficiency, or, to put it another way, to make up for reduced federal funding.[1] The Florida Seminoles opened the first reservation bingo parlor in 1974. A hundred tribes soon followed suit, with pull tabs, lotto, punch boards, tip jars, card games, and instant bingo being added to traditional bingo fare. Some set up or wanted to set up the higher stake games of blackjack, craps, slot machines, and pari-mutuel wagering. What's more, electronics were pushing bingo to more sophisticated heights.

The advent of tamperable video gaming in the mid-1980s triggered bureaucratic alarms. Indian gaming had become so dicey, various governments felt the need to set parameters in order to protect both the tribes and the patrons from criminal activity. In 1982, the Fifth Circuit upheld a ruling of the Federal District Court that the Seminole Tribe of Florida could engage in bingo gambling free of state licensing and regulation (*Seminole v. Butterworth*). While the state had civil and criminal jurisdiction over the reservations in agreement with the Supreme Court's decision in *Bryan v. Itasca County* (1976), the ruling did not give states general regulatory power over Indian tribes.

The question of whether Florida had the right to license and regulate bingo operations on the Seminole Reservation turned on whether Florida's existing bingo law was criminal/prohibitory or civil/regulatory in nature. The operation of bingo games in Florida was not prohibited by the state law, but merely regulated, and therefore the court held that the law was not applicable to bingo operations on the Indian reservation.

The Florida court sentiment was echoed in similar decisions handed down in the cases of *Oneida Tribe of Indians v. Wisconsin* (1981) and

Barona Group of the Capitan Grande Band of Mission Indians v. Duffy (Ninth Circuit, 1982). Finally, in 1987, the rationale of the lower Federal courts was upheld by the Supreme Court in *California v. Cabazon Band of Mission Indians*. Cabazon declared that whether a certain activity is against the public policy of the state depends on whether such gambling activity is legal under the Organized Crime Control Act of 1970. That act prohibits gambling businesses from operating in states where they are in violation of the laws of that state. In other words, if a state does not allow video gambling off the reservation, it does not have to allow it on the reservation. This is as far as *California v. Cabazon* could go without congressional guidelines. This was a coup for the tribes. For after all, the churches were already using bingo as fundraisers.

Congress waited for *California v. Cabazon* to be decided before finalizing its Indian Gaming Regulatory Act (IGRA) in 1988. Basically, the act provides a statutory basis for gaming activities as a means of promoting economic development, self-sufficiency, and strong tribal government. It also establishes regulation to protect tribal government from organized crime, ensures that tribes are the primary beneficiaries of gaming operations, and ensures that games are conducted fairly and honestly.

The act still allows the tribes to operate any form of gambling that is legal in the state where the reservation is located, but specifically gives tribes the okay to operate bingo halls regardless of state law. The IGRA set up the National Indian Gaming Commission to regulate bingo and other forms of Class II gambling, such as pull tabs, lotto, punch boards, tip jars, card games, and instant bingo. Exempt from legislation is Class I gaming, which includes the social or traditional gaming that is played in connection with tribal ceremonies and celebrations discussed in this book.

Class III gaming is quite another story and the brunt of the controversy. Pari-mutuel racetrack wagering and such casino games of chance as slot machines, blackjack, and craps fall into this category. Again, if casino-style betting is not legal in the state, it is not legal on the reservation. But under the IGRA, such betting can be negotiated in a compact between the states and the tribes, allowing states to put a cap on the betting and to control, somewhat, criminal temptation. A compact is an agreement between the sovereigns (tribes and states) similar to a treaty. A tribal/ state Class III compact deals with sovereign powers (such as application of laws, jurisdiction, and enforcement of laws) of the parties to the compact. Federal law requires states to negotiate in good faith.

The tribes assume that the language "to negotiate in good faith" means state governors are obligated to entertain all compacts brought to their capital steps. Compacts do not have to be negotiated, some states say. In states where casino games are already legal, compact agreements are generally not a problem. When states don't sign the compact, the tribes sue. The Eleventh Amendment limits federal court jurisdiction by providing that the citizens of one state cannot bring suit in federal court against the government of another state except by its consent, and this would include the sovereign tribes. The National Indian Gaming Association (NIGA) reported the following states who claimed immunity under the Eleventh Amendment in 1992: Alabama, Florida, Michigan, Mississippi, Montana, New Mexico, New York, North Dakota, Oklahoma, South Dakota, and Washington.

Tribes have found a loophole in state legislation, however. Although casino gaming is illegal in some states, they may allow various charities to hold "Las Vegas nights" a couple times a year. This has opened the door for the legal operation of the same activity on the reservations. Furthermore, states wishing to legalize video keno gambling, or electronic lotteries, are paving the way for any kind of video gambling on reservations. The tribes have won some lawsuits and lost others according to which way the loopholes were played out. The Mashantucket Pequot Tribe, for instance, won their case on the Las Vegas–night technicality (*Mashantucket Pequot Tribe v. Connecticut*, 1991) and opened a $200 million casino.

In 1995, of the twenty-three states whose governors had signed compacts approved by the Secretary of the Interior, twenty had not been approved by the state legislatures.

Tribes are hoping to circumvent the issue by adding specific language on the Eleventh Amendment to the IGRA. Tribes would like to be able to appeal to the Secretary of Interior to impose a compact on a state when it fails to negotiate with a tribe. That, in effect, would take away states' rights.

But in June 1994, the chair and vice-chair of the Senate Indian Affairs Committee proposed to strengthen state rights under the IGRA.[2] They proposed that tribal casinos adhere to much stricter federal regulations, including licensing of games, background checks of key casino employees, and audits of revenues and profits. The proposal would also let states refuse to allow Indian gaming within their borders—a right they don't explicitly have now. Tribes in those states could appeal to the Department of the Interior, but the department would not have to approve gaming requests. The proposal would also better arm the National Indian Gaming Commission, giving them exclusive authority to license Indian casinos. Tribes called the proposal a deliberate attack on Indian gaming. But the proposal was patterned after laws in Nevada and New Jersey, say its introducers, Hawaii Democrat Daniel K. Inouye, the Senate committee's chair, and Arizona Republican John McCain, the vice-chair.

Gambling proponents say reservation gambling doesn't attract organized crime. However, agencies have found evidence of organized crime involvement in Indian gaming on California, Florida, and New York reservations, plus lesser counts of embezzlement and theft in other states.[3] In New York, for instance, the FBI found evidence that reputed mobster boss John Gotti was involved in supplying slot machines to casinos on the St. Regis reservation, which is illegal under the Johnson Act in the absence of a compact. In Florida, associates of the late mob money man Meyer Lansky have been linked to reservation gambling. Associates of Anthony Accetturo have been identified by law enforcement officials as a leader in the Luchese crime family. A federal indictment charged nine men with attempting to take over gambling operations at the Rincon Indian Reservation south of San Diego.

Furthermore, eighteen non-Indian management contractors and video bingo vendors have taken a few reservations to the cleaners for a total of $62.2 million. In at least thirteen cases, gaming equipment that could have been leased for $3.2 million was leased for $40.3 million. The U.S. Attorney in the Eastern District of Wisconsin identified several cases where tribes lost a half-million dollars through theft and embezzlement in their gaming operations. The 1993 audit by the Department of Interior identified thirty-seven gaming operations that did not have approved compacts.

But a spokesman for the Attorney General Criminal Division said, "The Department of Justice believes that to date there has not been a widespread or successful effort by organized crime to infiltrate gaming operations."[4] Under the IGRA, criminal acts are referred to (and monitored by) the FBI and the Department of Justice. The U.S. Attorney's office is responsible for enforcing the compacts and with prosecuting criminal activity connected to Indian gaming. It took some time to properly organize the National Indian Gaming Commission, but now in place, it is responsible for approving management contracts and compacts and for regulating bingo. As the tribes themselves grow more solvent and experienced, they can police themselves. Furthermore, if states negotiate their compacts correctly, they can write their own tickets. But the issue, say gaming proponents, is not criminal enforcement.

"The issue is not 'gaming' itself—it is the vital economic benefit, which the Pueblos desperately need, and our sovereign rights," said Frank Chavez, a spokesperson for the New Mexico Indian Gaming Association and a member of Sandia Pueblo, one of fourteen tribes in New Mexico who signed compacts with the governor in 1995, only to find them deemed illegal by the Supreme Court until ratified by the legislature.[5] "For most tribes, gaming represents the first successful tribal enterprise which provides the confidence to venture into other businesses," Chavez believed.

The tribes see the Indian gaming issue as a struggle between two sovereigns. In the U.S. federal system of government, states are recognized as independent, sovereign entities with the right and responsibility to generate and collect revenues, enact and enforce laws, protect and defend their people, and prosecute and punish violators. "Indian nations are also federally recognized as independent, sovereign entities with the same rights and responsibilities as these states," wrote reporter Elizabeth Gannon.[6] "However, the same states that have historically fought to protect and defend their own independence and self-reliance are now fighting to take these rights away from Native American nations." The struggle is not new, she said. "Throughout U.S. history, state governments have been hostile to the concept of recognizing and dealing with tribes as sovereign governmental entities. . . . Instead of land, minerals, and other environmental assets, the struggle this time is centered on the tribes' economic assets—in the form of gaming revenues."

Soon after opening their casino near the Rhode Island border in 1992, the Mashantucket Pequot began pumping money into the local economy: $20.4 million in payroll-related income and taxes, $85 million in salaries and benefits, $40 million in goods and services, and $1 million in tourist advertising. The bingo operation alone grosses $20 million and nets $4 million annually. Profits nationally have gone to expanding the reservations and to building or upgrading water and sewer systems, roads, tribal community centers, wellness centers, and educational and child care facilities. Health insurance for all tribe members is another benefit provided by the operations. Many tribes are learning to emphasize economic impact and the services for the tribe rather than report actual income.[7] The success stories of tribe after tribe flood the airwaves, print media, wire services, and congressional testimony.

Indian gaming's most visible adversary is Atlantic City casino mogul Donald Trump, who during animated testimony before the House subcommittee in October 1993 accused the Indian gaming industry of being riddled with organized crime, although he was unable to provide evidence.[8] In his prepared statement he said his three casinos made him the largest individual casino operator in the world, in all modesty. He runs his casinos under the most restrictive regulatory standards in the country, yet the casinos on reservations would operate under different, less restrictive regulations through their negotiated compacts. If tribes were allowed to build on disputable reservations closer to New York City, "it would be the economic death knell to Atlantic City."

"History, at least history taught in most American schools, has instilled in [journalists] the image of the downtrodden Indian, beaten into submission, and taken advantage of at every turn," wrote Tim Giago in his regular column, Notes From Indian Country.[9] They see the casinos and immediately assume that whites have found a new way to get rich off of Indians: "Never mind that it is the Indian tribes who have finally discovered a way to get rich off Whites," Giago attested. The general thrust of his column is that the road to sovereignty is paved with the small steps of hiring tribal rather than white employees, consultants, and public relations firms. So that tribal dignity is not compromised, members should make sure that barmaids are not wearing short, color-ful buckskin skirts with turkey feather headbands and distributing "wampum cards," which misconstrues their original religious intent.

A National Park Service employee whose heritage includes Pima and Tohono O'odham in Arizona and who prides himself on his self-reliance, fears his tribe's involvement in the gaming business. "People were dependent on government programs in the 1970s, and when that was taken away, the people were devastated," he said in a personal con-versation. "Now, we'll make big money on gambling, but we will become dependent in the same way. When Arizona legalizes gambling off the reservation, it will all be gone again."

Appendix II
Noqoìlpi, the Great Gambler
(A Navajo Legend)

The Great Gambler legend is embodied in the Navajo origin legend, which Washington Matthews said was divided into four parts: the Story of the Emergence; Early Events in the Fifth World; the Twin War Gods, and the Growth of the Navajo Nation. The Chaco gambler saga drops in soon after the people began exploring the Fifth World.[1] The version Matthews recorded was a combination of several accounts told to him by Navajo shamen.

One informant was Hatáli Natlói, or Smiling Chanter, priest of the *klédzi hatál*, or Night Chant, who had a good standing in his community. Tall Chanter, Hatáli Nez, also a priest of the Night Chant, was the first to explain ceremonies and relate rite-myths to Matthews. Before he would confide in Matthews, he said, "The chanters among the Navajos are brothers. If you would learn our secrets you must be one of us." Another informant was Old Torlino, a priest of *hozóni hatál*, or Beauty Way. "My tale says the world is flat, and that there are five worlds, one above another," Old Torlino told Matthews. "You will not believe my tale, then, and perhaps you do not want to hear it." After Matthews assured him he wanted the story despite white man's theories, Torlino chanted the following:

> I am ashamed before the earth; I am ashamed before the heavens; I am ashamed before the dawn; I am ashamed before the evening twilight; I am ashamed before the blue sky; I am ashamed before the sun; I am ashamed before that standing within me which speaks with me [conscience!]. Some of these things are always looking at me. I am never out of sight. Therefore I must tell the truth. That is why I always tell the truth. I hold my word tight to my breast.

The chanters were not men of unlimited leisure, "as many suppose Indians to be." During the winter months—the only time when these tales are permitted to be told—the chanters were heavily engaged in telling the healing stories for their patients and in tending their own farms and stock. The shamen found it difficult to take two or three weeks out of their heavy schedule to devote to Matthews. Further was the danger to the shamen of telling the myths. When Hatáli Nez began telling the creation myth, he was agitated. As long as he told the story about the ancestors in the nether world, he said, he and Matthews traveled literally in that land of the dead, a place of evil and potent ghosts.

Near sunset one afternoon, and an hour or more before his suppertime, Hatáli Nez concluded his story of the subterranean wanderings of the Navajos and brought them safely through the "Place of Emergence," in the San Juan Mountains, to the surface of this world. Then he stopped talking, rolled a cigarette, and said he was tired and could not tell any more story. After Hatáli Nez took his leave, Matthews learned that he had told some of his friends that he would have to pray that night to counteract the evil effects of his journey through the lower worlds. The shaman ate his supper and then retired to his assigned room among the old adobe huts at Fort Defiance. Matthews followed, and after waiting out in the hall for more than a half hour, he heard the voice of the old man rising in the monotones of formulated prayer. "Knowing that the rules of the shaman forbade the interruption of any prayer or song, I abruptly entered the room and sat down on the floor near the supplicant." Matthews didn't indicate whether this interruption was acceptable or not.

Matthews did not publish the myths verbatim but took "Biblical license" in translating Navajo to English, adding the necessary words for clarity. He says he never exceeded the metaphor or descriptive force of the original and never added his own thoughts. For one thing, the stories were often embellished with pantomime and vocal modulation, which was lost in the translation. "If [I have] erred in rendering the spirit of the savage authors," he wrote, "it has been by diminishing rather than by exaggerating. [I have] endeavored to 'tune the sitar' rather low than high." In the following retelling of the Great Gambler myth, I have retuned the sitar for modern readers.

* * *

Some time before the Diné arrived in Chaco, a divine gambler had descended from the heavens and moved in among the Kisáni.[2] His name was Noqoìlpi, or He Who Wins Men (at play). He challenged the Kisáni to all sorts of games and contests and profited tremendously. He won first their property, then their women and children, and finally some of the men themselves. Noqoìlpi told them he would return part of their property in payment for building him Kĭntyél, or Broad House. So when the Diné arrived, the Kisáni were busy constructing the house in order to release their relatives and belongings. At Noqoìlpi's bidding, the Kisáni also made a race track and prepared for games of skill and chance so that the gambler could challenge people from neighboring communities and thus win their property as well.

When all was ready, an invitation to the games was extended to the people of Kĭndotlĭz, or Blue House. After waiting the proper four days, twelve men arrived at Broad House to win back some of their relatives. They promptly lost themselves to Noqoìlpi in the bargain. Five more groups of Blue House Kisáni arrived after their four-day waiting periods and soon counted themselves among the work crew. The games depleted the Blue House people, twelve at a time, beginning with able-bodied men, then their wives and children, and finally the important men and chiefs.

The Diné watched all of the proceedings from the sidelines and kept count of Noqoìlpi's holdings. But when people from other pueblos came in such numbers to play—and lose—the Diné lost count. In addition to their persons, the later victims gambled away their beads, shells, turquoise, and all sorts of valuables. With the labor of all these slaves, it was not long before the great house was built.

All this time, the Diné had been spectators and had not become involved; then one day a beneficent god came to the hut of a young Diné couple and appropriated their help. The cry of Hastséyalti (Talking God) was first heard four times in the distance, "wu'hu'hu'hu," growing louder and nearer each time. The god told the childless couple, through sign language, that among the possessions the Blue House people had gambled away to Noqoìlpi were two great shells. These were the greatest treasures of the Kisáni, and the Sun coveted them so much he had begged Noqoìlpi for them. The gambler's refusal insulted

the Sun. On orders of the Sun, Hastséyalti invited the young husband
to attend a counsel of divine personages at the summit of a certain
mountain in twelve days.

The Diné youth kept his appointment.[3] Assembled on the mountain
were Hastséhogan (House God); Nĭ'ltsi, the Wind; Tsalyél, the Darkness; Tsápani, the Bat; Lĭstsó, the Snake; Tsĭlkáli, the Little Bird, Nasĭ'zi,
the Gopher, and Hastséyalti, among others. Also present were the dis-
satisfied pets and domesticated animals of the gambler, who were anx-
ious for liberation—as well as a share of the spoils should the gambler
be defeated. All night the gods sang and danced and performed mystic
rights to purify and bestow gambling powers upon the young Diné.
When morning came, they bathed the neophyte and disguised him to
look exactly like Noqoìlpi.

But before the gods could send the young Diné to gamble with
Noqoìlpi, they had to decide the best approach. To do that, they
needed to discover Noqoìlpi's level of remorse for refusing the Sun the
great shells. Wind volunteered for the mission, saying he was able to
infiltrate the gambler's home; but although he could not be seen, he
certainly could be heard. Darkness, the quieter candidate, entered the
gambler's room as he slept, and ransacked his mind, thus ascertaining
that Noqoìlpi was saddened by his insult to the Sun. Not believing it,
Wind did his own spying, turning up with the same answer. Noqoìlpi
was indeed sorry for not giving the shells to the Sun.

Next, the counsel of gods planned their gaming strategy. The first
game they proposed to play was taka-thad-sáta, or thirteen chips. The
chips, painted red on one side and white on the other, would be tossed
into the air; winning depended on the number of chips that would fall
white side up. When the Diné threw his chips in the air, Bat would
catch them from his hiding place in the ceiling and exchange them for
a set painted white on both sides.

The second game was nánzoz, played with two poles and a single
hoop. The object of the game was to roll the hoop down the track
toward the pole designated for the player, either red or black, and hope
that the hoop got entangled in the many-tailed "turkey claw" attached
to the pole. Snake said he would hide in the hoop and make it fall to
their champion's advantage.

In the third game, *tsĭ'nbetsil*, contestants would push against a tree until it was torn up by its roots. Gopher said he could gnaw the roots of the tree so that the Diné could push it over with ease. In the fourth game, *tsol*, the object was to hit the ball across a certain line. Little Bird said all the Diné would have to do is tap the ball, and the bird would fly it to the line.

When they were in agreement, the party of conspirators came down from the mountain to the brow of the canyon and waited for sunrise. Wind blew a strong gale to give the gambler's pets an excuse for not warning him of the approach of the strangers. There the conspirators waited for one of Noqoìlpi's two wives, who were in the habit of going for water every morning. At sunrise, they spotted a woman leaving the gambler's house with a water-jar on her head. The Diné, disguised as Noqoìlpi, descended into the canyon and followed her to the spring. She didn't become aware of his presence until she bent to fill the jug. She was not alarmed by his approach, but soon discovered her error. She said nothing and allowed him to follow her into the house under the safety of the ruse.

When the Diné entered the great house, the slaves had already assembled, perhaps sensing the impending doom for the game master. Noqoìlpi became immediately angry and jealous when he spotted the imposter accompanying his wife. But rather than mention this, he instead asked the important question, "Have you come to gamble with me?" He asked the question four times, and each time the young Diné declined. Thinking the stranger was afraid to play, Noqoìlpi began challenging him recklessly. He bet an eye for an eye, tooth for a tooth, legs for legs, person for person. The Diné refused all wagers.

Finally, the young Diné pointed to the two Pueblo boys who had been quickly dressed by the gods to look like women. "I'll bet my wives against your wives in a game of thirteen chips." The great gambler smiled and accepted the wager. His two wives queued up against the wall with the wife impersonators and watched the game. With Bat's assistance, the Diné won the game and the wives.

The games adjourned outside, where the contestants next played hoop-and-pole. The prepared track laid east-west, but Wind instructed the hero to change the direction of the course to north-south. Then, at the bidding of the Wind, he chose the red stick. When he rolled the hoop, it looked as though it would become entangled in Noqoìlpi's stick-and-claw. But to the gambler's chagrin, the hoop extricated itself and continued rolling until it fell on the hero's pole, thanks to Snake. The gambler was so angry, he threw his stick, thereby forfeiting the game to the Diné. There followed a variety of games on which Noqoìlpi staked and lost his wealth in precious stones, houses, and slaves.

The last game was the game of ball. All the people were assembled near the line over which the balls were to be hit. On one side of the line stood the gambler's remaining slaves, and on the other side stood the freed people. Noqoìlpi added himself to the bet. He hit his ball as hard as he could with the club, but the ball did not reach the line. The Diné hit his ball with a light tap, and it sailed far beyond the line with the aid of Little Bird flying within it. With shouts of joy, the captives jumped over the line and joined the freed people.

The victor distributed the booty among the gods who helped him free the people. Most importantly, he gave the two great shells to the Sun.

Noqoìlpi sat to one side, bitterly bemoaning his fate and cursing his enemies. He threatened to strike with lightning and to send war, disease, freezing temperatures, fire, and flood. "He has cursed enough," whispered Wind to the hero. "Put an end to his angry words."

So the son of Hastséhogan said to Noqoìlpi, "You have bet yourself and lost. You are not a god, for my power has prevailed over yours." The victor took out the magic *Etĭ'n Dĭlyĭ'l*, or bow of darkness, pulled back the string aiming upwards, and shot Noqoìlpi into the air like an arrow. As Noqoìlpi flew he muttered in the angry tones of abuse, but no one could understand what he said. Up and up he went, growing smaller and smaller, until he faded to a mere speck and disappeared from view.

Noqoìlpi came to the home of *Begochídí* (*Békotsĭdi*), the god who carries the moon and who is synonymous with the God of the Americans. He is very old and dwells in a long row of stone houses. Noqoìlpi related to Begochídí his sad story of poverty, misery, and failure. Begochídí took pity on him and gave him new stock, the likes of which the world had not seen: sheep, asses, horses, swine, goats, and fowl. He also gave him *bayeta* and other cloths of bright colors more beautifully woven than by his own Kisáni slaves. He made a new people, the Mexicans, and gave them to the gambler to rule over. Then he sent Noqoìlpi back into the world, far to the south of his former abode, landing in old Mexico.

Noqoìlpi's people increased greatly in Mexico, and after a long while they began to move north and build towns along the Rio Grande. Noqoìlpi came with them until they arrived at a place north of Santa Fe, New Mexico. There they ceased building, and he returned to old Mexico, where he still lives and where he is now *Nakaí Dìgíni*, or God of the Mexicans.

After the Diné youth shot Noqoìlpi into the sky, he returned to his people and told them of all he had seen. He then went back to *Tse'gìhi*,[4] the home of the *yéi* (gods).

Appendix III

Gaming-piece Distribution Among Prehistoric Peoples of the Southwest: Anasazi Gaming Pieces, Listed by the National Park Service, Chaco Center

New Mexico Anasazi Chaco Canyon	Gaming Piece	Room Designation or Excavation Location	Date (C.E. unless otherwise noted)
SJ29116 Archaic campsite north of Pueblo Bonito	1 bone die (also 2 balls and 4 stone disks which are possible gaming pieces)	Trench 3	600–800
29SJ1649 (Bc256) Shabik'eshchee Village, late Basket Maker	1 bone die	Pithouse Y, antechamber	550–700
29SJ299 Basket Maker village north of Fajada with kiva, hearth from later periods	1 bone die	Not given	600s
29SJ628 Basket Maker III to early Pueblo I pithouses in Marcia's Rincon	1 sepiolite die (1 azurite ball)	Pithouse C Pithouse A	700–1020 600–820

Site	Artifacts	Context	Dates
29SJ627 Early Pueblo I to mid-Pueblo II community in Marcia's Rincon	9 bone dice 2 limonite	Room 8 (levels 2 & 3), Room 10 (subfloor), Room 23 (level 1), Kiva E, Test Trench 20, Test Trench 5	2 from 1000–1040/50; 2 from 900–1000; 5 from 920–1120 (Kiva E, only 2 found in same area); 2 undated
29SJ629 Late Pueblo I to Pueblo III in Marcia's Rincon	1 bone	Plaza grid 16	920–1020
29SJ625 (Bc243) Three-C Site, Early Pueblo II in South Gap	2 bone dice	Not given	1 from 920–1020, 1 undated
29SJ1928 Chetro Ketl, Pueblo III, Bonito Phase greathouse	"None found"		
29SJ410 (Bc250) Penasco Blanco, Pueblo III, Bonito Phase greathouse	"None found"		

Site	Gaming pieces	Provenience	Dates
29SJ389 Pueblo Alto, Pueblo III, Bonito Phase (1000 to 1200) greathouse	5 bone dice, 3 calcite dice, 1 limonite (1 azurite ball)	Rooms 103/floor 3, 139/floor 2, & 143; Kiva 10, Plaza, Kiva WC, TM 211, TM 210, TM 239, TM 260	1 (920–1020), 4 (1020–1120), 2 (920–1220), 1 (1020–1220), 1 (1120–1220) ball (920–1020)
29SJ387 (Bc253) Pueblo Bonito, Pueblo III, Bonito Phase largest greathouse. Primitive and extensive digging makes accurate dating difficult.	28 bone dice	Rooms 67, 78, 102, 109, 173, 149, 154, 162, 204, 205, 267, 273, 287, 290, 322, 323 (2 die), 326 (2 die), 334, 348 (3 die), Kiva X, West Court trench, and 3 misc.	Not given
29SJ947 (Bc254) Pueblo del Arroyo, Pueblo III, Bonito Phase, greathouse	1 shell die, 2 bone dice	Rooms 46a, 51, 54	1020–1220
29SJ391 (Bc259) Una Vida, Pueblo III, Bonito Phase greathouse	"None found"		
29SJ396 (Bc53) Pueblo III, Hosta Butte Phase, small house village near Casa Rinconada	1 bone die, 1 stone die	Room 6, Kiva B	1020–1220

29SJ398 (Bc58) Pueblo III, Hosta Butte Phase, small house village near Casa Rinconada	11 bone dice	Unknown	Undated
29SJ399 (Bc59) Pueblo III, Hosta Butte Phase, small house village near Casa Rinconada	8 bone dice	1 in Room 8, 7 in Refuse	1020–1220
29SJ1930 (Bc257) Talus Unit No. 1, Pueblo III, Hosta Butte Phase, small house between Chetro Ketl and Pueblo Bonito	2 bone dice	Room 10 and East of Kiva J	920–1220, 1070–1220
29SJ2385 Turkey House, Pueblo III, Hosta Butte Phase, small house near Shabik'eshchee	2 bone dice	Unknown	Undated
29SJ400 (Bc52) Pueblo III, McElmo Phase, small talus ruin south of Casa Rinconada	1 bone	Not given	Not given

29SJ1921 (Bc55) Pueblo III, McElmo Phase, small house site between Chetro Ketl and Hungo Pavi	1 bone die	Room 45	920–1220
29SJ393 (Bc248) Kin Kletso, Pueblo III, McElmo Phase, small house site in Rinconada area	3 bone dice	Room 41, Room 45 ash refuse	1120–1220
Other New Mexico Anasazi			
Salmon Ruin, East of Farmington, Bonito greathouse, circa 1080 (from 1985 survey)	4 bone dice	Not given	1 in primary occupation, 3 in secondary
Artificial Leg Site II, Rio Rancho Basket Maker III to Pueblo I (from 1967 survey)	1 bone die	Pithouse 3	Not specifically dated
Colorado Anasazi			
Mesa Verde (from 1937 survey)	1 bone die	Structure 3, main room	c. 640

(Compiled by author from Mathien 1982, 1985, and 1992)

Gaming Pieces Among Various People Listed by Early Archaeologists

New Mexico	Gaming Piece	Room Designation or Excavation Location	Date (C.E. unless otherwise noted)
Pueblo Bonito (Pepper, 1920)	57 cylindrical wooden sticks, 20 cms × 1.2 cm, debarked, grounded smooth with squared ends and incised spirals, used for gaming or cutting buckskin; 17 smaller sticks, 3 to 5 cms × 1.2 cms, no spirals, flattened ends, poss. gaming use (1 hourglass shape); 1 stick 10.5 cms × 2.7 cms (for kicking game?); 26 wooden dice, flat on one side, rounded edges & tips, 1.7 to 7 cm long with varying widths; 1 meal or gambling tray basket, two-rod coil type, 1½ foot in diameter.	Room 2	Not given

Gaming Pieces, continued

Room 9	1 flattened, cylindrical antler, 4.5 cms long (pos. gambling stick); 25 small, water-worn pebbles.
Room 24	1 cedar kicking stick, 8 × 3.5 cms; 3 arrow pieces, cut for gambling (1 painted red); 3 worked walnuts.
Room 25	1 worked antler, 8.3 × 1 cms (pos. gaming); 2 kicking sticks, 7 × 3 to 4 cms. 6 wooden dice, 2 × 1.3 cms, styles vary; 1 cylindrical gaming stick, 17 × 1 cms; 18 reed arrow sections, cut for gaming w red, green color bands, feather bits (8 w notched ends, 2 w burned holes).

Room 32	54 pos. gaming sticks, up to 1.2 cms thick w "spatula blades" up to 3.4 wide, wrapped w feathers, cotton, buckskin, or yucca cord. No length given; "Pos. Zuni golf clubs?" look like shovels; 1 13 × 4 cms kicking stick; (400 wooden objects in room).
Room 33	2 racing batons (?), 1 petrified wood, 1 chalcedony, 9 × 2 cms; 4 wooden billets, 6 × 2.5 cms for gaming or racing; 1 gaming stick sim. to Rm 2.
Rooms 10 & 33	1 wooden ball, 1 pumice ball.
Rooms 24, 39, 83, 109, 110, 171, 173	7 bone dice, size, style not discussed.
Rooms 2, 25, 106, 171	6 drilled walnuts.
Rooms 70, 106	kicking sticks listed, no detail.

Gaming Pieces, continued

Pueblo Bonito (Judd, 1954)	16 bone dice, 12 elliptically-shaped but varied pointed ends, 8 flat both sides, 8 flat-round sides, markings generally on flat side; 5 incised wooden cylinders; 3 bone counters, equally sized, semiglobular, 1 backed with resinous pellet.	Pueblo Bonito "debris," previously dug rooms, and miscellaneous	3 from Old Bonito, 7 from Late Bonito, 2 from mixed periods, and 4 from miscellaneous periods.
Swarts Ruin Mimbres Site near Silver City (H. S. & C. B. Cosgrove, 1932)	"A few bone dice and gaming chips similar to those found in Kiboko Canyon & White Dog Cave, Ariz., Pueblo Bonito, Rio San Francisco, & other Mimbres." Describes: 1 oblong die, reverse sides marked, no pitch, ¾" long; 1 round piece, drilled center on one side, marked on reverse, 7⁄16" long; 1 oblong disc, not scored; 1 rectangular piece; 1 rib fragment.	Bulk found in excavated houses not specified.	Not given.

Site			
SU Site Mogollon Village, western New Mexico (Martin, 1940)	1 bone die, similar to Anasazi, rectangular, curved edges, scratched diagonally on smooth side, other side left rough.	Pit House S	Assumes post 700 C.E.
	Found 3 of the latter in one place, 2 of which were bound together by cord.	Doolittle Cave, a Mimbres Shrine.	
Fresnal 1 Shelter, near Alamogordo (Irwin-Williams, 1979)	Bone dice.	Not given	Jornada Mogollon, Hueco Basket Maker, c. 1 C.E. (culture dates from 2000 B.C.E.)
Arizona			
Mogollon site in Whitewater District, near Allantown (Roberts, 1940)	Unspecified no. of bone dice, tabular with marks on one side, high polish on other, ochre rubbed into lines of some, ash or charcoal rubbed into others; also small, peculiar stones (toys?); 2 miniature mauls, & simple stone balls.	Refuse pile (?)	Great Pueblo Period

Gaming Pieces, continued

Hohokam ballcourt village at Snaketown (Haury, 1976)	2 shell discs, pos. dice, or inlay. "Bone, shell dice rare in Hohokam." 5 purposely rounded stone balls, from 1.6 to 15.8 cm in diameter, of sandstone, caliche, basalt, and diorite. The diorite weighed 12.427 lb, pos. anvil or shot put.	Not given.	Shells: Possibly Colonial Period (700–900) to Sedentary Period (900–1100) Balls: Gila, Sacaton, & Civano Phases (550 to 1450)
	Dark green diorite ring, weighing 3.49 kg, 18.1 cm in diam., 5.6 cm thick, flat outer edge. Hole tapers in diam. 5 to 3.7 cm. Wear and dents suggest use as target in hoop/pole game. (Mentions others found, 1 near Tucson, imported from Mexico in 900–1100.)	Sacaton Phase houses Block 10G	900 to 1100 C.E.
	Smaller lava rings, from 3.4 to 8.6 cm in diam.; also pos. game target or for shucking dried kernels from corn cobs.	Example given: Pit 3:10F; Level 4, north test	Vahki Period (300 B.C.E. to 500 C.E.)

Basket Maker and Pueblo I sites at Kayenta (Kidder & Guernsey, 1919)	Kinboko Cave I, Cist I, Sayodneechee burial cists, & small cave near "Monuments"	Basket Maker to Pueblo I	Describes 6 peeled cottonwood gaming sticks: 3 exactly alike, 3⅛″ × 8⁄16″ smooth, flat sides marked, rough round sides, ends flat, rounded edges; 3 plain round cylinders with round edges of varying size. 2 other worked sticks also found: 1 is ¾″ × ⅜″, flat side & round side, the other is 1″ × ¼″. Describes cottonwood ball & billet, a short section of branch with 1 squared end, 1 arched; another oval ball, cedar bark wrapped around sandstone, covered with prairie dog hide; set of 8 lenticular & 3 round bone pieces contained in skin pouch secured by fiber string; lenticular dice 11⁄16″ × ¼″ with flat/round sides; round pieces coated with pitch on covex sides and

Gaming Pieces, *continued*

Location	Description	Site	Phase
	pitch-filled perforated centers; 1 lenticular die found in nearby cist, and another in empty cave.		
Basket Maker caves near Kayenta (Guernsey & Kidder, 1921)	Unspecified number of circular bone pieces, pitch-coated on flat side, cemented to small stone drums. Included: 3 sets of 7 circular compound dice (two in small skin bags), and 1 set of 4.	White Dog Cave	Basket Maker II

Utah

Location	Description	Site	Phase
Alkali Ridge, near Blanding (Brew, 1946)	9 polished bone "sporting pieces," 1 circular, the others elliptical 2.2 to 2.4 cm long, no cross-hatching.	Site 13	Pueblo I phase

Colorado

Location	Description	Site	Phase
Ackerman-Lowry site 26 miles northwest of Cortez in Montezuma County (Martin, 1939)	4 elliptical-shaped slips of bone dice, cross-hatching on 2, other 2 has rough vs. polished sides, range from 2.7 to 3.3 cm long.	Not given	Pre-pottery Basket Maker

Early Pueblo Ruins in the Piedra District, southwestern Colorado (Roberts, 1930)	Unspecified number of flat, incised, oblong discs of varying size.	Not given	Early Pueblo (?)
Basket Maker II sites near Durango (Morris, 1954)	97 scored circular, rectangular, & lenticular bone pieces the size of a man's thumbnail, often found scattered in same area, or together. Occurrences in sets: single, 7 times; pairs, 3 times; 4, 4 times; 6, 7, 9, 10, 13—1 time each. Mammal shafts ground down to thin pieces, one side scored randomly or in pattern; round pieces have shallow holes in center on convex, unscored side.	67 from Talus Village, 29 from North Shelter, 1 from South Shelter; the set of 13 was found in Burial 18, and set of 9 in Cist 21, Floor 4d.	Basket Maker II

(Compiled by author. See also Culin, 1907; Roberts, 1936; Hough, 1914.)

Notes

Introduction

1. Culin, *Games of the North American Indians*, 250–52. This Captain Jack should not be confused with the famous Kintpuash, also known as Captain Jack, one of the Modoc leaders in the war of 1872–73 against the U.S. Army in northern California.

2. Ford, "Inter-Indian Exchange in the Southwest," 717.

3. The total revenue from all forms of commercial gaming in the United States in 1994 was $40 billion, reportedly more than what is spent on movies, video games, concerts and Major League Baseball combined. In a poll conducted by Yankelovich, Inc. for Harrah's, a major casino (reported by Gene Sloan, "New Pastime: The Money Is on Gambling," *USA Today*, February 11, 1994), Americans spent thirteen billion dollars during their ninety-two million visits to gaming establishments in 1993. Out of the 100 thousand households surveyed, 27 percent said they had gambled at least once that year, an increase of 10 percent from 1990. Gamblers tended to be well educated and to hold higher paying white-collar jobs. More than half (54 percent versus 46 percent) were women. By June of 1993, 149 tribes had initiated 296 gaming operations, according to an audit report by the U.S. Department of Interior Office of Inspector General, "Issues Impacting Implementation of the Indian Gaming Regulatory Act," November 1993. In March 1995, the National Indian Gaming Commission estimated that 115 tribes operated casinos under 131 tribal/state agreements in 23 states. Anne Constable, in "High Noon: Scrambling Over Gambling," *Santa Fe Reporter*, January 17–23, reported that of the 555 federally recognized tribes, 120 have casinos and another 80 offer bingo and pull tabs. See Appendix I.

4. *Myths of the Cherokee*, Bureau of American Ethnology (henceforth, BAE) 19, LXVIII–LXIX.

5. *Calendar History of the Kiowa Indians*, BAE 17, 348.

6. *Chungké* is a corruption of a Creek word (by early southern traders) and is used to denote the game in other cultures as well. "Chunkey" and other variations are also found in the literature.

7. Culin, "American Indian Games," 58–64.

8. In *Anthropology*, 495, 417–18, Kroeber showed that when gambling was restricted, cul-

tural diffusion was stagnant. The Chinese began printing playing cards in 969 C.E. The Egyptians began block-printing one-page charms around 1200. Printing technique was known in Islam, but not used seriously until 1307 when some brave Arab published a description of the Chinese printing process. But the Europeans didn't establish the process until 1350, and they did so independently when they produced single-sheet block prints on devotional themes. The Mohammedan countries were the likely roadblocks between China and Europe. Islam forbade images and gambling. Furthermore, printing was not sanctioned by Mohammed, and there was a fear of impiety if even the Koran was printed. Then suddenly playing cards appeared simultaneously in Spain, Italy, and Germany between 1377 and 1379. The timing is more than coincidental, and the likely transmitters were several Mongol overlords or *khantes* of the black market.

9. Avedon and Sutton-Smith, *The Study of Games*, 60.

10. Culin, *Games*, 34–5.

11. Culin, *Games*, 486.

12. Culin, *Games*, 174–75.

13. Culin, *Games*, 105.

14. Culin, *Games*, 238.

15. Culin, *Games*, 324.

16. Morgan, *League of the Iroquois*, 291.

17. Culin, *Games*, 109–10.

18. Tylor, "The History of Games," 735–47.

19. Huizinga, *Homo Ludens*, 57–58.

20. The paraphernalia on the Zuñi altar (Culin, *Games*, 34) included a set of four cane dice; a set of four long cane dice; a set of four wooden cylinders for hidden-ball game; two corncob feather darts with ball made of yucca leaves; and sticks for kicked-billet game. Similar objects were found on the altars of the Hopi Flute ceremony. For example, on the altar of the Drab Flute from Oraibi, four small flower-like cups, yellow, green, red, and white, rest upon the floor at the base of the effigy. Between them are two wooden cylinders, painted black, corresponding to the kicking sticks of the Zuñi race game. A cornhusk ring, tied to a long stick, precisely like one used in certain forms of the ring-and-dart game, stands on each side of the principle figure. The altar is carried by two girls in a public ceremony on the ninth day, the ring being tossed with the stick. Culin also mentioned a bundle of gaming reeds being placed with other objects upon the Tewa kiva altar erected at the winter solstice at Hano (Hopi), implying the Tewa Pueblos in New

Mexico would have similar altar effects. War instruments are gaming instruments. At Hopi, the word for the dice basket means shield.

21. Culin, *Games*, 34–35.

22. Huizinga, *Homo Ludens*, 1–27.

23. Avedon and Sutton-Smith, *Study of Games*, 21.

24. Stuart, "The Timeless Vision of Teotihuacan," *National Geographic*, 18.

25. Huizinga, *Homo Ludens*, 53.

26. Puche and Velasco, "Ball game in Mesoamerica," 253–54.

27. Ortiz, *New Perspectives on the Pueblos*, 153, 155.

28. Huizinga, *Homo Ludens*, 61.

29. Allison, *A Structural Analysis of Navajo Basketball*; Cliff, "Navajo Games," 18; Culin, *Games*, 789–90.

30. Franciscan Fathers, *An Ethnological Dictionary of the Navajo Language*, 478.

31. Definition from Gill and Sullivan, *The Dictionary of Native American Mythology*, 59.

32. Kirk, *Myth*, 31.

33. Eliade, *Myth and Reality*, 5–6.

34. Kirk, *Myth*, 8–12.

35. Kluckhohn, "Myths and Rituals: A General Theory," 45–79.

36. Hultkrantz, *Belief and Worship in Native North America*, 3–19.

37. Eliade, *The Myth of the Eternal Return*, 27–28.

38. Allen, *The Sacred Hoop*, 239–44.

39. Allen, *The Sacred Hoop*, 239–44.

40. Malcom Jones's introduction to Dostoevsky, *The Gambler*, xvii–xviii.

41. Navajo officials continue to lobby their members to establish gambling facilities despite the vote. See "Navajo Council Backs Lottery," Mark Engler, July 22, 1995, *Albuquerque Journal*.

42. Associated Press, "Navajo President Vetoes Gambling: Zah Wants Tribe to Vote on Casinos," *Albuquerque Journal*, August 6, 1994.

43. Aberle, "Mythology of the Navaho Game of Stick Dice," 144–54.

44. Evers, "The Great Gambler," 61; Ration, "A Navajo Life Story," 63–71.

45. Too late, I discovered Janet Cliff's article "Navajo Games," which cites 163 works on Navajo games or mythology, with a summary for each reference in the bibliography.

46. The people near Tucson who used to be the Papago voted to revert back to their ancestral name of Tohono O'odham. Papago was a foreign word that meant "bean."

47. Kirk, *Myth*, 1–7.

Chapter 1

1. Recorded by George Catlin, in Culin, *Games*, 365.

2. Waldman, *Atlas of the North American Indian*, x.

3. Thompson, "The Conquering Gambler," 194, cites Livingston Ferrand, *Traditions of the Chicoltin Indians*, Jessup North Pacific Expedition ii, No. 23 (New York, 1909) 38.

4. Culin, *Games*, 237, cites Rev. A. G. Morice, "Notes on the Western Dénés," *Traditions of the Canadian Institute*, v. 4 (Toronto, 1895) 79.

5. Funeral games among the Lakotas of South Dakota were a way of dispensing the property of the dead, in Culin, *Games*, 183. The Sioux (Beauchamp, "Iroquois Games," 275) played a dice game using seven plumstones which was called the "ghost gamble." One player represented the ghost of the dead.

6. Swanton, "How the Seaward-Sqoā'ḷadas Obtained the Names of Their Gambling Sticks," *Haida Myths and Texts*, 322–24.

7. Boas, "The Four Cousins," *Chinook Texts*, 220–22.

8. Frachtenberg, "Wind-Woman and Her Children," *Alsea Texts*, 23–33.

9. Swanton, "Sounding-Gambling-Sticks," *Haida Myths and Texts*, 52–56.

10. Boas, "Giant Gambles with Gull," "Giant Obtains the Olachen," *Tsimshian Myths*, 65, 653–55.

11. Boas, *Tsimshian Myths*, 712.

12. Boas, "Thunderbird Steals the Wife of Another Bird," *Tsimshian Myths*, 712–14.

13. Boas, "Okulā'M Her Myth," *Chinook Texts*, 31–36.

14. Frachtenberg, "The Universal Change," *Alsea Texts*, 35–55.

15. Dixon, "Winning Gambling Luck," in "Shasta Myths," 24–25.

16. Dixon, "The Race with Thunder," in "Shasta Myths," 368.

17. Campbell, *Where the Two Came to Their Father*, 84.

18. Dixon, "Coyote and the Road River People," in "Shasta Myths," 25–27.

19. Sapir, "Coyote and Rabbit Gamble," *Yana Texts*, 226–27.

20. Sapir, "Gopher and Rabbit Gamble," *Yana Texts*, 227.

21. Gifford, "Prairie Falcon's Contest with Meadowlark," in "Western Mono Myths," 352–54.

22. Barrett, "Falcon's Contest with Ki'lak," "Falcon Escapes the World," "Coyote and

Falcon Create People," *Myths of the Southern Sierra Miwok*, 7–10. Recall a similar theme in an Alsea myth in the Pacific Northwest region.

23. Kroeber, "Coyote's Adventures and the Prairie Falcon's Blindness," *Indian Myths of South Central California*, 231–40.

24. Kroeber, "The Prairie Falcon Loses," *Indian Myths of South Central California*, 240–42.

25. This is similar to the Haida myth "Sounding-Gaming-Sticks."

26. Barrett, "Yayil's Journey to the South World," *Myths of the Southern Sierra Miwok*, 9–10.

27. Fowler, *Willard Z. Park's Ethnographic Notes*, 239.

28. Lowie, "Wolf's Son," in "Shoshonean Tales," 105–109.

29. Lowie, "Cŭnā´Bⁱ," in "Shoshonean Tales," 160–61. Lowie also refers to Tobats as TŏBa´ts.

30. Lowie, "The Gamblers," in "Shoshonean Tales," 174–76.

31. Recall that Prairie Falcon also used an egg for a stick-pushing ball in the California region myths.

32. Lowie, "Cottontail Gambles Against the Sun," in "Shoshonean Tales," 198.

33. Lowie, "Wildcat," in "Shoshonean Tales," 199.

34. Lowie, "Centipede," two versions, in "Shoshonean Tales," 229–332.

35. This sequence also parallels the Prairie Falcon myth of California.

36. Teit, "The Gambler," in "Traditions of the Lillooet Indians," 338–39.

37. Sapir, "Eagle, A Klamath Man, Goes to the Columbia River to Gamble," *Wishram Texts*, 292–94.

38. Teit, "The Ball," *Traditions of the Thompson River Indians*, 32–34.

39. Teit, "The Story of the Man Who Travelled to the Sun," *Traditions of the Thompson River Indians*, 54–55.

40. For another Thompson River gambling myth, "The Skunk and the Badger," see Teit, *Traditions of the Thompson River Indians*, 85–87.

Chapter 2

1. O'Bryan, "The Story of Noqoil pi, The Great Gambler," *The Dîné*, 48–63.

2. Lowie, *Crow Texts*, 70.

3. It was archaeologist Gerard Fowke (*Archaeological History of Ohio, The Mound Builders and Later Indians*) who dubbed the disks "chung-kee" stones in 1902. They were most plentiful in the lower ranges of the Appalachians and more or less numerous throughout the central Missis-

sippi Valley and eastward. Many were taken from the mound at Hopewell, while others were found in New York and Pennsylvania. Similar gaming stones have been discovered at Ohio and Kentucky Mound Builder sites, especially near the Ohio River. Gaming stones were also reported among the Oneota culture of Iowa and were among the offerings in a common burial in North Carolina. They varied in shape, material, and degree of finish. Some of the finer grades, as chalcedony and quartz, received the highest finish through grinding or rubbing and bear no signs of hammering. Other sources report figurines in Mississippian sites of players on their knees rolling stones shaped like bowls. Meanwhile, the elite burial in the same mound included handsomely engraved shell gorgets, shell beads, copper beads, breast plates, and chisels of iron. One of some fifty mounds along the Georgia Coast on Creighton Island yielded 220 skeletons in "pockets" and urns. Burial inventory includes discoidal gaming stones of more abundance than in other places of the coastal region. See also Shetrone, *The Mound Builders*.

4. Mooney, *Myths of the Cherokee*, 311–15.

5. Lawson, *History of Carolina*, 57.

6. Culin, *Games*, 486–88.

7. See Schoolcraft, *The Indian in His Wigwam*, 188–90; Williams, *Schoolcraft's Indian Legends*.

8. Culin, *Games*, 82–83.

9. The Eskimo of Alaska believed the northern lights were boys playing a different game of ball, while others say the light is a game being played by shades using walrus skulls as balls (Culin, *Games*, 701).

10. Culin, *Games*, 82–83.

11. Curtin, "Geha Aids a Deserted Boy," *Seneca Indian Myths*, 16–21.

12. He kills the bear by aiming at a white spot in a right hind foot. White patches are commonly vulnerable in other gambling myths.

13. Curtin, "The Grandmother and Grandson," *Seneca Indian Myths*, 167–75.

14. In a number of Pueblo and Navajo myths, butterflies flutter out of the decapitated gambler.

15. Curtin, "Hodadeio and His Sister," *Seneca Indian Myths*, 334.

16. Curtin, "The Thunder Boy," *Seneca Indian Myths*, 110–15. See "The Adventures of Wolf-Marked" in the same book (22–33) for another Seneca gambling myth. See also Curtin and J.N.B. Hewitt, *Seneca Myths and Fiction*, 1918, for similar myths.

17. Swanton, "The Cannibal Woman," *Myths and Tales of the Southeastern Indians*, 219–22.

18. Mooney, "Ûñtsaiyi´, the Gambler," *Myths of the Cherokee*, 311–15.

19. The word translates as "brass" and is applied to any metal.

20. Mooney said that "play ball against them" is a Cherokee figure of speech for a contest of any kind, particularly a battle. Thunder is always personified in the plural, as in *Ani´Hyûñ´tikwalâ´ski*, the Thunderers. Mooney assumes that the boy's father and brothers are *Kana´ti* and the Thunder Boys. But Kana´ti is the Lucky Hunter, and his wife is *Selu*, or Corn. They live in the east, not the west, although they are indeed the parents of the Thunder Boys.

21. Mooney noted the tree was thought to be in the home of the Thunder Man and that there was an occult connection between the pinnated leaves and lightning.

22. Swanton, "Thunder and Laigatonōhana," *Myths and Tales of the Southeastern Indians*, 184.

23. Swanton, "Lodge Boy and Thrown-Away," *Myths and Tales of the Southeastern Indians*, 222–26.

24. Swanton, "The Men Who Went to the Sky," *Myths and Tales of the Southeastern Indians*, 139–41.

25. Swanton, *Myths and Tales of the Southeastern Indians*, 123–24. The game was played with two teams; the representative from one team hides a "bullet" under one of four deerhide swatches on a big bearskin (hairside up), and the representative from the other team must guess its location.

Chapter 3

1. Lesser, in *Pawnee Ghost Dance Hand Game*, said the Arapaho prophet Sitting-Bull continued the spread of the Ghost Dance through 1891. Lesser was probably not referring to the legendary Sioux warrior, Sitting Bull, who was killed the previous year. Lesser made no further distinction between the two.

2. Warrior societies of the horse culture performed public ceremonials, particularly the Sun Dance ritual. Initially, individual power was first sought through the vision quest, self-mutilation, and deprivation; it was furthered by participation in raids and the counting of war honors, or coups, against enemies. This is where the Ghost Dance later found a dangerous home.

3. Lesser, in *Pawnee Ghost Dance*, 64, cites D.J.M. Woods, *Annual Reports of the Commissioner of Indian Affairs*, 1891–92.

4. Mooney, *The Ghost-dance Religion*, 915.

5. Culin, *Games of the North American Indians*, 438–40.

6. Lesser, *Pawnee Ghost Dance*, 182.

7. Dorsey, "Origin of the Basket Dice Game," *The Pawnee, Mythology, Part 1*, 44–46. The myth, told by Woman-Cleanse-the-People, an old Skidi woman and keeper of the Skull bundle, probably predates the Ghost Dance era.

8. Dorsey, *Traditions of the Skidi Pawnee*, 235, describes a different mythic origin of six plumstone dice. In the tale of Scabby Bull, the stones are each particularly marked. The first has a new moon and little black star. The second bears a half moon, the third a full moon, the fourth a great star, the fifth two stars, and the sixth is marked with seven stars. The man holds the stones up to the sky, and through the power of the moon and stars, the stones are painted black.

9. Ponca legend says the plum-stone game is invented by Ukiaba, a tribal hero of the Ponca, who sends five plum stones to a young woman whom he secures by magical arts. He tells her that if she gambles with the stones, she will always win. See J. Owen Dorsey, *The Çegiha Language*, 617.

10. Lesser compared the old games to the new game rituals in no less than 175 pages.

11. Lesser said women never participated in the old hand games because they didn't participate in the warpath. They did, however, participate in the new games and even owned a few ritual formats. For instance, Murie in *Ceremonies of the Pawnee, Part 1*, 75, said that White Star Woman, or Old Lady Washington of the Morning Star Band, was a Ghost Dance prophetess and a prominent player in the first Ghost Dance in the early 1900s. She was responsible for breaking down some of the prohibition against women taking part in the bundle ceremonies and had sought to introduce them to Ghost Dance ideas. In some forms of the game, men were pitted against women, with men on the north and women on the south, to determine which sex had the greater power.

12. Murie, *Ceremonies, Part 1*, 124–25.

13. Murie, *Ceremonies, Part 2*, 195–99.

14. Murie, *Ceremonies, Part 2*, 199–200.

15. Murie, *Ceremonies, Part 2*, 278–79.

16. The pole was more of a "claw" or stick with strings attached that easily snagged the hoops. The Navajos played with a similar "turkey claw."

17. Dorsey, *Skidi Pawnee*, 343, said the ring was traditionally made from the skin of the buffalo vulva.

18. Dorsey, *Skidi Pawnee*, 84.

19. Dorsey and Murie, "Buffalo Gaming Sticks," *The Pawnee*, 104–05, n. 1.

20. Dorsey and Murie, "Buffalo Gaming Sticks," *The Pawnee*, 104–05, n. 1.

21. See Grinnell, "The Girl who Wanted to Be a Ring," *Harper's Magazine*, 425.

22. Dorsey, "Coyote Rescues a Maiden," *Skidi Pawnee*, 257.

23. Dorsey and Kroeber, "Found-in-Grass," *Traditions of the Arapaho*, 364. See 181 for myth titled, "Light-Stone," about big wheel, running wheel, and medicine wheel; and 275, "The White Crow," for reference to the wheel game.

24. Dorsey and Murie, "The Gambler and the Gaming Sticks," *The Pawnee*, 185–91.

25. A similar warning was issued by Tobats to his gambling/creator brother, Cunawabi, in a Shoshonean tale in the Great Basin region.

26. Dorsey and Murie, *The Pawnee*, 185, n.1.

27. Dorsey reported similar gambler myths involving the buffalo for the Wichitas and Arikaras. See "The Buffalo Wife and the Javelin Game," *Traditions of the Arikara*, 189, "Brothers Who Became Lightning and Thunder," *Traditions of the Caddo*, 35 (both in Culin, *Games*, 462–63); and "Half-A-Boy, Who Overcame the Gambler," *The Mythology of the Wichita*, 194–99 (in Culin, *Games*, 470–71).

28. Dorsey and Murie, "The Basket Game, or the Woman in the Moon," *The Pawnee*, 233–36.

29. Rarely is the hero a female. But in "The Girl, Spider-Woman, and the Ball Game" (Dorsey and Murie, *The Pawnee*, 236–39), a young girl beats the gambling Spider Woman with the help of her arthritic uncle who could fly on a set of twin (or double) balls. See Dorsey's *Wichita Tales*, Journal of American Folk-Lore, v. 15, 215, and *The Mythology of the Wichita*, 27, 92, for a report of similar shinny and double ball myths. Both in Culin, *Games*, 626–28.

Chapter 4

1. Matthews, "The Navaho Origin Legend: The Story of the Emergence and Early Events in the Fifth World," *Navaho Legends*, 63–104.

2. Navajos played the moccasin (or shoe game as it was later called) until sunrise to ceremoniously reenact the mythic event, according to Matthews in "Navajo Gambling Songs," 1–19. Designated players lose intentionally so that the sun would continue to reign over half the day. Eight moccasins are buried in the ground up to their tips in two rows side by side. The players are divided in half and given control of one row of moccasins. They toss a chip to determine which party starts first—daylight animals would

play if the chip landed white-side, as opposed to black-side, up. Those players, concealed by a screen, hide the stone in a shoe. With a stiff yucca switch, a selected member of the opposing team strikes the shoe he believes holds the stone. If he chooses correctly, his team goes next, but if he fails, the other team wins a portion of the 102 counters, depending on the position of the moccasin struck in relation to the moccasin containing the stone. The system of counting was so intricate that Matthews was unable to comprehend it fully. The game is over when one side holds all the counters. The final two notched sticks are called grandmothers, which when received are stuck in the rafters of the hogan so that they can "go seek their grandchildren," and for luck. Many songs are sung between innings to assist the gamblers in their work, harkening back to the first game that was played with the primeval animals. Animals dug the tunnels to the moccasins or clutched the stone in their claws to aid, or waylay, the game. Here are two examples recorded by Matthews:

Gopher Song
Gopher sees where the stone is,
Gopher sees where the stone is,
Strike on! Strike on!

Dove Song
Coo coo picks them up,
Coo coo picks them up,
Coo coo picks them up,
Red moccasin picks them up,
Glossy-lock picks them up,
Coo coo picks them up.

3. Matthews first published the gambler account in 1889 as "Noqoìlpi, the Gambler: A Navajo Myth," in *Journal of American Folk-Lore*, 89–94, and then incorporated it into the 1897 *Navaho Legends*. See Appendix II for a fuller account based on these two versions.

4. Cliff, in "Navajo Games," 9, counts a total of fifteen different games cited in the different versions of the Great Gambler. The four most common games, often in the same order, are seven-card dice or thirteen chips, hoop and pole, push on the wood, and racing. "Holy People" aid the challenger in winning the following games: ball game (Rat/Mouse/Bird), ball race, baseball, foot race (Wind/Breeze and Frog), Guessing Game (Wind/Breeze), a guessing game (Wind), hoop and pole (Snake), kicked stick (Woodpecker), Measuring Worm (Measuring Worm), push on the wood (Wind and Worm/Gopher), seven-card dice (Bat/Wind), Shinny

(Bird), stick dice (Lightning/Wind), thirteen chips (Bat/Canary), and wrestling (Wind).

5. Key sights in the Navajo gambler accounts are Pueblo Bonito, Chetro Ketl, and Peñasco Blanco in the canyon itself, plus Pueblo Alto on the canyon's north mesa. They are joined by Pueblo Pintado, ten miles east of Chaco Canyon, and Aztec Ruin, about fifty miles to the north. The other great houses in and around the canyon and the smaller housing projects clustered in Chaco's major drainages are not listed by name here because they do not apply to the gambler mythology directly.

6. Archaeologists believe the kivas evolved from the sacred preservation of the ancestral pithouses. Modern Pueblos use kivas for ceremonial purposes and it is assumed that the practice began during Anasazi times, although this is not necessarily so.

7. The Zuñi, Hopi, and Keresan-speaking Pueblos, such as Acoma, Zia, and Laguna, show evidence of being derived, at least in part, from the Chacoan Anasazi, while the Tanoans are descendants of the Mesa Verde Anasazi. Precise heritage is difficult to trace because of the centuries of intermarriage, political divisiveness, and multiple relocations.

8. The literature on the Homeric poems and their relationship to history is, of course, vast. For the interested reader, two modern classics to start with are M. I. Finley, *The World of Odysseus*, rev. ed. (Harmondsworth: Penguin Books, 1956) and G. S. Kirk, *Homer and the Epic* (Cambridge: Cambridge University Press, 1965).

9. See Vivian, "Navajo Archaeology of the Chacra Mesa, New Mexico"; Brugge, "Tsegai: An Archeological Ethnohistory of the Chaco Region," and A *History of the Chaco Navajos*; and Lister and Lister, *Chaco Canyon: Archaeology and Archaeologists*.

10. Brugge, *History of the Chaco Navajos*, 1–2.

11. Evers, *Between Sacred Mountains*, 83.

12. Evers, *Between Sacred Mountains*, 89.

13. Eliade, *The Myth of the Eternal Return*, 42–47.

14. Hosta may have been derived from the Navajo word *hosteen*, meaning man, and sometimes used as "Mister," although the caption below his portrait translates Hosta as "the Lightning."

15. Jackson, "Report on the Ancient Ruins Examined in 1875 and 1877," in *Tenth Annual Report of the United States Geological and Geographical Survey*, 447.

16. Pepper, *Pueblo Bonito*, 26.

17. Matthews may have been mistaken about Chetro Ketl. The Navajo word *Kîntyél* (or *Kin Teel*) usually refers to Pueblo Pintado. O'Bryan, "The Story of Noqoil pi, the Great Gambler," *The Dîné: Origin Myths of the Navaho Indians*, 48–63, locates *Kin ty eli* at Aztec Ruin. The Navajo name for Chetro Ketl is actually *Kin Klizin or Kin Lizin*, meaning Black House, which is not to be confused with another Chaco great house by the same name.

18. Pepper, *Pueblo Bonito*, 36.

19. Gabriel, *Marietta Wetherill: Reflections on Life with the Navajos in Chaco Canyon*, 153–60. The ceremony was supervised by Hatáli Nez (Tall Chanter), one of the medicine men who relayed a version of the gambler story to Matthews.

20. Brugge, *History of the Chaco Navajos*, 1–3.

21. Gabriel, *Marietta Wetherill*, 156–57.

22. Wetherill and Cummings, "A Navaho Folk Tale of Pueblo Bonito," *Art and Archaeology*, 132–136.

23. Blue gum is associated with Navajo witchcraft, according to Kluckhohn in *Navajo Witchcraft*, and helps with one's gambling prowess, among other desires. He identifies it as the root of one of three plants: Lygodesmia juncea (pursh), stephanomeria pauciflora, or datura (jimsonweed), a hallucinogenic. In Chapin's version, "A Navajo Myth from Chaco Canyon," *New Mexico Anthropologist*, the Gambler controls the players by having them smell a weed, which makes them obsessed with gambling. This is discussed in further detail in Chapter 5.

24. See Judd, *The Material Culture of Pueblo Bonito*, 342–54, for different versions of the gambler myth.

25. Windes, *Investigations at the Pueblo Alto Complex, Chaco Canyon, New Mexico 1975–1979*, 20–22.

26. See Gabriel, *Roads to Center Place: A Cultural Atlas of Chaco Canyon and the Anasazi*, for details on the National Park Service survey of Pueblo Alto.

27. O'Bryan, *The Dîné*, 48–63.

28. Chapin, "A Navajo Myth from Chaco Canyon," 63–67.

29. See Tedlock, *Popol Vuh: The Definitive Edition of the Mayan Book of the Dawn of Life and the Glories of Gods and Kings*, 38, 358.

30. Only ten percent of Pueblo Alto's ruins, plaza, and trash mound have been excavated.

31. For a list see Lister, "Mesoamerican Influence at Chaco Canyon, New Mexico," in

Across the Chichimec Sea: Papers in Honor of J. Charles Kelley, 233–41.

32. Kelley and Kelley, "An Alternative Hypothesis for the Explanation of Anasazi Culture History," in *Collected Papers in Honor of Florence Hawley Ellis*, 178–223.

33. Prescott, *The Conquest of Mexico*, 84–86.

34. Reyman, "Pochteca Burials at Anasazi Sites?" in *Across the Chichimec Sea: Papers in Honor of J. Charles Kelley*, 242–59.

35. Besides skeletons, the contents of Rooms 32 and 28 included painted board; small balls of red and yellow paint; two or three bundles of arrows, 81 with points still attached; remains of woven decorated garments and textiles; a large number of locally made jars, bowls and pitchers; flute; a piece of hammered copper; 121 jar covers; turquoise matrix; 93 turquoise beads; non-Chacoan pottery shards; a shark's tooth; calcite and quartz crystals; more than 400 shell beads; and hundreds of other items. The arrows and board may have had something to do with gaming. Contents of Room 33 included 8 flageolets (end-blown four-holed flutes), one of which was painted like cloisonné, 43 ceremonial sticks or canes of several types, hundreds of turquoise beads and pendants—503 with Skulls 2 and 3 alone, large numbers of shell jewelry, iron pyrite inlay, local ceramic dishware, one or two turquoise-encrusted mouthpieces for shell trumpets, and several hundred other artifacts. Room 38 contained the remains of fourteen imported macaws.

36. Due to decomposition, it was impossible to tell how many sticks had been lying beneath the surface, but from the fragments found in the sand, Pepper estimated there must have been 375 sticks in all.

37. Sahagún, *A History of Ancient Mexico*. In *General History of the Things of New Spain, Florentine Codex: Book 9, The Merchants*, Sahagún talked about the traveling canes being covered by paper that never burned as a gift to the god *Yiacateculti*.

38. Pepper found approximately 225 possible gaming pieces in and near the pochteca mortuary suite, including a sundry collection of worked antler, reed, and arrow pieces; more long and short gaming and kicking sticks; walnut shell, wooden, and bone dice; wooden billets; wooden and pumice balls; and racing batons. (An inventory of Pepper's find is listed in Appendix III.)

39. Kelley and Kelley, "An Alternative Hypothesis," 178–223.

40. See Lekson, *Great Pueblo Architecture of Chaco Canyon, New Mexico*, for more information on kivas in Chaco Canyon.

41. Ellis and Hammack, "The Inner Sanctum of Feather Cave: A Mogollon Sun and Earth Shrine Linking Mexico and the Southwest," *American Antiquity*, said the sipapu was probably delivered to the Anasazi from Mexico through the Mogollon culture. The rich contents of Feather Cave in the Mogollon district of south-central New Mexico point to rapid diffusion from Mesoamerica to the Southwest of numerous religious concepts and specific gods at various periods.

42. The solstices and the north-south axis became primary, as already portrayed by the Great North Road, in the latter half of the eleventh century. Pueblo Bonito was realigned to within a quarter degree east of north, just prior to the construction of the roads. The orientation is underlined by a north-south wall sixty-five meters long which roughly cuts the great house in half. The other cardinal direction pair was represented in Pueblo Bonito's long east-west wall. Pueblo Alto and its counterpart on the south mesa, Tsin Kletzin, were built within view of each other to hold a bearing of a half degree east of north. The northerly orientations were repeated in other Chacoan features. Nine out of ten great houses in the canyon, and three out of four great houses outside the canyon, were intentionally aligned with cardinal and solar bearings or with lunar minor and major standstill bearings. In addition, a number of these houses also shared common internal geometry which also correlated with solar and lunar cycles. A formal study was performed by the Solstice Project (Sofaer, Sinclair, and Donahue, "Solar and Lunar Orientations of the Major Architecture of the Chaco Culture of New Mexico"), and is briefly outlined in Gabriel, *Roads to Center Place*.

43. See Mayer, "An Examination of Miller's Hypothesis," *Native American Astronomy*, 180–201.

44. See Brandt et al., "Possible Rock Art Records of the Crab Nebula Supernova in the Western United States," *Archaeoastronomy in Pre-Columbian America*, 45–58, and Brandt and Williamson, "Rock Art Representations of the A.D. 1054 Supernova: A Progress Report," in *Native American Astronomy*, 171–77.

45. Solar and lunar temples oriented to cardinal directions or celestial events are no stranger to the Americas. For example, Aveni said in "Possible Astronomical Orientations in

Ancient Mesoamerica," *Archaeoastronomy in pre-Columbian America*, that the near 17 degrees east of north orientation of the Street of the Dead at Teotihuacán may have aligned with Dubhe, the brightest pointer star on the Big Dipper. The east-west orientation (16 degree 30′ south of true east) as emphasized by a major street and a canal may have been triggered by an actual event in the sky. On May 18, 150 C.E., the Pleiades underwent helical rising, that is, it appeared in conjunction with the sunrise and then crossed the zenith on the same day. The day would have been traditionally significant because it was the first of two annual days when the sun cast no shadows at noon, demarcating a change in the seasons. These two coordinates are marked by large crosses within circles that may have also served as a playing board for a dice game called *patolli*.

46. Brandt and Williamson, "Rock Art Representations of the A.D. 1054 Supernova: A Progress Report," *Native American Astronomy*.

47. Ellis, "A Thousand Years of the Pueblo Sun-Moon-Star Calendar," *Archaeoastronomy*, 59–87.

48. For a succinct list of works in both areas, see Judge, "Chaco: Current Views of Prehistory and the Regional System," in *Chaco & Hohokam*, 29–30.

49. Sahagún, *Florentine Codex, Book 8, Kings and Lords*, 29–30.

50. Refers to prehistoric inhabitants of Mexico who developed elaborate urban centers.

51. Leyenaar, *Ulama: The Perpetuation in Mexico of the Pre-Spanish Ball Game Ullamaliztli*, 1.

52. Castillo, "Pre-hispanic Ball Game and the Origin of the Game on the Central Mexican Plateau," in *El Juego de Pelota en El México Precolumbino y su pervivencia en la actualidad*, 259.

53. Leyenaar, *Ulama*, 3–4.

54. Archaeologists have found traces of Quetzalcóatl icons in the ball court architecture throughout Mesoamerica after 900 C.E. For this reason they consider the ball court built in the City of Quetzalcóatl at Toltec Tula to be the prototype for later courts.

55. See Haury, *The Hohokam: Desert Farmers and Craftsmen; Excavations at Snaketown, 1964-1965*, for detailed information of his ballcourt findings.

56. Wilcox, "Hohokam Social Complexity," in *Chaco & Hohokam*, 25–375.

57. Great kivas were centerpieces of the Anasazi and Mogollon communities, but the ballcourts lay on the Hohokam fringe. "What

conclusion may be drawn from this I do not know, but it could be a hint of intervillage competition of the kind still existing in the kickball races of the Papago [Tohono O'odham]," wrote Haury in (Reid and Dayel) *Haury's Prehistoric Southwest*, 428. Those villages with courts may have been divided in half into moiety groups, from which teams were drawn, and also the referees, whether religious or secular.

Hohokam descendants do not have formal ball courts, but historical Tohono O'odham (Papago) gambled to "place a claim" upon the goods possessed by each other. Hackenberg, "Pima and Papago Ecological Applications," *Handbook of the North American Indians*, 164, said a needy village would challenge a richer neighbor to compete against its champion runners, kickball players, or race horses. The challenging village would bet its real property, such as horses and blankets, against the equivalent value of food supplies. If they lost, they faced being wiped out. Tohono O'odham etiquette required that challengers received consolation prizes if they lost, and if a village had nothing to stake, they could always sing for their supper. In the "begging dance," lasting several nights, spectators were expected to feed the performers.

58. Crown and Judge, "Synthesis and Conclusions," *Chaco & Hohokam*, 296–97.

59. One specimen (from Sacaton Period, 900 to 1100 B.C.E. at Snaketown, the capital of the Hohokam in the Phoenix valley) of excellent workmanship deserves attention. Made of dense, dark greenish diorite and weighing in at nearly eight pounds, it measures seven inches in diameter and two inches thick. It is flat on the outer edge with a cone-shaped hole through the center. The abrasions in the hole are at right angles to the face of the stone, suggesting that something was thrust through it, yet persistent misses wore smooth the surface near the hole. The rock ring was hit more on one side than the other. The weight and wide edge were necessary to achieve any length of roll in the soft desert soil. This violent wear lead Haury to speculate that the ring was a chungké stone similar to those found in Mound Builder sites (Haury, *The Hohokam*, 293).

60. A few historical tribes listed in Culin's catalogue played hoop and pole with traditional stone rings, flat stone spheres, or bowls, some of which had perforated centers. The Cheyenne of Oklahoma played with a limestone medicine wheel, four and a half inches in diameter with deep grooves simulating buckskin, as if the buckskin hoop was the prototype. A star and a moon

were engraved on opposite sides. The Bellacoola of British Columbia played with lava rings two and a half to three and a half inches in diameter. The five-and-a-half-inch lava rings of the Kwakiutl of British Columbia more closely resembled the ancient rings of the Hohokam. Boas says the Kwakiutl called these rings "mist-covered gambling stone," "cloud-covered gambling stone," "rainbow gambling stone," and "carrier of the world." The Eno played with highly polished bowl-shaped disks of white quartzite, up to five and a half inches in diameter, and stained yellow.

61. Haury also found five purposely rounded stone balls in the Hohokam sites. Four were made from sandstone, caliche, or basalt, were up to two and a half inches in diameter, and dated between 975 and 1150 C.E., and 1300 and 1350 C.E. The fifth ball proved to be the most interesting because of its exceptional finish and size. Made from diorite, it was more than six inches in size and a concentrated 12.427 pounds in weight. Balls of this size are not common in the Southwest. There was no scarring to imply use, but there were several pitted areas to make him think it was used as an anvil. "A comprehensive review of stone spheres states that most of them were gaming pieces and that they may have been in more-or-less continuous use for 6,000 years," Haury says. (Haury, *The Hohokam*, 290–93).

Early Anasazi (Basket Maker III) also played ball. At Kayenta, Arizona (Kidder and Guernsey, *Archaeological Explorations in Northeastern Arizona*, 186, 190), archaeologists found an oval ball five and a half inches in diameter, made by winding cedar bark about a flat piece of sandstone and covering the whole with prairie-dog hide, skin side out. They also found a cottonwood ball and billet of excellent workmanship for possible use in a Pima-style kicking game. In the Whitewater District of Arizona (Roberts, *Archaeological Remains in the Whitewater District*, 125–26), a number of simple stone balls appeared that were about the same size and character as those used by the Zuñi Indians in their hidden ball game. Several of the older men from Zuñi visited the excavations on various occasions and when they were shown the stone balls exclaimed, I'yänkolo'we, which was apparently the name for a hidden ball game. The game is part of a ceremony for rain and a petition for abundant crops. "While it is not known that these earlier peoples had similar beliefs and ceremonies, it seems logical to conclude that they did and that the present specimens were for use in that connection," said Roberts.

Culin, *Games*, 728, lists two examples of tribes throwing stone spheres at targets. The Bannock of Idaho called the game involving a two-and-a-half-inch ball, *tin-bin ter-ow-a-ko*. At the Tewa pueblo of Santa Clara, the game of *kou-wa-di* was close to extinction.

62. It isn't clear whether the Mound Builders played dice. Among the flint flake and points, stone axes and hematite pendants found in the fields near the six mounds of Poverty Point in Louisiana (which emerged in the lower Mississippi Valley around 1500 B.C.E. and peaked between 1200 to 800 B.C.E.), were sixty-seven baked clay objects of various shapes, some resembling deer ankle bones or astragali. The astragalus was used as a die by many ancient cultures around the globe. Scholars believe the earthenware objects were heated in the coals and dropped into food for cooking, but Shetrone, *The Mound Builders*, said they were "authoritatively regarded as gambling cones." Such pottery disks were also found in the shell deposits which contained burials near mounds at Mobile Bay, Alabama.

63. Haury, *The Hohokam*, 293.

64. Roberts, *Additional Information on the Folsom Complex*, 31, plates 9, fig. e, makes this conjecture, but also doubts it.

65. Irwin-Williams, "Post-Pleistocene Archeology, 7000–2000 B.C.E.," in *Handbook of the North American Indians*, vol. 9, 42. This was a Jornado Mogollon site.

66. See Appendix III for reports of gaming pieces in the Southwest.

67. See Spencer, *Mythology and Values: An Analysis of Navaho Chantway Myths*, 58–59, for specific information on gambling in these chants. For Navajo names and ceremonies associated with Anasazi sites, see Franstead, "An Introduction to the Navajo Oral History of the Anasazi Sites in the San Juan Basin Area"; and Franstead and Werner, "The Ethnogeography of the Chaco Canyon Area Navajo"; York, Frederick, "An ethnographic survey of localities of significance to the Navajo population in the vicinity of the NMGS impact area"; and Kluckhohn, *Navajo Witchcraft*.

The story of the Moccasin Game, played between nocturnal and diurnal animals to determine night and day, has been associated with the Beauty Way and the Dead Spirit ceremony. Offerings of turquoise were made to the yucca plant that furnished the ball and counters by the chanter in charge of the ceremony. At the end of the game, the same chanter hid the ball and counters and made another offering and said a prayer for a patient. Contestants who scored ten points customarily prayed or blew smoke through the smoke hole for the patient's recovery (Cliff, "Navajo Games," 6).

68. Brugge, Chaco Navajos.

69. Evers, Between Sacred Mountains, 99.

70. In addition to the previously mentioned versions by Evers, Matthews, and O'Bryan, the following allude to Mexico: Goddard, "The Emergence," Navajo Texts, 140–47; Pousma, He-Who-Always-Wins and Other Navajo Campfire Stories, 57–69; Zolbrod, Diné bahane', 99–122. Incidentally, the versions collected by Goddard (in 1923–24) and by O'Bryan (in 1928) appear to have come from the same informant. Zolbrod is based on Matthews, and Evers is based on O'Bryan. The following two versions have unique endings. In Wetherill and Cummings, "A Navaho Folk Tale of Pueblo Bonito," the gambler is never challenged by a hero, but his slaves eventually murder him and bury him under a rock. In Pousma's version, the gambler widow challenges the victor to a guessing game. Other versions not included in this book are Hogner, Navajo Winter Nights; and Whitman, Navaho Tales (also based on Matthews); both are children's books. The Navajo gambler myth has also been mentioned in the following texts: Coolidge and Roberts, The Navajo Indians, 71, 86, 111; Haile (1902 letter) in Culin, Games, 668, 790; Fishler, In the Beginning: A Navaho Creation Myth, 62–66, 105; Lavine, The Games the Indians Played, 22, 54; Reichard, Navajo Religion, 59, 77, 198, 209, 275, 383, 388, 474, 499, 502, 522, 526, 601; Spencer, Reflection of Social Life in the Navaho Origin Myth, 9–95; Ten Broeck, "Manners and Customs of the Moqui and Navajo Tribes in New Mexico," Information Respecting the History, Condition, and Prospects of the Indian Tribes of the United States, 91.

71. Chapin, "A Navajo Myth from Chaco Canyon," 67.

72. Ration, "A Navajo Life Story," The South Corner of Time; 67–69. Interestingly, Ration said the wizard gambler was a white man who could only be beaten by his twin. The people decided that the gambler's next opponent would be his identical twin who lived at Bird Knoll, identifiable only by the fact that he was the honest one. A match with his twin would change the bad gambler's luck. A real brother could win only after having sex with his sister-in-law. That was what he was doing when the gambling wizard's brother came to his home. He was not to greet his wizard brother as "my dear brother," but as

"my opponent" or shake his hand. He was to begin singing a song from the Prostitution Way.

73. Matthews served as assistant surgeon at Fort Wingate near Gallup, New Mexico, for the U.S. Army in the 1870s and 1880s. Fort Wingate was isolated but it rendered passage to Navajo country and rich opportunity for a man like Matthews. He immersed himself in Navajo customs and in the next few years wrote several essays on the Navajos. Matthews was a nineteenth-century-style Indian sympathizer. In 1888, he joined colleagues in protesting federal neglect of the Cherokees, who had been removed from North Carolina to Oklahoma in 1837–38. He introduced remedial measures to check their abnormally high death rate. Perhaps the Navajos traded ceremonial information for amnesty. Marietta Wetherill maintained that the Navajos shared religious secrets with her in order for her to relay the information to the white man, with the thought that understanding would lessen his fear of the Indians and he would stop trying to remove them from the land (Judd, The Bureau of American Ethnology: A Partial History).

74. Zolbrod, Diné bahane': The Navajo Creation Story, 112.

75. Windes, Investigations at the Pueblo Alto Complex, 21–22.

76. Two wooden dice and a gaming disk made from a Jemez black-on-white pottery shard were found in a seventeenth century Navajo-Pueblo refugee camp north of Chaco Canyon. (Keur, "Big Bead Mesa, an Archaeological Study of Navaho Acculturation, 1745–1812," Supplement to American Antiquity, 81.)

77. McNitt, Navajo Expedition: Journal of a Military Reconnaissance from Santa Fe, New Mexico to the Navajo Country Made in 1849, 19–22.

78. He based his ideas on the writings of Prescott, Conquest of Mexico, and Humboldt, Vues des Cordillères et Monuments des Peuples Indigènes de l'Amerique, both popular authors of the times.

79. Olguín, "The Sacred Ball Game in the Capital of the 'Mexicas,'" in El Juego, 293–94.

80. Foreword to Architecture and Dendrochronology of Chetro Ketl, Chaco Canyon, New Mexico. Maize originated in the Valley of Tehuacan between 1000 and 2000 B.C.E. Many Southwestern ethnologists agree that the Puebloan culture acquired most of its gods from Mexico by the tenth century, including Quetzalcóatl. Casas Grandes (in Northern Mexico) may have fallen under the Quetzalcóatl sign of the feathered serpent between 1060 and 1340 C.E. Kelley and Kelley, "An Alternative Hypothesis for the

224 NOTES TO CHAPTER 5

Explanation of Anasazi Culture History," believed that pochteca refugees, cut off from their homeland after 1150, or Pueblo IV, may have fled to new developing centers on the Hopi mesas, at Zuñi, and the eastern Pueblos where they would have intensified the Quetzalcóatl cult. Elements implying the presence of the Quetzalcóatl cult in Anasazi culture include the macaw carcasses and their colorful feathers, the plumed serpent motif on pottery and gaming sticks, and conch shells. Historical Pueblos practiced the kachina cult (and still do), which some Southwestern investigators believed to be the outgrowth of the Mexican deities such as the Quetzalcóatl cult making its way into New Mexico sometime in the fourteenth century.

Chapter 5

1. Luckert, The Navajo Hunter Tradition, 133 ff.
2. Reichard, Navajo Religion, 461, 482–83.
3. His name was originally Motecuhzuma or Motecuhzoma, but was changed to Montezuma by Spanish chroniclers. His name supposedly meant "sad, severe man," but Bandelier, "The 'Montezuma' of the Pueblo Indians," American Anthropologist, 319, says the name meant "Our Wrathy Chieftain." He was grandson of Moctezuma Ilhuicamina (1440–68). For the purpose of the Montezuma tales, we will use the misnomer here.
4. Puche and Velasco, "Ball game in Mesoamerica," El Juego, 255.
5. Puche and Velasco, "Ball game in Mesoamerica," El Juego, 255.
6. Sahagún, Florentine Codex, Book 8, 29.
7. Durán, Historia de las Indias.
8. In patolli five or ten black beans served as two-sided dice, distinguishable by a hole drilled into one side of each bean. Players kept track of their rounds with six or so stone counters on a checkered cross-shaped field made of cloth. The cross was drawn onto the mat with a diluted rubber called olli. In Náhuatl, ollin refers to the movement of the sun, further symbolized by the rubber ball volleyed between opposing ball-game teams representing light and dark. According to Castillo ("Pre-hispanic Ball Game and the Origin of the Game on the Central Mexican Plateau," El Juego, 256), the two opposing players in patolli may have indirectly implied the same antagonism.
9. Ometochtli, or Two Rabbits, bestowed the deuce throw and accommodated games in general.
10. Tylor, "On American Lot-Games, as Evidence of Asiatic Intercourse Before the Time of Columbus," 82–88, cites Spanish writers Gomora, Durán, and Sahagún for the information on patolli given here.
11. Prescott, The Conquest of Mexico, 168–78. His sources were such sixteenth-century chroniclers as Sahagún, Torquemada, Diaz, and Durán.
12. Leyenaar, Ulama, 38–39.
13. Diaz del Castillo, The Discovery and Conquest of Mexico, 1517–1521, 323–24.
14. Prescott, Conquest, 361–65.
15. Prescott, Conquest, 493.
16. Surviving Pueblos today are divided into six different languages. These include: Hopi (in Arizona); Zuñi; Keresan (Acoma, Laguna, Zia, Santa Ana, San Felipe, Santo Domingo, and Cochiti Pueblos); and the three Tanaon dialects: Tiwa (Taos, Picuris, Sandia, and Isleta Pueblos); Tewa (San Juan, Santa Clara, San Ildefonso, Tesuque, Pojoaque, and Nambe Pueblos); and Towa (Jemez Pueblo and the extinct Pecos Pueblo). The Hopi and Tanoan are tentatively classified in the Aztecan-Tanaon phylum, and the Zuñi and Keresan belong to the Uto-Aztecan phylum, although this is not confirmed. Gambling myths cited here typically belong to the Zuñi and to the Keresan- and Tewa-speaking Pueblos. Each pueblo is an autonomous unit of government, and although lifestyles, cultures, and beliefs within each are similar, they are distinctive. For purposes of this chapter, however, some generalities will be made.
17. Spanish soldiers and clergy began hearing Montezuma stories as early as 1664 in northern Mexico, where ruins were referred to as "montezumas." In Arizona, a 1745 Tohono O'odham story claimed Montezuma as Elder Brother, who brings misfortune to the people, but who establishes a new people, and all attempts to kill him fail because he can raise from the dead. The Arizona Pima regarded themselves as his descendants and attached him to the Hohokam ruins.
18. The reference was a letter by Governor Atonio de Otermín to the king of Spain in 1680.
19. Among the Keresans, the culture hero's name is Boshayanyi or Poshaiyanne. At Zuñi he is Poshayanki, who is associated with their curing societies as the benevolent curer. He was probably known to the Hopi in connection with the now extinct Pobösh curing society. The Hopi culture hero is Pahana, whose return is still awaited today. I mentioned Poseyemu to a Hopi man, and he responded, "Yes, the gambler." The recognition may have been the result of living

near the Hopi villages occupied by Tewa Pueblo immigrants. Since each pueblo has a different spelling and pronunciation for this culture hero, I will refer to all of them as Poseyemu.

20. In *Pueblo Nations: Eight Centuries of Pueblo Indian History*, 65–67, Joe Sando, from Jemez Pueblo, said the story was a subterfuge on the part of the prisoners. Keresan captives reported the ringleader to be *Payastiamo*, and pointed to the mountains in one direction; a Tewa said the leader's name was *Poheyemo* and pointed in another direction; and a Towa man said his name was *Payastiabo*. "The joke" is that these three names are the "deities whom the Pueblos address their prayers to intercede with the One who lives above beyond the clouds," said Sando. "He generally lives to the north, in the highest mountain, or in the clouds. But the Spaniards concluded that he was indeed the leader of the revolt." Although many Pueblo leaders were involved in organizing the revolt, Popé, from San Juan Pueblo, stands out in history as the hero. He was one of forty-seven religious leaders flogged in 1676 for practicing witchcraft. He fled to Taos and over the years worked to unify the pueblos and convince them to rebel, while working a strategy to do so, says Chilton, et al., in *New Mexico: A New Guide to a Colorful State*, 26–28. Interestingly, Bandelier said the mythical Montezuma was born at Ojo Caliente, north of San Juan Pueblo, the home of Popé.

21. Parsons, *Pueblo Indian Religion*, 179, confirmed that Poseyemu at various pueblos had fused with Montezuma.

22. Bandelier, "The 'Montezuma' of the Pueblo Indians," *American Anthropologist*, 319–26, said the document could not have been written anywhere else but Mexico, but inspiration for it may have come from New Mexico, namely Hosta's pueblo. He claims Jemez possessed a printed book called "History of the Pueblos," complete with illustrations. In actuality, the book was a copy of Cortés's letters, but all the Pueblos knew of its existence. Bandelier never saw either document himself.

23. Although General Kearny's arrival into Santa Fe in 1846 was not trumpeted by celestial fanfare, he was also thought to be the returning Montezuma. One Jemez man told Lt. Simpson that "the children of Montezuma were to be delivered by a people who would come from the East." Simpson added, "In consequence of the good treatment they were receiving from the Americans, they were beginning to believe that that people had come; that General Kearny had

told them they would believe this more and more, because they would continue to be treated well by the Americans, and they were finding it so." (McNitt, *Navajo Expedition*, 24–25) Apparently, the Pueblos had not read Prescott.

24. See Sando, *Pueblo Nations*.

25. Actually, the Pueblos do not have a "heaven" per se. When Keres Pueblos die, for example, they return to Iyatiku, the Earth Mother, who lives in the underworld, which is represented by the kiva and its rituals.

26. Xólotl was the legendary leader of the Chichimecs, who became the Aztecs in the fourteenth century. The Aztecs absorbed the Toltec culture, who also influenced the Highland Mayas. (Miranda, "Game in the Mythological Cities of Quetzalcóatl," *El Juego*, 268)

27. Parmentier, *Handbook of the North American Indians*, vol. 9, 609–22.

28. Ortiz, *New Perspectives on the Pueblos*, 143.

29. Gunn, "The Moki Tradition," *Shat-Chen: History, Traditions, and Narratives of the Queres Indians of Laguna and Acoma*, 167–72. Moki could be a reference to Moqui, associated with the Hopis.

30. The myth may have been an attempt to explain the subtle infiltration of the Kachina cult by Mesoamerican merchants who took refuge with the Keres. It may have also been a recording of the dispute between the traditional people and the progressive people, which caused the "Laguna break," resulting in some clans moving to Isleta Pueblo in 1880.

31. The Pueblos did not throw away their heritage in favor of the Christian religion imposed upon them. Instead, they incorporated the new into the old, much of which is still practiced underground today. Each pueblo has a Catholic patron saint and feasts are held on that saint's day in conjunction with native dances. See White, *The Pueblo of Sia*, 263–281, for references to Santiago and Boshayanyi (Poseyemu).

32. Stevenson, *The Sia*, 59–67. Stevenson said she heard the story repeated at Jemez.

33. White, *The Pueblo of Sia*, 5, said Stevenson claimed to have been the daughter of Poseyemu (Po'shaiyänne) and used flashlight powder to demonstrate her power. As a medicinewoman herself (referring to her pre-med classes), Stevenson claimed a right to attend sacred ceremonies. Daughter of Po'shaiyänne may have been an appropriate title considering that, commendably, Stevenson was the first woman ethnologist to work in the Southwest. She was a pioneer in the young science of

anthropology and was the first to see value in collecting data on the Pueblo religion.

34. The dice game was counted on a square circuit of forty pebbles, ten to a side representing the cardinals. Players smacked the center stone with four wooden blocks; the count depended on how they fell. Players' markers moved in opposite directions starting at the corners. At Laguna, the center stone sometimes wears a painted face and is wreathed in evergreen, representing Spider Woman (and perhaps the climbway from the underworld).

35. This may be a reference to Malinche, the Indian woman from Coatzacualco who served Cortés as interpreter and concubine. In one Tewa Pueblo story, Montezuma, guided by the Great Spirit, marries Malinche, said to be the daughter of the leader of the Pueblo of Zuñi. In the allegedly concocted "History of Montezuma," according to Bandelier, she is born to Montezuma in the Pueblos and later marries Cortés with New Mexico as her dowry. All of this is documented in a book containing the letters of Cortés, a copy of which was supposedly in the possession of Jemez Pueblo, according to Bandelier, in "The 'Montezuma' of the Pueblo Indians."

36. Culin, Games, 120. He may be referring to the Kopot brothers discussed later in this chapter.

37. Boas, "The Gambler," Keresan Texts, 253–54.

38. In O'Bryan's Navajo gambler episode in The Dîné, 65, the champion is asked to guess the identity of the figure on the wall. The figure is Ash'ke chili, the Guard of Water Jars, the Zuñi God of Dew. He has a bill like a crow and holds four pretty flowers in each hand. Next to the figure are nine circles; the first four are jars containing the Male Rains (black, blue, yellow, and white); the next four contain the vapors or Female Rains (black, blue, yellow, and white). The ninth jar contains all the bad medicine or black magic that the gambler uses. The champion is told to make an offering of mixed stone chips to the little breeze that would sit on his right ear and help him guess correctly.

39. Gunn, "Pais-Chun-Ni-Moot, The Fire-brand Boy," Schat-Chen, 161–66.

40. The story is one explanation for El Malpais, the volcanic rock around Laguna pueblo. Other traditions claim the rock to be the blood of the monster killed by the twins.

41. Tyler, Pueblo Gods and Myths, 25, 150.

42. Malotki, "Maasaw niqw Orayit Naat-sawinaya—How Maasaw and the People of Oraibi Got Scared to Death Once," Hoptu-

tuwutsi/Hopi Tales: A Bilingual Collection of Hopi Indian Stories, 109–117.

43. Malotki, "Maasaw," 208–09.

44. Tyler, Pueblo Gods and Myths, 143–48.

45. Parsons, Pueblo Indian Religion, 1090–91.

46. See Gunn, Shat-Chen, 72–73, for a similar story.

47. Parmentier, The Mythological Triangle, 610.

48. Tyler, Pueblo Gods and Myths, 215.

49. Culin, Games, 32–33.

50. Twins at Zuñi are identified as Áhaiyuta and Mátsailema and collectively referred to by the elder brother's name, Áhaiyuta.

51. See Cushing, "Outlines of Zuñi Creation Myths," for a full account of tournaments played during the semiannual festivals of the twins at Zuñi.

52. Stevenson, "Zuñi Games," American Anthropologist, 480, claimed a slightly different account of the game. Legend says the stick-dice game was played for rain by the Gods of War and the Ah'shiwanni (rain priests) soon after coming to this world. The Ah'shiwanni organized a fraternity at Zuñi which they called Shówekwe, or arrow-reed people, for the express purpose of playing the game for rain. Each player takes the side of one of the Gods of War, two pieces of split reed representing the side of the elder God of War, and two the younger God of War.

53. Ortiz, New Perspectives, 144.

54. Boas, "Cliff Dweller," Keresan Texts, 104–11, 257–58. Among the Keresans, the twins are generally called Masewa, the older, and Oyoyewi, the younger. The Sun Youth parallel is Boas, "The Gambler," Keresan Texts, 253–54.

55. Ration, "A Navajo Life Story," called the gambler's laborers Cliff Dwellers.

56. Boas, Keresan Texts, 277, said the kachina, or Ko'ko (masked spirits) other than the gambler, murder women or kill people they have overcome by gambling. In a Zuñi myth, the Bow Priest's spinster daughter locks herself in a room grinding corn. The priest sponsors competitions for her hand, but she only accepts the elder brother of the twins. This so angers the other suitors that they challenge him to a race. Being supernatural, he wins, and the bride takes cornmeal to the twins' mother at Corn Mountain. Gill and Sullivan, The Dictionary of Native American Mythology, 6–7.

57. Spider Woman is the Pueblo creator who thinks the world into being with her thoughts. Prayers are sent to the tiny spiders in the underworld to push the cornplants upward.

58. Gunn, "Sutsu-Nuts, the Ruler of the Ka-Tsi-Na (Kachina)," Schat-Chen, 127–33.

59. Boas, *Keresan Texts*, 258, points to another version claiming that Yellow Woman's sons are the result of an encounter with the Sun and they guess that the contents in the bag are birds rather than stars. Birds are often associated with star gods.

60. Culin, *Games*, 792.

61. Boas, *Keresan Texts*, 237; Parmentier, "The Mythological Triangle," 614.

62. Her sister is usually *Naosete* or *Uresete*, and Iyatiku is interchangeable with both. (Spellings and attributes vary widely between pueblos.) They are usually, though not always, the daughters of *Sustinako* (spelling varies), grandmother Spider Woman, or Thinking Woman. Sustinako also has a sister in some manifestations named *Shrotunako*, personifying memory and instinct.

63. Gunn, "Ko-Pot Ka-Nat," *Shat-Chen*, 115–19. The reed may refer to gaming. In Gunn, "Pais-Chun-Ni-Moot, The Firebrand Boy," *Schat-Chen*, 161–66, players cast reed dice. In Boas, "The Gambler," *Keresan Texts*, 253, the gambler lives at Reed-Leaf-Town.

64. Boas, *Keresan Texts*, 254, said the Kopot brothers were once described to Boas as stars or assistants to the twin heroes.

65. Gunn said the story was about the sinking of Atlantis, which he believed was the home of the first Kush Kutret. The Keres people call themselves *Hanno*, meaning "from the east." Hanno, according to Gunn, sounds like the Phoenician word for man, as in Hannibal, Kush Kutret refers to Carthage, and the water animal is actually a whale. Curiously the end of the episode is suspiciously similar to Gunn's "Pais-Chun-Ni-Moot, The Firebrand Boy." Gunn believed that the myths were told in a particular order to describe the migration phases from Atlantis through Florida to New Mexico. Mythically speaking, the stories are about the destruction of the three or four underworlds or past worlds, and the subsequent evacuation from each. They emerged into this world somewhere in northern New Mexico.

66. Culin, *Games*, 201–204. The Maricopa live with the Pima on the Arizona reservation.

67. This could be a hidden image of string games like Cat's Cradle so popular among North American tribes. The Zuñi found the center of the universe by stretching the legs of a water strider to the four oceans.

68. This is an image of the kicking-stick race the Pima played.

69. Hundreds of hieroglyphic books had been written by the Mayas, but only three and part of a fourth survived the bonfires of the Spanish Conquest in the 1500s. Christian priests worked out a Maya alphabet to teach prayers to the natives in their own language. Quiché Maya noblemen took advantage of the new alphabet and recorded the *Popol Vuh* to preserve an ancient culture of temple calendars now in ruins. In 1901–03, a friar named Francisco Ximénez made the only surviving copy with a Spanish translation. The sacred text was translated from Spanish into English in 1950 and translated from the original Quiché Maya by a native speaker named Andrés Xiloj, which Tedlock published as *Popol Vuh: The Definitive Edition of the Mayan Book of the Dawn of Life and the Glories of Gods and Kings*.

70. Tedlock, *Popol Vuh*, 34–46.

71. Pasztory, *Religión en Mesoamérica*, 441–55.

72. Leyenaar, *Ulama*, 10–13.

73. Goddard, *Navajo Texts*, 140; O'Bryan, *The Dîné*, 48–63; and Reichard, *Navajo Religion*, 77.

74. Zolbrod, *Diné bahane'*, 371, n. 28, said this shows how highly the deities value jewels. In other versions of the gambler myth, offerings of precious stones are made to the gods in exchange for their help. Their help is not a one-sided supplication but a transaction; the offerings commit the deities.

75. Reichard, *Navajo Religion*, 389.

76. Begochídí creates the principle mountains and their vegetation in the first underworld. Black God quarrels with him and sets the world on fire, forcing the people to escape to the next world. Begochídí creates the second world and creates the twin males and females, called One-Who-Follows-The-Other, whom he destroys and then restores. Black God burns this world, too, and the people move to the third world (Reichard, *Navajo Religion*, 569, 571). This parallels the destruction of the world by fire in Gunn's "Pais-Chun-Ni-Moot, The Firebrand Boy," and Boas's "The Gambler."

77. Matthews notes that in one story, Begochídí, sitting in the north side of the room, and Sun, sitting in the south side of the same room, make all the animals. While the former makes a horse, the latter makes an antelope, and this is why the two animals look the same. Matthews said Begochídí means "he tried to catch it," a name the deity attained while hunting (in Zolbrod, *Diné bahane'*, 372–73, n. 33).

78. Reichard, *Navajo Religion*, 389.

79. Zolbrod, *Diné bahane'*, 372–73, n. 33.

80. Reichard, *Navajo Religion*, 386–87.

81. Zolbrod, *Diné bahane'*, 111.

82. It was Matthews, *The Night Chant*, 9, who first translated *Hastséyalti* as Talking God, or Talking Elder of the Gods. He is otherwise called *Yéibichai* (*Yébitsai*), or the Maternal Grandfather of the Gods, and is the principal character in the *klédzi* or Night Chant. A yéibichai dance is held the last night of this nine-day ceremony. Hastséyalti is a beneficent character, always ready to rescue the humans from peril, and he is often associated with the mist or clouds which appear in the mountains. He is also called *Bĭtsís Lakaí*, or White Body. In other versions of the gambler legend, the offended deity is Sun—one can see how the two can be easily confused in the mind of the recorder. In this case, he is Sun's messenger. Reichard, *Navajo Religion*, 502–3, said Hastséyalti (*xa·cĭcé·ó´yan*, or *xa·ctcéó´yan*), an "untranslatable name," is represented as Yellow Body in the third world and is said to have been created by Whiteshell Woman from a yellow ear of corn. Water Boy is his son, who may be an aspect of the young husband who ousts the gambler. Cliff, "Navajo Games," referred to Talking God as Red God or Racing God. Matthews said *Hastséhogan* is a house or farm god and is one of the leading personages in the group of yéi or divine beings who dwell in caves and old cliff-dwellings. He is also beneficent to humans, and farm songs are sung to him during the Night Chant. Zolbrod, *Diné bahane'*, 364, n. 12, said Matthews was wrong in calling *Hashch'éoghan* a house god and that his name was Growling God; he was more or less an equal to Talking God. The two were helpful to the humans as they populated the fifth world and today are considered powerful gods.

83. Zolbrod, *Diné bahane'*, 348, n. 6, referring to Matthews's unpublished ms.

84. See Goddard, *Navajo Texts*, 140–146. Zolbrod, *Diné bahane'*, 372, n. 28, said the young husband is the precursor to Reared in the Earth, who overcomes the evil caused by the trickster Coyote. Reichard, *Navajo Religion*, 461, 482–83, said Monster Slayer, Reared in the Earth, and Came Down on a Sunbeam are all the same entity. The younger boy likewise has three manifestations: Child of the Water, Changing Grandchild, and Cuts Around It. The afterbirths of Monster Slayer and Child of the Water were buried in the ground, and new beings grew into Reared in the Earth (the first afterbirth) and Child of the Water (the second afterbirth).

85. Cliff, "Navajo Games," 23–26.

86. Huizinga, *Homo Ludens*, 52.

87. Spencer, *Mythology and Values*, 58–59.

88. Eleven Navajo chantways include gaming: Game Way, Hail Way or Chant, Water Way, Night Way, Plume Way, (Big) Star Way, Beauty (or Blessing) Way, Wind Way, Mountain Way, Enemy Way, and Prostitution Way. Just as there is no one patented version of the Great Gambler, chantways also vary between tellers and ethnologists. The hero is exiled because of excessive gambling in the following chantway versions: Goddard, "The Emergence" (a Game Chant), *Navajo Texts*, 161; Reichard, *The Story of the Navajo Hail Chant*, 3; Wheelright, *Hail Chant and Water Chant*, 100, 3; Curtis, Night Way in *The North American Indian*, vol. 1, 111; Wyman, Plume Way and Star Way in *The Sandpaintings of the Kayenta Navaho*, 40–41, 88; and Reichard, Feather Chant in *Navajo Religion*, 68. The games the exiled hero is obsessed with vary from story to story and include ball, dice, foot racing, hoop and pole, kickstick, *ne'ji*, Seven Card Dice, and Straddlesticks. See Cliff's notes and bibliography, "Navajo Games," for a thorough index to the vast library of chants as they pertain to gambling mythology.

89. Reichard, *Navajo Religion*, said Prostitution Way is an odd translation and should be called Endurance, Excess, Rashness, or Recklessness Chant. The plot is similar to the Water Way. See Haile, *Waterway, a Navajo Ceremony*, 110; Wheelwright, *Hail Chant and Water Chant*: 55–90, 91–100, for two versions of Water Way. See Spencer, *Mythology and Values*, 106–16 and 134–148, for abstracts.

90. This aspect of the chantway is probably the original form of the gambler legend reported by Wetherill and Cummings, "A Navaho Folk Tale of Pueblo Bonito."

91. Kin Teel was the setting for the Great Gambler's exploits in Matthews, "Noqùlpi, the Gambler."

92. Whether as part of a chantway or as an independent episode, the method of defeating the gambler is fairly consistent.

93. A rebounding ax is one that turns on whoever uses it.

94. In Eubank's gambler legend, "Legends of Three Navajo Games: The Moccasin Game, Thirteen Chips, and Forty Stones," *El Palacio*, 138–39, the gambler of Pueblo Bonito changes himself into a butterfly in order to steal the embroidery of the Rain God's ladies who live at Rainbow Bridge. The ladies are interested in the butterfly's pattern for their embroidery and allow him into their house. Once inside, the gambler abducts the ladies, and Rain God is compelled

to challenge him to a game of Thirteen Chips. He wins with the help of Little Canary.

95. Boas, "Turkey Woman," *Keresan Texts*, 255–56.

96. Tyler, *Pueblo Gods and Myths*, 142–48.

97. The theme of excess gambling is carried into myths involving Coyote, Toad, Frog, among others. One source is Hill and Hill, "Frog Races a Lewd Woman," and "The Legend of the Navajo Eagle-Catching Way," in "Two Navajo Myths," *New Mexico Anthropologist*, 6–7: 31–36, 111–14. See Cliff, "Navajo Games," for bibliography on Navajo gambling animal mythology.

98. It is the general assumption that Navajos did not practice witchcraft until after they were forced to live with their linguistic cousins the Apache on the reservation at Fort Sumner. However, I have not found evidence of gambling witchcraft stories in Apache mythology. This does not mean it does not exist. Mooney, "The Jicarilla Genesis," *American Anthropologist*, 198, reported a typical gambling story in which the hoop and pole game was invented by *Yolkaiistsun*, the White-Bead Woman, for her two sons by the Sun and the Moon, respectively. She tells them not to roll the wheel north, and for three days, the Sun's son obeys, and rolls it only toward the east, south, and west. Then, the Moon's son persuades him to roll it north. An adventure with an owl follows, which prepares them for other dangerous feats, after which they live in the western ocean.

99. Kluckhohn, *Navajo Witchcraft*, 185–86.

100. Kluckhohn, *Navajo Witchcraft*, 180.

101. Goddard, *Navajo Texts*, 40–57, 140–47.

102. Reichard, *Navajo Religion*.

103. Culin, *Games*, 435.

104. Matthews, *Night Chant*, 15.

105. Zolbrod, *Diné bahane'*, 370, n.26, said the Hopi Gambler, *Hasootkata*, is much more sinister than the Navajo Noqoìlpi in Malotki's version of the gambler story, "*Tsorwukiqulö—Tsorwukiqulö and His Eagles*," *Hoptutuwutsi/Hopi Tales*, 151–201. Hasootkata seems no more sinister than most of our gamblers. Tsorwukiqulö's sister kills one of his pet eagles, so he flies away in ceremonial clothing on the back of another eagle. The eagle takes him through a hole in the sky and strands him on a butte as punishment for his sister's mistreatment of eagles. The boy eventually squeezes into the home of Grandmother Spider and begins to hunt for her in the east and west. She warns him not to go north of the hunting place in the west for fear of the evil gambler (Hasootkata), but he goes anyway and loses to

him in a game of *totolospi*, dice. Having wagered his life, Tsorwukiqulö is shaved, stripped, and tied up in a blizzard to freeze to death. Grandmother Spider calls the kachinas to help free him. They play totolospi with Hasootkata in his kiva, while they dance, until they win all of his belongings. A clown kachina called *Kwikwilyaqa*, "Striped Nose," hits Hasootkata on the head. Hasootkata challenges them to a crop-planting contest. The dancing kachinas make the rains come, and their crops outgrow the gambler's. It rains so much, the water comes into the kiva and drowns him. Liberated, Tsorwukiqulö kills the eagle who left him on the butte and the Spider drops him back to earth on a thread.

106. Haile, "Navaho Games of Chance and Taboo," *Primitive Man*, 1938.

107. Cliff, "Navajo Games," 15; and Haile, "Navaho Games of Chance and Taboo."

108. Cliff, "Navajo Games," 15–16. Allison, "A Structural Analysis of Navajo Basketball," however, attests to a high use of witchcraft and other forms of "medicine" for basketball players on the Navajo reservation. Sings were performed to counter fears that basketball players were bewitched.

Chapter 6

1. J.A.B. van Buitenen, *Mahābhārata, The Book of the Assembly Hall*, 1975.

2. We can only assume the Urim and Thummim was a two-sided lot, as opposed to the four-sided astragalus used by the Greeks.

3. Kirk, *The Iliad: A Commentary*, Vol. I, Book 3, 318–23.

4. Kirk, *The Iliad*, Vol. II, Book 7, 257–59.

5. Huizinga, *Homo Ludens*, 79–81.

6. David, *Games, Gods and Gambling: The Origins and History of Probability and Statistical Ideas from the Earliest Times to the Newtonian Era*, 6–7.

7. David, *Games, Gods and Gambling*, 8.

8. The reference depends upon the translation. Samuel Butler and George Chapman refer to dogs and vultures; Richard Lattimore, to the delicate feasting of dogs and of all birds; Andrew Lang, Walter Leaf, and Ernest Myers, as dogs and all winged fowls; Robert Fables, William Cullen Bryant, and Robert Fitzgerald, simply as dogs and birds.

9. Richardson, *The Iliad: A Commentary*, Vol. VI; Book 23, 175–76.

10. Classical literature, for instance, speaks of girls tossing the astragali in the air and catching them on the back of the hand, much like the modern game of "jacks." Alexander of

Athens painted the five goddesses playing the same game of knucklebones, referring to the back of the hand.

11. David, *Games, Gods and Gambling*, 2–7.

12. However, the lots cast by the Trojans were not necessarily astragalus dice.

13. David, *Games, Gods and Gambling*, 16. Numerology in dice is an interesting trend to consider. Two astragali were often used for Egyptian board games. Four and sometimes five astragali were used in Roman temples, but when dice began to be used for prediction, three seems to have been the preferred number, although two were still used for games of chance, such as hazard or backgammon. The number three became mystical, as in the beginning, the middle, and the end; body, soul, spirit; spirit, water, blood; father, son, holy spirit. This superseded the four elements of the Greek: earth, air, water, fire; and the additional fifth element of the Orientals, ether. "Pythagoras taught that three was the perfect number, the symbol of all deity, and the new Christian sect appropriated his idea," said David. Sir John Falstaff, in the Merry Wives of Windsor, said, "There's a divinity in odd numbers, either in nativity, chance and death." The Aztecs, however used four beans as dice but petitioned Five Flowers to bring them luck in the game of patolli, while the game of five and twenty, or pachisi, was played with five cowry shells (although six and seven shells have also been reported). The North American Indians relied mainly on the numbers two and four and tended to use four two-sided lots in their games.

14. David, *Games, Gods and Gambling*, 17.

15. David, *Games, Gods and Gambling*, 16.

16. There is evidence of intercontinental diffusion of gameplaying, gambling, and divination. The object in the Greek *plinthion* or *polis* was for two pieces, or dogs, of the same color to trap and capture the dog of the other color as they moved along the squares on a board. Likewise, the men or counters in the Arabic game of *tab*, a kind of *backgammon*, were called dogs. The game still existed a century ago when Tylor saw "donkeyboys of Cairo" move their dogs, bits of stone and red brick, around in the dust ("The History of Games," reprinted in *The Study of Games*, 73). Although the practice of divination by dice did not show up in the Mediterranean until after the Greek infiltration, it is possible that it spread westward from India and Tibet.

17. David, *Games, Gods and Gambling*, 16–18. Oracle bones were put to similar use by the rulers of the Shang dynasty (circa 1600–1027 B.C.E.). Augerers poured blood into the underside of the tortoise shells or on the shoulder blades of cattle and then seared it with a hot metal tool. The diviner foretold the future from the shapes of the cracks that appeared. Sometimes the questions or answers were inscribed next to the cracks. Another system was based on the *I Ching*, or Book of Changes, one of the central texts of Confucianism. Coins or yarrow sticks were cast to come up with a combination that corresponded with one of sixty-four hexagrams listed in the *I Ching*. The hexagrams provided advice using symbolism seen in nature, particularly the yin and yang. The Book of Changes was first created at the end of the second millennium B.C.E.

18. David, *Games, Gods and Gambling*, 6–7.

19. David, *Games, Gods and Gambling*, 24.

20. Cowries are mollusks which may have been used as money in Asia and Africa.

21. "Backgammon Among the Aztecs," *Macmillan's Magazine*, 145, reprinted in *The Games of the Americas*.

22. Huizinga, *Homo Ludens*, 57, added that the seasons were depicted as six men playing with gold and silver dice.

23. See Dimmit and van Buitenen, *Classical Hindu Mythology: A Reader in the Sanskrit Purāṇas*, 148–54, for analysis of Shiva and Shakti and their association with Kali and Kala. Incidentally, Vishnu's consort, Laksmi, is the goddess of fortune who sways between benevolence and malevolence.

24. From *Mārkaṇḍeya Purāṇa*.

25. In *The Mahābhārata: Book of the Forest*, 182–93, van Buitenen argued that King Nala's gaming sequence mirrors the gaming sequence that gets the hero exiled in the first place. It may also be a parallel to the story of the frenzied gambler in the *Rig Veda* discussed later in this section.

26. Eliade, *Images and Symbols: Studies in Religious Symbolism*, 62–66; Dimmit and van Buitenen, *Classical Hindu Mythology*, 19–22. Kal or *cal* refers to limestone pebbles (as in calcium) presumably used for counting and thus is the root of words like calculate and calendar.

27. I assume the four-sided astragalus is being referred to in this analogy, as opposed to the throw of five, six, or seven two-sided cowry shells.

28. Each age also includes two twilight or intermittent periods which are equal to one-tenth the length of each age. The intermittent periods add 800, 600, 400, and 200 years to each age respectively for a total of 12,000 divine years, equal to 4,320,000 human years.

29. MacCulloch, *Eddic Mythology*, 342–46. Two collections of Old Norse writings, known

as the *Edda*, form the most authoritative source for ancient Nordic mythology. The *Elder*, or Poetic, *Edda* is a collection of thirty-four anonymous Icelandic poems, interspersed with prose dating from the 9th to the 12th century, mostly dealing with Norse mythology and legend.

30. The runes contained the alphabet and corresponded with magic spells, which evolved into divination.

31. McCulloch, *Eddic Mythology*, 344–45; Huizinga, *Homo Ludens*, 57, 81.

32. See Ram, *With the Three Masters*, 23–24. The original author is Soami Ji Maharal, a spiritual leader of *Surat Shabda Yoga*, the discipline of the Sound Current, or as Plato called it, the music of the spheres. For a more modern explanation of this teaching, see Dennis Holtje, *From Light to Sound, The Spiritual Progression* (Albuquerque, New Mexico: MasterPath, Inc., 1995).

33. Bose, *Hymns from the Vedas*, 195. The Vedas (Sanskrit: "knowledge"), the most sacred books of Hinduism and the oldest literature of India, presumably date from between 1500 and 500 B.C.E. This literature was preserved for centuries by an oral tradition in which particular families were entrusted with portions of the text for preservation. As a result, some parts of the texts are known by the names of the families they were assigned to. In its narrowest sense, the term Veda applies to four collections of hymns: *Rig Veda, Sama Veda, Yajur Veda*, and *Atharva Veda*. These hymns and verses, addressed to various deities, were chanted during sacrificial rituals.

34. Miller, *The Vision of Cosmic Order in the Vedas*, 2. No single date or authorship can be assigned to the *Mahābhārata*, compiled by many anonymous poets and Hindu priests beginning around 400 B.C.E. and ending around 400 C.E. This work is not just a story, but a library of classical Indian religious thought, and many of the eighteen books were woven into the central plot as the politics changed, so that the core 24,000 couplets grew to nearly 100,000. The religious/historical context of the *Mahābhārata* may explain its eclecticism.

In the second millennium B.C.E., the Indo-Europeans, a legendary blonde race of Aryans, began a series of massive migrations from their home north of the Black Sea. They eventually dominated most of Europe, the northern Near East, and the Indian subcontinent, absorbing or eliminating antagonist cultures along the way. Vedism may have originated with the Aryans in India. As the political and cultural center of India shifted from the Indus to the Ganges River Val-

ley, Buddhism, Jainism, and mystical revisions of orthodox Vedism into Brahmanism all developed around 500–300 B.C.E. Vedism remained the preserve of the priestly Brahmin caste. In contrast, Buddhism, founded by Siddhartha Gautama (circa 563–483 B.C.E.), appealed to merchants in the growing urban centers and took hold at first, and most lastingly, on the geographic fringes of Indian civilization. Buddhism and Jainism sought to replace some of the rigidity of Brahamical rules. The *Mahābhārata* was conspired and reworked over eight centuries as these changes took place. A major agenda was a changing of the guard in the old Vedic pantheon, particularly to promote Krishna as a god and to elevate Brahma to supreme deity. This stands to reason since the Krishna sect is based on the *Purāṇas*, which postdate the *Mahābhārata*. (See van Buitenen, *The Mahābhārata: The Book of the Assembly Hall*, 24–26, for this hypothesis.)

Scholars sometimes distinguish Vedism, the religion of ancient India based on the *Vedas*, from Hinduism, although it is difficult to pinpoint a time that demarcates them. The period from roughly 500 B.C.E. to 1000 C.E. is sometimes spoken of as that of classical Hinduism. The Vedic deities were somewhat different from those which dominate in Hinduism, although scholars have traced the origins of Vishnu and Shiva back to Vedic counterparts. Vedic principles and such Veda hymns as the *Bhagavad Gita* are embodied in the *Mahābhārata*. The relation of Vedism to the Hinduism of later centuries is complex and not well understood. The Vedas are preserved in traditional fashion in certain parts of India, and the tendency is widespread to look to them as expressions of the fundamental genius of Hindu thought and aspiration. Hinduism itself is complex. It is associated with the cast system based on dharmic law and karma from which liberation can be attained through certain practices or yogas, though less so today, through one of six philosophical thoughts, or through various cults.

35. Dimmit and van Buitenen, *Classical Hindu Mythology*, 64.

36. The Kurukeṣtra kingdom was most likely based on the powerful Magadha kingdom formed around 542 B.C.E. At that time, Northern India was divided into a large number of monarchies and aristocratic republics derived from tribal groupings. The Maurya dynasty, founded by Chandragupta circa 321 B.C.E., expanded the kingdom, uniting most of Northern India into a centralized bureaucratic empire. The third Mauryan king, Asoka (ruled circa 274–236

B.C.E.) conquered most of the subcontinent. He converted to Buddhism and inscribed its tenets on pillars throughout India. He downplayed the caste system and tried to end expensive sacrificial rites. (See van Buitenen's introduction to *The Mahābhārata: The Book of the Beginning*, 1–16, for synopsis and religious/political analysis.)

37. The Vedas hadn't quite grasped reincarnation or *karmic* law, an exact system of rewards and punishments based on a previous life or on behalf of the next one, which takes dharmic law a step further. The promise in the Vedas was an afterlife in heaven. If things didn't go right in heaven, then one fell slightly from grace as a "twice-born" on earth. The principle characters in the *Mahābhārata* are the twice-born. (Belief systems of traditional Native American tribes do not tend to embrace the concept of reincarnation.)

38. Maya says she is a divine architect and offers to build the hall as a reward for being saved from a fire. That Maya made the offer in the first place seems out of character to van Buitenen (*The Book of the Assembly Hall*, 6–9), unless one considers this alleged contractor a foreigner. Maya's building materials come "from the north" where the gods go every thousand eons to worship; hence, says van Buitenen, the architecture for the palace most likely comes from the north(western) country of Persia (Iran). Maya was an *asura*, which in sanskrit means a demon adversary of the good spirits, or *devas*. But in the Iran of the prophet Zoroaster (Zarathustra), the Ahura Mazda (god of wisdom) battles the *daeva*, Ahiram. The words, nearly phonetically the same, have reverse meanings. Furthermore, Persia has the same Aryan heritage as does India. Aryan peoples (Persians, Medes) dominated the area of present Iran by the beginning of the first millennium B.C.E.

That this Maya was also an architect supports the theory that he was Persian, van Buitenen says. Early Indian stone architecture was an off-shoot of the Achaemenids Empire of ancient Persia. After the Achaemenids were defeated by Alexander of Macedon and further dismembered by the Seleucids, the old Zoroastrian dominion abandoned its creative talent, including architects, to the outer world, notably India. At this time, an India-based empire was being established at Magadha, reaching the borders of Afghanistan. Magadha employed the Persian-style architecture in building its capital, Pataliputra, where the "sumptuous palaces" similarly displayed "the designs of Gods, Asuras, and men," as ambassador of the Seleucids noted in 302 B.C.E., conceivably the true date of the

Mahābhārata. Thus, the asura Maya builds a Persian temple for the five Pandava brothers.

39. Van Buitenen, *Mahābhārata: The Book of the Assembly Hall*, 10–11.

40. The assembly hall has "golden pillars covering the sky like mountains or monsoon clouds." Pillars are an important concept in India. Dharma, as religious duty, has four feet or pillars to better support it: truth, mercy, purity, and charity. The Navajos say sixteen pillars, four each of white shell, abalone, turquoise, and red shell, were placed in the four directions to support the sky. At the center, opposite the Place of Emergence from the underworld, is the skyhole through which the Twins climbed to gamble with their father.

41. The king takes five steps like a counter on a gameboard—four in each direction and a fifth toward the sky to ceremonially enact the conquest. In the vedic manuals, the ceremonial enactment is called *digvyavasthāpana*, or "separate establishment of the quarters." The number five sums up the universe: each one associated with the components of the Veda (ritual text), the pantheon, the people, and the year, which is the old symbol of the cycle of life. Five is also an important element of pachisi. Like the architecture, the ritual, as well as the game, may have originated in Persia. (Van Buitenen, *Book of the Assembly Hall*, 18–19.)

42. Van Buitenen, *Book of the Assembly Hall*, 19–30.

43. Van Buitenen, *Book of the Assembly Hall*, 123.

44. Van Buitenen, *Book of the Beginning*, 153–54.

45. Van Buitenen, *Book of the Assembly Hall*, 124, 129.

46. Van Buitenen, *Book of the Assembly Hall*, 128.

47. Van Buitenen, *Book of the Assembly Hall*, 126.

48. Van Buitenen, *Book of the Assembly Hall*, 129. Apparently, it is possible to cheat at throwing the dice. An expert "patol" player at Isleta Pueblo could throw the number of stick dice he desired almost unfailingly by his arrangement of the sticks in his hand and the manner and force with which he struck them down. "It is a dexterity which anyone may acquire by sufficient practice, and only thus. The five throw is deemed very much the hardest of all, and I have certainly found it so." (Culin, *Games*, 191.)

49. Huizinga, *Homo Ludens*, 57.

50. Huizinga, *Homo Ludens*, 59.

51. Huizinga, *Homo Ludens*, 82.

52. So say Avedon and Sutton-Smith, *The Study of Games*, 55. Culin, *Chess and Playing Cards*, said the first writer to compare American Indian games to those of the Old World, as an argument in favor of the Asiatic origin of the American race, was P. Lafitau in his *Moers de Sauvages Ameriquains Comparees aux Moeurs des Premiers Temps*, Paris, 1874.

53. Tylor, "Backgammon Among the Aztecs," *Macmillan's Magazine*, 142.

54. See Tylor, "Backgammon Among the Aztecs," 142–50; "On the Game of Patolli in Ancient Mexico and Its Probably Asiatic Origin," *Journal of the Anthropological Institute of Great Britain and Ireland*, 116–31; "The History of Games," *The Fortnightly Review*, 735–47; "On American Lot-Games, as Evidence of Asiatic Intercourse Before the Time of Columbus," Supplement to *International Archives for Ethnographie* 9, 56–66.

55. Tylor, "On American Lot-Games," 56, read Alexander von Humboldt, who believed as John Gunn did (see Chapter 5), in a connection between Atlantis and Mexico.

56. Pachisi and backgammon may have developed from the colloquial Arabic game of *tab*, meaning "game." Two players threw slips of split palm branches, white on the inside, green on the outside, against the wall or an upright stick. They kept count of their "dogs" on a tab board divided into four rows of an odd number of squares, and the object was for all pieces to reach the adversary's row. The counter was called a Christian or Nazarene, until it was able to go out and fight, becoming a Moslem. A throw of one-white was called a dog, a six-throw a Sultan, and a four-throw a Wezir. The unfortunate soul who threw them received two blows on the soles of his feet with a palmstick. (Tylor, "On the Game of Patolli," 118.)

Indians in Peru, Argentina, and Bolivia played a game called *taba* with a cow or llama astragalus. "By far the greater weight of evidence points to the conclusion that the taba game, i.e., with use of the astragalus, is an importation from Spain," as early as 1789, wrote Cooper in "Games and Gambling," 503–24. He said taba in Spanish meant astragalus, although *tauva* or *tahua* in Quechua, the language of Peru, means four—as in four sides of the astragalus. The same game among the Tarahumara Indians, who live below the Arizona–Mexico border, was called *la taba* or *tábatci*. Consider the distance between the Tarahumara in Chihuahua, Mexico, and the

Quechua in Cuzco, Peru. However, taba probably does not directly refer to the astragalus, but has its root in the word of tables, tablet, and tabulate. This points to the import of the Moslem game of tab into Spain and also into England, where it is called tables. Tabalera in Spanish means to shake or drum, and that also could refer to the throw of the dice. Some of the Quechua game words sound hauntingly Hindi. Peruvians played with a six-sided, dotted die called *huayru*, meaning uncertain. Other names, while keeping pachisi (meaning five and twenty) in mind, included *posca* or *pichka*, when meant five; *chunkara*, meaning ten; and *pasa*, meaning one hundred. They also played multiple-dice games, using blocks of wood or beans and simple boards marked with three to seven dots.

57. Kroeber, *Anthropology*, 550–52.

58. One of Culin's sources noticed similarly carved figurines of ivory at Plover Bay in Eastern Siberia but was unable to tell if they were used for gaming. (Culin, *Games*, 103.)

59. In *The Song of Hiawatha*, for instance, the Ojibwa/Chippewa bowl and counters game of *pugasaing* consisted of thirteen fetishes: two *Ininewug* (related to the word for wandering gambler); one Great Serpent, or *Gitshee Kenabik*; two dragon-like water serpents; one war club or *Pugamágun*; four circular brass pieces, slightly concave, called *Keego*, the generic name for fish; and four ducks, or bird-shaped *Sheshebwug*. Scoring depended on how the pieces landed in specific combinations when tossed from a bowl. The highest score in one play, in this mathematically sophisticated game, was 158. This occurred when all the pieces landed vermilion-side up, and one of the Ininewugs stood upright on the bright side of one of the brass pieces (Culin, *Games*, 67).

60. Besides the Aztec, board-playing tribes included: Hopi, Pima, Apache, Navajo, Tohono O'odham (Papago), Hano, Havasupai, and Walapai of Arizona; Acoma, Cochiti, Laguna, Zia, Santo Domingo, Sandia, San Felipe, Santa Clara, San Ildefonso, Nambe, Tesuque, Isleta, and Taos of New Mexico; Tarahumara and Tepehuan of Chihuahua, Mexico; and Kekchi of Maya stock in North Guatemala, Mexico. The Kiowas of Oklahoma, linked linguistically with one Pueblo tribe (Tanoan Tewas), also played dice board games.

61. In pachisi, and possibly patolli, the free spaces were safe havens for opposing counters, but in New World games, these were penalty areas. The Oklahoma Kiowas called the spacings rivers, and if a counter fell into one, it was obliged

to return home and forfeit a point. However, at Isleta Pueblo a player who fell into the river was entitled to another throw, and the Tewa-speaking Pueblos considered the rivers or gates to be neutral areas. If a counter landed on an opponent's counter in a game played by the Kekchi of Guatemala, that counter was taken prisoner, and the captor reversed its direction in order to escape the same fate. At Zuñi, the spaces were called passageways or canyons, through which the counters entered the game, like modern Parcheesi.©

62. In Murr, *Verschiedenen Ländern des Spanischen America*, part I, 256.

63. Culin, *Games*, 160–65.

64. Erasmus, "Patolli, Pachisi, and the Limitation of Possibilities," *Southwestern Journal of Anthropology*, 369–87.

65. Culin, "American Indian Games," *American Anthropologist*, 58–66.

66. See Avedon and Sutton-Smith, *The Study of Games*, 61–62, for an outline of the paths on which Culin and other diffusionists thought games in general traveled back and forth around the globe. Briefly, they apparently originated in Sumer, Mesopotamia, Egypt, and India, working their way in all directions through time, eventually arriving on the North American continent via Scandinavia or the Pacific Islands. The American Indians taught the games to the European colonists, who in turn took them back home.

67. Erasmus, "Patolli, Pachisi, and the Limitation of Possibilities," 124.

68. Boas, *Mythology and Folk-Tales of the North American Indians*, 409–10.

69. Boas, "The Classification of American Languages," *American Anthropologist*, 216.

Epilogue

1. Allen, *The Sacred Hoop*, 45.

Appendix I

1. Historical background for this section from Hearing before the House Committee on Interior and Insular Affairs on the Indian Gaming Regulatory Act, June 25, 1987. Another interesting source is the National Indian Gaming Association's homepage on the World Wide Web: http://dgsys.com/~niga. NIGA claims to serve 141 sovereign Indian nations.

2. Tracey A. Reeves, "Congress May Reshuffle Indian-Gambling Deck," *Albuquerque Journal*, January 14, 1994.

3. Mike Gallagher, "Mob Already Involved on Some Reservations," *Albuquerque Journal*, January 14, 1994.

4. Laurence A. Urgenson, Acting Deputy Assistant General Criminal Division, Oversight Hearing on the Implementation of the Indian Gaming Regulatory Act, P.L. 100–497, and related law enforcement issues, before the House Subcommittee on Native American Affairs, October 5, 1993.

5. Elizabeth Gannon, "Struggle Between Two Sovereigns," special section of the *New Mexico Business Journal*, December 1993, paid for by the New Mexico Indian Gaming Association.

6. Gannon, "Struggle Between Two Sovereigns."

7. Testimony of G. Michael Brown, IGRA Hearing (See note 3). Tribes state that Indian gaming is only a $5 billion industry, or just five percent of the entire industry. One magazine estimated that gross wagering at reservation casinos ran as high as $28.9 billion for 1993.

8. Testimony of Donald Trump, IGRA Hearing. See note 3.

9. Tim Giago, "Indian Tribes Must Mold Own Public Relations Images," *Notes from Indian Country*, column, *Albuquerque Journal*, April 1, 1994.

Appendix II

1. Matthews's "Noqoìlpi, the Gambler: A Navajo Myth" was first published in 1889 (pp. 89–94) and was reprinted as part of "The Navaho Origin Legend, Early Events of the Fifth World," in 1897 (pp. 81–87). Spellings for Navajo words here were taken from the second version. Other gaming references in *Navaho Legends* include: gambling songs, 24; stick dice, 77, 219, n. 47; eye juggling, 90; Coyote and rolling stone game, 97; Coyote and hoop and pole game, 97–98; Changing Woman's sons race, 106, 134; hoop and pole and moccasin game, 141, 240, n. 176, 226, n. 76; excessive gaming, 191, 193; and a racing god, 254, n. 271.

2. *Diné* is the Navajo name for themselves, the people. *Kisáni* is Navajo for Pueblos, according to the Matthews version of the Navajo gambler legend. The original names are retained here. In a Navajo dictionary, *Kiis'áanii* is the word for Hopi.

3. From now on, the narrative refers to the young man as the son of Hastséhogan. He is otherwise anonymous.

4. Canyon de Chelley, Arizona, an Anasazi site.

Bibliography

Aberle, David. "Mythology of the Navaho Game of Stick Dice." *Journal of American Folklore* 55 (1942): 144-54.

Allen, Paula Gunn. *The Sacred Hoop: Recovering the Feminine in American Indian Traditions.* Boston: Beacon Press, 1986.

Allison, Maria T. "A Structural Analysis of Navajo Basketball," Ph.D. diss., University of Illinois at Urbana-Champaign, 1980.

Avedon, Elliott M., and Brian Sutton-Smith. *The Study of Games.* New York: John Wiley & Sons, Inc., 1971.

Aveni, Anthony. "Possible Astronomical Orientations in Ancient Mesoamerica." In *Archaeoastronomy in Pre-Columbian America*, edited by Anthony F. Aveni, pp. 163–90. Austin: University of Texas Press, 1975.

Bancroft, Hubert. *Native Races of the Pacific States of North America*, vol. 1. San Francisco: Bancroft and Company, 1874–1876.

Bandelier, Adolf F. "The 'Montezuma' of the Pueblo Indians." *American Anthropologist*, vol. 5, No. 4 (1892): 319–26.

Barrett, S. A. "Falcon's Contest with Ki'lak," "Yalil's Journey to the South World," "Falcon Escapes the World," "Coyote and Falcon Create People," *Myths of the Southern Sierra Miwok*, University of California Publications in American Archaeology and Ethnology, vol. 16, no. 1, (March 27, 1919): 7-10.

Beauchamp, W. M. "Iroquois Games." *Journal of American Folk-Lore*, vol. 9, no. 35 (December-January 1896): 269–77.

Boas, Franz. "Okulā´M Her Myth," "The Four Cousins," *Chinook Texts*, Report of the Bureau of American Ethnology, no. 20, pp. 31–36, 220–22. Washington: Smithsonian Institution, 1894.

———. "Mythologies and Folk-Tales of the North American Indians." *Journal of American Folk-Lore*, Vol. 1914, pp. 409–10.

———. "Giant Gambles with Gull," "Giant Obtains the Olachen," "Thunderbird Steals the Wife of Another Bird," *Tsimshian Myths*, Report of the Bureau of American Ethnology, no. 31, pp. 65, 653, 712–13. Washington: Smithsonian Institution, 1916.

———. "The Classification of American Languages." *American Anthropologist*, 22 (1920): 216.

———. "Cliff Dweller," "The Gambler," "Turkey Woman," *Keresan Texts*, vol. III, part I, pp. 104–11, 253–54, 255–56, 257–58. Publication of the American Ethnological Society, edited by Franz Boas, issued as vol. 8. New York: AMS Press, 1928.

Bose, Abinash Chandra. *Hymns from the Vedas.* New York: Asia Publishing House, 1966.

Brandt, John C., et al. "Possible Rock Art Records of the Crab Nebual Supernova in the Western United States." In *Archaeoastronomy in Pre-Columbian America*, edited by Anthony F. Aveni, pp. 45–58, Austin: University of Texas Press, 1975.

Brandt, John C., and Ray A. Williamson. "Rock Art Representations of the A.D. 1054 Supernova: A Progress Report." In *Native American Astronomy*, edited by Anthony F. Aveni, 171–77. Austin: University of Texas Press, 1979.

Brew, J. O. *Archaeology of Alkali Ridge, Southwestern Utah.* Papers of the Peabody Museum of American Archaeologoy and Ethnology, vol. 21 (1946).

Brugge, David, "Tsegai: An Archeological Ethnohistory of the Chaco Region." Manuscript, Chaco Center, Albuquerque, 1977.

———. *A History of the Chaco Navajos.* Reports of the Chaco Center, no. 4. Albuquerque: Division of Cultural Research, National Park Service, 1980.

Butler, Samuel, trans. *The Iliad of Homer.* Encyclopaedia Britannica's Great Books of the Western World, vol. 4. Chicago: William Benton, 1952.

Campbell, Joseph. Commentary in *Where the Two Came to Their Father: A Navaho War Ceremonial Given by Jeff King.* Compiled and edited by Maude Oaks. Princeton: Princeton University Press, 1991.

Castillo, Patricia Ochoa. "Pre-hispanic Ball Game and the Origin of the Game on the Central Mexican Plateau." In *El Juego de Pelota en El México Precolumbino y su pervivencia en la actualidad,* edited by Fundació Folch, 256–58. Catátogo de Museu Etnològic. Ajuntament de Barcelona, 1992.

Chapin, Gretchen. "A Navajo Myth from Chaco Canyon." *New Mexico Anthropologist* 4:4 (1940): 63–67.

Chilton, Lance, et al. *New Mexico: A New Guide to a Colorful State.* Albuquerque: University of New Mexico Press, 1984.

Cliff, Janet. "Navajo Games." *American Indian Culture and Research Journal* 14:3 (1990): 1–81.

Coolidge, Dane, and Mary Roberts. *The Navajo Indians.* Boston: Houghton Mifflin, 1930.

Cooper, John M. "Games and Gambling." Bulletin of the Bureau of American Ethnology, vol. 5, no. 143, pp. 503–24. Washington: Smithsonian Institution, 1949. Reprinted in *The Games of the Americas: A Book of Readings,* edited by Brian Sutton-Smith. New York: Arno Press, 1976.

Cosgrove, H. S., and C. B. Cosgrove. *The Swarts Ruin, a Typical Mimbres Site in Southwestern New Mexico, Seasons of 1924–1927.* Papers of the Peabody Museum of Archaeology and Ethnology, Vol. 15, No. 1. Cambridge, Mass: The Museum, 1932.

Crown, Patricia L., and W. James Judge. "Synthesis and Conclusions." In *Chaco & Hohokam: Prehistoric Regional Systems in the American Southwest,* edited by Patricia L. Crown and W. James Judge. Santa Fe: School of American Research Press, 1991.

Culin, Stewart. *Chess and Playing Cards.* Report, United States National Museum for 1896 (1898).

———. "American Indian Games." *American Anthropologist,* n.s., 5, (1903): 58–64. Reprinted in *The Study of Games,* edited by Elliott M. Avedon and Brian Sutton-Smith, 103–08. New York: John Wiley & Sons, Inc., 1971.

———. *Games of the North American Indians.* Report of the Bureau of American Ethnology, no. 24, 1902–1903. Washington: Smithsonian Institution, 1907. Reprint. 2 vols. Introduction by Dennis Tedlock. Lincoln: University of Nebraska Press, 1992.

Curtin, Jeremiah. "Geha Aids a Deserted Boy," "The Thunder Boy," "The Grandmother and Grandson," "Hodadeio and His Sister." *Seneca Indian Myths,* pp. 16–21, 110–15, 167–75, 334. New York: E. P. Dutton & Company, 1923.

Curtin, Jeremiah, and J.N.B. Hewitt. *Seneca Fiction, Legends, and Myths.* Report of the Bureau of American Ethnology, no. 11, Washington: Smithsonian Institution, 1910–11.

Curtis, Stewart. *The North American Indian: Being a Series of Volumes Picturing and Describing the Indians of the United States and Alaska,* vol. 1, edited by Frederick W. Hodge. Norwood, Mass: Plimpton Press, 1907–1930. Reprinted: Johnson Reprint, New York, 1970.

Cushing, Frank Hamilton. "Outlines of Zuñi Creation Myths." Report of the Bureau of American Ethnology for the Years 1891–1892, no. 13. Washington: Smithsonian Institution, 1896.

David, F. N. *Games, Gods and Gambling: The Origins and History of Probability and Statistical Ideas from the Earliest Times to the Newtonian Era.* New York: Hafner Publishing Company, 1962.

Diaz del Castillo, Bernal. *The Discovery and Conquest of Mexico, 1517–1521,* edited by Genaro Garcia. Translated by A. P. Maudslay. Mexico City: Mexico Press, 1918.

Dimmit, Cornelia, and J.A.B. van Buitenen. *Classical Hindu Mythology: A Reader in the Sanskrit Purāṇas.* Philadelphia: Temple University Press, c. 1978.

Dixon, Ronald. "Winning Gambling Luck," "Coyote and the Road River People," "The Race with Thunder," in "Shasta Myths." *Journal of American Folk-Lore* 23:87, (January–March 1910): 24–27, 368.

Dorsey, George Amos. *Traditions of the Skidi Pawnee.* Memoirs of the American Folk-Lore Society, vol. 8. New York: Houghton, Mifflin, 1904.

Dorsey, George Amos, and A. L. Kroeber. "Light-Stone," "The White Crow," "Found-in-Grass," *Traditions of the Arapaho,* pp. 181, 275, 364, Field Columbian Museum, *Publication* 81, Anthropological Series 5, 1903.

Dorsey, George Amos, and James R. Murie. "Origin of the Basket Dice Game," "Buffalo Gaming Sticks," "The Gambler and the Gaming Sticks," "The Basket Game, or the Woman in the Moon," "The Girl, Spider-Woman, and the Ball Game," *The Pawnee, Mythology, Part 1,* pp. 44–46, 104–05, 185–91, 233–39. Washington: Carnegie Institute of Washington, 1906.

Dorsey, J. Owen. *The Ǭegiha Language*. Contributions to North American Ethnology, vol. 6, Washington, 1890.

Durán, Diego. *Historia de las Indias*. 2 vols. Mexico, 1867-80.

Dostoevsky, Fedor. *The Gambler*. [1864]. Introduction by Malcom Jones. Oxford: Oxford University Press, 1991.

Eliade, Mircea. *Images and Symbols: Studies in Religious Symbolism*. [1952]. Princeton: Princeton University Press, 1991.

———. *The Myth of the Eternal Return*. Bollingen Series XLVI. New York: Pantheon Books, 1954.

———. *Myth and Reality*. Translated by Willard R. Trask. New York: Harper Torchbooks, 1963.

Ellis, Florence Hawley. "A Thousand Years of the Pueblo Sun-Moon-Star Calendar." In *Archaeoastronomy in Pre-Columbian America*, edited by Anthony F. Aveni, 59–87. Austin: University of Texas Press, 1975.

———. Foreword to *Architecture and Dendrochronology of Chetro Ketl, Chaco Canyon, New Mexico*, edited by Stephen H. Lekson. Reports of the Chaco Center, no. 6. Albuquerque: National Park Service, 1983.

Ellis, Florence Hawley, and Laurens Hammack. "The Inner Sanctum of Feather Cave: A Mogollon Sun and Earth Shrine Linking Mexico and the Southwest." *American Antiquity* 33:1 (1968): 25–44.

Erasmus, Charles John. "Patolli, Pachisi, and the Limitation of Possibilities," *Southwestern Journal of Anthropology* 6, Winter 1950, pp. 369–87. In *The Study of Games*, edited by Elliott M. Avedon and Brian Sutton-Smith. New York: John Wiley & Sons, Inc., 1971.

Erdich, Louise. *The Bingo Palace*. New York: HarperCollins, 1994.

Eubank, Lisbeth. "Legends of Three Navajo Games: The Moccasin Game, Thirteen Chips, and Forty Stones," *El Palacio* 52 (1945):138–40.

Evers, Larry, editor. "The Great Gambler," *Between Sacred Mountains: Navajo Stories and Lessons from the Land*, 63–69. Chinle, Arizona: Rock Point Community School, 1982.

Fishler, Stanley A. *In the Beginning: A Navaho Creation Myth*, University of Utah Anthropological Papers, 13 (1953):62–66, 105.

Ford, Richard I. "Inter-Indian Exchange in the Southwest." In *Handbook of the North American Indians*, vol. 9, p. 717. Alfonso Ortiz, volume editor, William C. Sturtevant, general editor. Washington: Smithsonian Institution, 1979.

Fowke, Gerard. *Archaeological History of Ohio: The Mound Builders and Later Indians*. Columbus: Press of Fred J. Heer, 1902.

Fowler, Catherine. *Willard Z. Park's Ethnographic Notes on the Northern Paiute of Western Nevada, 1933–1940*, Salt Lake City, Utah: University of Utah Press, 1989.

Frachtenberg, Leo J. "Wind-Woman and Her Children," "The Universal Change," *Alsea Texts and Myths*, Bulletin of the Bureau of American Ethnology, no. 67, pp. 23–33, 35–55, Washington: Smithsonian Institution, 1920.

Franciscan Fathers. *An Ethnological Dictionary of the Navajo Language* [1910], pp. 154–155, 478–89, 495–97, St. Michael's, Arizona: St. Michael's Press, 1968.

Franstead, Dennis. "An Introduction to the Navajo Oral History of the Anasazi Sites in the San Juan Basin Area," 1979. Manuscript, Chaco Center, Southwest Cultural Resources Center, National Park Service, Albuquerque.

Franstead, Dennis, and Oswald Werner. "The Ethnogeography of the Chaco Canyon Area Navajo," 1974. Manuscript, Chaco Center, Southwest Cultural Resources Center, National Park Service, Albuquerque.

Gabriel, Kathryn. *Roads to Center Place: A Cultural Atlas of Chaco Canyon and the Anasazi*. Boulder: Johnson Books, 1991.

———, editor. *Marietta Wetherill: Reflections on Life with the Navajos in Chaco Canyon*. Boulder: Johnson Books, 1992.

Gifford, Edward Winslow. "Prairie Falcon's Contest with Meadowlark." In "Western Mono Myths," *Journal of American Folk-Lore*, Vol. 36, No. 141, pp. 352–54, January-September 1921.

Gill, Sam D., and Irene F. Sullivan. *The Dictionary of Native American Mythology*, New York: Oxford University Press, 1992. First published by ABC-Clio, 1992.

Goddard, Earle Pliny. "The Emergence" and "Game Story," *Navajo Texts*, Anthropological Papers, American Museum of Natural History, New York, pp. 40–57, 140–46, 161, vol. 34, 1933.

Grinnell, George Bird. "The Girl who Wanted to Be a Ring," *Harper's Magazine*, vol. 102, p. 425, February, 1901.

Guernsey, S. J., and A.V. Kidder. *Basket-maker Caves of Northeastern Arizona*. Papers of the Peabody Museum of American Archaeology and Ethnology, Vol. III, No. 2. Cambridge, Mass.: The Museum, 1921.

Gunn, John. "Ko-Pot Ka-Nat," "Sutsu-Nuts, the Ruler of the Ka-Tsi-Na," "Pais-Chun-Ni-Moot, the Fire Brand Boy," *Schat-Chen: History, Traditions, and Narratives of the Queres Indians of Laguna and Acoma*, pp. 115–119, 127–33, 161–66, 168–72. Albuquerque: Albright and Anderson, 1917. Reprint: AMS, 1977.

Hackenberg, Robert A. "Pima and Papago Ecological Applications." *Handbook of the North American Indians*, vol. 10, p. 164, Alfonso Ortiz, volume editor, William C. Sturtevant, general editor. Washington: Smithsonian Institution, 1983.

Haile, Rev. Berard. "Waterway, a Navajo Ceremony," *American Tribal Religions*, vol. 5, Museum of Northern Arizona Press, 1979; based on unpub. ms. "Ceremony in the Water Way," 1932.

———. "Navaho Games of Chance and Taboo." *Primitive Man*, 1928–1937, Catholic Anthropological Conference, Washington, D.C., vols. 1–10, pp. 35–40, 1938.

Haury, Emil W. *The Hohokam: Desert Farmers and Craftsmen; Excavations at Snaketown, 1964–1965*. Tucson: The University of Arizona Press, 1976.

Hayes, Alden C. "A Survey of Chaco Canyon Archeology." In *Archeological Survey of Chaco Canyon, New Mexico*, by Alden C. Hayes, David M. Brugge, and W. James Judge, pp. 1–68. Publications in Archeology 18A, Canyon Cayon Series, Chaco Center, National Park Service, Albuquerque, 1981.

Hill, W. W., and Dorothy Hill. "Frog Races a Lewd Woman," and "The Legend of the Navajo Eagle-Catching Way." In "Two Navajo Myths," *New Mexico Anthropologist*, 6–7 (1943):31–36, 111–14.

Hogner, Dorothy Childs. *Navajo Winter Nights: Folk Tales and Myths of the Navajo People*, New York: Thomas Nelson, 1935.

Hough, Walter. *Culture of the Ancient Pueblos of the Upper Gila River Region, New Mexico and Arizona*. Annual report of the United States National Museum for 1901, and issued separately in 1903 as archeological field work in northeastern Arizona, Bulletin 87. Washington: Smithsonian Institution, 1914.

Huizinga, Johan. *Homo Ludens: A Study of the Play Element in Culture*. Boston: Beacon Press, 1950.

Hultkrantz, Åke. *Belief and Worship in Native North America*. Syracuse, New York: Syracuse University Press, 1981.

Humboldt, Alexander von. *Vues des Cordillères et Monuments des Pueples Indigènes de l'Amerique*. Paris N. Maze, 1816.

Irwin-Williams, Cynthia. "Post-Pleistocene Archeology, 7000–2000 B.C." In *Handbook of the North American Indians*, vol. 9, Alfonso Ortiz, volume editor, William C. Sturtevant, general editor. Washington: Smithsonian Institution, 1979.

Jackson, William H. "Report on the Ancient Ruins Examined in 1875 and 1877." In *Tenth Annual Report of the United States Geological and Geographical Survey of the Territories Embracing Colorado and Parts of Adjacent Territories, Being a Report of the Progress of the Explorations for the Year 1876*, by F. V. Hayden, pp. 411–50. Washington: Government Printing Press, 1878.

Judd, Neil M. *The Material Culture of Pueblo Bonito*. Smithsonian Miscellaneous Collections, vol. 124. Washington: Government Printing Office, 1954.

———. *The Bureau of American Ethnology: A Partial History*. Norman: University of Oklahoma Press, 1967.

Judge, W. James. "Chaco: Current Views of Prehistory and the Regional System." In *Chaco & Hohokam: Prehistoric Regional Systems in the American Southwest*. Edited by Patricia L. Crown and W. James Judge. Santa Fe: School of American Research Press, 1991.

Kelley, J. Charles, and Ellen Abbot Kelley. "An Alternative Hypothesis for the Explanation of Anasazi Culture History." In *Collected Papers in Honor of Florence Hawley Ellis*. Theodore R. Frisbie, editor. Papers of the Archaeological Society of New Mexico 2, Santa Fe, 1974, pp. 178–223. Norman, Oklahoma: Hooper Publishing Company, 1975.

Keur, Dorothy Louise. *Big Bead Mesa: an Archaeological Study of Navaho Acculturation, 1745–1812,* Supplement, Memoirs of the Society for American Archaeology; no. 1, Menasha, Wis.: The Society for American Archaeology, 1941. (Note: On cover: Supplement to American Antiquity, volume VII, no. 2, part 2, 1941.) Issued also as diss., (Ph.D.) Columbia University. Reprinted as *Tchefuncte Culture* by James A. Ford and George Irving Quimby, Milwood, N.Y.: Kraus, 1974.

Kidder, A.V., and S. J. Guernsey. *Archaeological Explorations in Northeastern Arizona.* Bulletin of the Bureau of American Ethnology, no. 65, Washington: Smithsonian Institution, 1919.

Kirk, G. S. *Myth: Its Meaning and Functions in Ancient Culture.* Cambridge: Cambridge University Press, 1970.

————. *The Iliad: A Commentary, Volume I: books 1–4, Volume II: books 5–8,* edited by G. S. Kirk, Cambridge: Cambridge University Press, 1985 and 1990.

Kluckhohn, Clyde. "Myths and Rituals: A General Theory," *Harvard Theological Review,* 35 (1942): 45–79.

————. *Navajo Witchcraft.* Papers of the Peabody Museum of American Archaeology and Ethnology, Harvard University, Vol. 22, No. 2. Cambridge, Mass., 1944, 1967.

Kroeber, Alfred L. "Coyote's Adventures and the Prairie Falcon's Blindness," "The Prairie Falcon Loses," *Indian Myths of South Central California,* University of California Publications, Vol. 4, No., 4, pp. 231–42, Berkeley, 1907.

————. *Anthropology.* New York: Harcourt, Brace and Company, 1948.

Lavine, Sigmund A. *The Games the Indians Played.* New York: Dodd, Mead, 1975.

Lawson, John. *History of Carolina.* London: 1701 or 1714.

Lekson, Stephen H. *Great Pueblo Architecture of Chaco Canyon, New Mexico.* Originally published 1984 by the National Park Service, U.S. Department of the Interior, Albuquerque, New Mexico, as Publications in Archeology 18B, Chaco Canyon Studies. Reprinted: Albuquerque: University of New Mexico Press, 1984.

Lesser, Alexander. *Pawnee Ghost Dance Hand Game.* Madison: University of Wisconsin Press, 1978.

Leyenaar, Ted J. J. *Ulama: The Perpetuation in Mexico of the Pre-Spanish Ball Game Ullamaliztli.* Leiden, The Netherlands: Riksmuseum voor Volenkunde, 1978.

Lister, Robert. "Mesoamerican Influence at Chaco Canyon, New Mexico. In *Across the Chichimec Sea: Papers in Honor of J. Charles Kelley,* edited by Carroll L. Riley and Basil C. Hendrick, pp. 233–41. Carbondale and Edwardsville, Ill.: Southern Illinois Press, 1978.

Lister, Robert, and Florence C. Lister. *Chaco Canyon: Archaeology and Archaeologists.* Albuquerque: University of New Mexico Press, 1981.

Longfellow, Henry Wadsworth. *The Song of Hiawatha.* The Minnehaha edition, New York: Federal Book Company, 1989.

Lowie, Robert H. "Wolf's Son," "Cúnä´Bⁱ," "The Gamblers," "Cottontail Gambles Against the Sun," "Wildcat," "Centipede," in "Shoshonean Tales," *Journal of American Folk-Lore,* January-June 1924, Vol. 37, No. 1, p. 105–09, 160–61, 174–76, 198, 199, 229–332.

————. *Crow Texts.* Berkeley and Los Angeles: University of California Press, 1960.

Luckert, Carl W. *The Navajo Hunter Tradition.* Tucson: University of Arizona Press, 1975.

MacCulloch, John A. *Eddic Mythology* [c.1930]. New York: Cooper Square Publications, 1964.

Malcolm, Roy, L. *American Antiquity.* 5 (1939): 4–20.

Malotki, Ekkehart. "*Maasaw niqw Orayit Naatsawinaya*—How Maasaw and the People of Oraibi Got Scared to Death Once," "*Tsorwukiqlö*—Tsorwukiqlö and His Eagles," *Hoptutuwutsi/Hopi Tales: A Bilingual Collection of Hopi Indian Stories,* pp. 109–117, 151–201. Flagstaff: Museum of Northern Arizona Press, 1978.

Martin, Paul S. *Modified Basket Maker Sites: Ackermen-Lowry Area, Southwestern Colorado,* 1938. Field Museum of Natural History Anthropological Series, Vol. 23, No. 3, publication 444, 1939, p. 421.

————. *The SU Site Excavations at a Mogollon Village in Western New Mexico.* Field Museum of Natural History Anthropological Series, Vol. 32, No. 1, fig. 31, 1940.

Mathien, Frances Joan. *Ornaments and Minerals from Chaco Canyon National Park Service Project, 1971–1978.* Manuscript, Division of Cultural Research, National Park Service, Santa Fe, New Mexico, 1985.

————. "Ornaments and Minerals from Pueblo Alto," in *Investigations at the Pueblo Alto Complex, Chaco Canyon, New Mexico 1975–1979*, Volume 1, 381–427, by Thomas C. Windes. Summary of Tests and Excavations at the Pueblo Alto Community, National Park Service, Santa Fe, New Mexico, 1987.

————. "Ornaments and Minerals from Site 29SJ627," in *Excavations at 29SJ627, Chaco New Mexico*, pp. 265–318, edited by Frances Joan Mathien. Reports of the Chaco Center, no. 11, Branch of Cultural Research, National Park Service, Santa Fe, New Mexico, 1992.

Matthews, Washington. "Noqoìlpi, the Gambler: A Navajo Myth." *The Journal of American Folk-Lore*, 2:5, pp. 89–94, April-June 1889.

————. "Navajo Gambling Songs," *American Anthropologist*, Vol. 2, No. 1, pp. 1–19, Washington, D.C., January 1889.

————. "The Navaho Origin Legend: The Story of the Emergence and Early Events in the Fifth World," *Navajo Legends*, pp. 63–104. Boston: American Folklore Society, 1897. Other gambling or games references, see pp. 24, 77, 81–87, 90, 97–98, 106, 134, 141, 160, 176, 191, 193, 219 n.47, 226 n. 76, 240 n. 176, 254 n. 271.

————. "The Night Chant, a Navaho ceremony," *Memoirs of the American Museum of Natural History*, vol. 6 (1902), pp. 15, 25.

Mayer, Dorothy. "An Examination of Miller's Hypothesis." In *Native American Astronomy*, edited by Anthony F. Aveni, pp 180–201. Austin: University of Texas Press, 1979.

McNitt, Frank. *Navajo Expedition: Journal of a Military Reconnaissance from Santa Fe, New Mexico to the Navajo Country Made in 1849.* Frank McNitt edited book from First Lt. James Hervey Simpson's "Journal of a Military Reconnaissance from Santa Fe, New Mexico to the Navajo Country, Made with the Troops under Command of Lt. Col. John M. Washington in 1849," for *Senate Executive Document No. 64, of 31st Congress 1st Session, 1852.* Norman: University of Oklahoma Press, 1964.

Miller, Jeanine. *The Vision of Cosmic Order in the Vedas.* London: Routledge & Kegan Paul, 1985.

Miranda, Frederica Sodi. "Game in the Mythological Cities of Quetzalcoatl." In *El Juego de Pelota en El México Precolumbino y su pervivencia en la actualidad*, edited by Fundació Folch. Catátogo de Museu Etnòlogic. Ajuntament de Barcelona, 1992.

Mooney, James. *The Ghost-dance Religion.* Report of the Bureau of American Ethnology, no. 14, Washington: Smithsonian Institution, 1896.

————. "The Jicarilla Genesis," *American Anthropologist*, vol. 11 (1898), p. 198.

————. *Calendar History of the Kiowa Indians.* Report of the Bureau of American Ethnology, no. 17. Washington: Smithsonian Institution, 1898.

————. "Ûñtsaiyi´, the Gambler," *Myths of the Cherokee.* Report of the Bureau of American Ethnology, no. 19, 1897–1898. Washington: Smithsonian Institution, 1900.

Morgan, Lewis Henry. *League of the Iroquois.* Rochester: Sage & Brother, 1851.

Morris, Earl H. *Basket Maker II Sites Near Durango, Colorado.* Publication 604, Carnegie Institution of Washington, Washington, D.C., 1954.

Murie, James R. *Ceremonies of the Pawnee; Part 1: The Skiri; Part 2: The South Bands*, Smithsonian Contributions to Anthropology; no. 27, Washington: Smithsonian Institution, 1981.

Murr, Nachrichten von. *Verschiedenen Ländern des Spanischen America*, Halle 1809, part I, p. 256.

O'Bryan, Aileen. "The Story of Noqoil pi, the Great Gambler," *The Dîné: Origin Myths of the Navaho Indians*, pp. 48–63. Bulletin of the Bureau of American Ethnology, no. 163, Washington: Smithsonian Institution, 1956.

Olguín, Felipe Solís. "The Sacred Ball Game in the Capital of the 'Mexicas.'" In *El Juego de Pelota en El México Precolumbino y su pervivencia en la actualidad*, edited by Fundació Folch, pp. 293–98. Catátogo de Museu Etnòlogic. Ajuntament de Barcelona, 1992.

Ortiz, Alfonso. *New Perspectives on the Pueblos.* Albuquerque: University of New Mexico Press, 1972.

Parmentier, Richard J. "The Mythological Triangle: Poseyemu, Montezuma, and Jesus in the Pueblos," in *Handbook of the North American Indians*, vol. 9, pp. 609–22, Alfonso Ortiz, volume editor, William C. Sturtevant, general editor, Washington: Smithsonian Institution, 1979.

Parsons, Elsie Clews. *Pueblo Indian Religion.* Chicago: University of Chicago Press, 1939.

Pasztory, Esther. "The Historical and Religious Significance of the Middle Classic Ball Game." In *Religión en Mesoamérica.* XII Round Table, SMA, pp. 441–55, Mexico, 1972.

Pepper, George H. "Ceremonial Objects and Ornaments from Pueblo Bonito, New Mexico." *American Anthropologist*, n.s. (1905), pp. 196–252.

———. "The Exploration of a Burial Room in Pueblo Bonito, New Mexico." Putnam Anniversary Volume, Anthropological Essays Presented to Frederic Ward Putnam in Honor of his Seventieth Birthday, pp. 196–252. New York: G. E. Stechert and Co., 1909.

———. "Pueblo Bonito." *Anthropological Papers of the American Museum of Natural History*, no. 27, New York, 1920.

Pousma, Richard H. *He-Who-Always-Wins and Other Navajo Campfire Stories*, pp. 57–69. Grand Rapids, Mich.: Eerdmans, 1934. See also 75–81, 89–92, 101–03, 109–10, 126–27, 135–36, 139–42 for other gaming myths and references.

Prescott, William H. *The Conquest of Mexico*. New York: The Modern Library, 1843.

Puche, Mari Carmen Serra, and Karina Rebeca Durand Velasco. "Ball game in Mesoamerica," *El Juego de Pelota en El México Precolumbino y su pervivencia en la actualidad*, Catátogo de Museu Etnològic, Ajuntament de Barcelona, 1992.

Ram, Rai Sahib Munshi. *With the Three Masters*, Vol. III. Punjab, India: Radha Soami Satsang Beas, 1967. (Third edition: 1987)

Ration, Tom. "A Navajo Life Story," *The South Corner of Time: Hopi, Navaho, Papago, Yaqui Tribal Literature*, pp. 63–71, edited by Broderick H. Johnson. Tsaile, Ariz.: Navajo Community College Press, 1977.

Reichard, Gladys A. *The Story of the Navajo Hail Chant*. New York: Columbia University Press, 1944.

———. *Navajo Religion*. Tucson: University of Arizona Press, 1974 [1950].

Reid, J. Jefferson, and David E. Doyel, editors. *Emil W. Haury's Prehistory of the American Southwest*. Tucson: University of Arizona Press, 1986.

Reifler, Sam. *I Ching: A New Interpretation for Modern Times*. New York: Bantam Books, 1974.

Reyman, Jonathan. "Pochteca Burials at Anasazi Sites?" In *Across the Chichimec Sea: Papers in Honor of J. Charles Kelley*, edited by Carroll L. Riley and Basil C. Hendrick, pp. 242–59. Carbondale and Edwardsville, Ill.: Southern Illinois Press, 1978.

Richardson, Nicholas. *The Iliad: A Commentary, Volume VI: books 21–24*, edited by G. S. Kirk. Cambridge: Cambridge University Press, 1993.

Roberts, F. H. *Early Pueblo Ruins in the Piedra District, Southwestern Colorado*. Bulletin of the Bureau of American Ethnology, no. 90, Washington: Smithsonian Institution, 1930.

———. *Additional Information on the Folsom Complex*. Smithsonian Miscellaneous Collections, Vol. 95, No. 10, 1936.

———. *Archaeological Remains in the Whitewater District: Eastern Arizona, Part 2, Artifacts and Burials*. Bulletin of the Bureau of American Ethnology, no. 126, Washington: Smithsonian Institution, 1940.

Sahagún, Fray Bernardino de. *A History of Ancient Mexico*. Nashville: Fisk University Press, 1932.

———. *General History of the Things of New Spain, Florentine Codex, Book 2, The Ceremonies; Book 4/5, Soothsayers and Omens; Book 8, Kings and Lords; Book 9, The Merchants*. Translated from the Aztec to the English by Arthur J. O. Anderson and Charles E. Dibble, Monographs of The School of American Research, Number 14, Parts III, IX, X. Santa Fe: School of American Research and University of Utah, 1954–1981.

Sando, Joe S. *Pueblo Nations: Eight Centuries of Pueblo Indian History*. Santa Fe: Clear Light Publishers, 1992.

Sapir, Edward. "Eagle, A Klamath Man, Goes to the Columbia River to Gamble," in *Wishram Texts, together with Wasco Tales and Myths, collected by Jeremiah Curtin and edited by Edward Sapir*, Publications of the American Ethnological Society, edited by Franz Boas, Volume II, pp. 292–94, Leyden, 1909.

———. "Coyote and Rabbit Gamble," "Gopher and Rabbit Gamble," *Yana Texts*, University of California Publications in American and Ethnology, Vol. 9, No. 1, pp. 226–27, February 19, 1910.

Schoolcraft, Henry Rowe. *The Indian in His Wigwam; or, Characteristics of the Red Race of America: from Original Notes and Manuscripts*. New York: AMS Press, 1978. Originally issued 1844–1845, bearing title: *Oneota; or, The Red Race of America*. New York: W. H. Graham, 1848.

Afterwards published under various titles: *The Red Race of America; The Indian in His Wigwam; The American Indians; Western Scenes and Reminiscences.*

Shetrone, Henry Clyde. *The Mound Builders.* New York: D. Appleton, 1931.

Silko, Leslie Marmon. *Storyteller.* New York: Arcade, 1981.

Sofaer, Anna, Rolf M. Sinclair, and Joey B. Donahue. "Solar and Lunar Orientations of the Major Architecture of the Chaco Culture of New Mexico," *Proceedings of the Colloquio Internazionale Archeologia e Astronomia,* held at the University of Venice, May 1989.

Spencer, Katherine. *Life in the Navaho Origin Myth.* University of New Mexico Publications in Anthropology, No. 3, Albuquerque, N. M., 1947.

———. *Mythology and Values: An Analysis of Navaho Chantway Myths,* Memoirs of the American Folklore Society, vol. 48, Philadelphia, 1957.

Stevenson, Matilda Coxe. *The Sia.* Report of the Bureau of American Ethnology, no. 11, Washington: Smithsonian Institute, 1889.

———. "Zuñi Games." *American Anthropologist,* n.s., 5, 1903.

Stuart, George E. "The Timeless Vision of Teotihuacan," *National Geographic,* Vol. 188, No. 6, December, 1995.

Sutton-Smith, Brian, editor. *The Games of the Americas: A Book of Readings.* New York: Arno Press, 1976.

Swanton, John R. "Sounding-Gambling-Sticks," "How the Seaward-Sqoā'ɫadas Obtained the Names of Their Gambling Sticks," *Haida Texts and Myths,* Bulletin of the Bureau of American Ethnology, no. 29, pp. 52–56, 322–24, Washington: Smithsonian Institution, 1905.

———. "How Water Was Lost and Recovered," "The Men Who Went to the Sky," "Thunder and Laigatonōhana," "The Cannibal Woman," "Lodge Boy and Thrown-Away," *Myths and Tales of the Southeastern Indians,* Bulletin of the Bureau of American Ethnology, no. 88, pp. 123–24, 139–41, 184, 219–22, 222–26, Washington: Smithsonian Institution, 1929.

Tedlock, Dennis. *Popol Vuh: The Definitive Edition of the Mayan Book of the Dawn of Life and the Glories of Gods and Kings,* with commentary based on the ancient knowledge of the modern Quiché Maya. New York: Simon & Schuster, 1895.

Teit, James A. "The Ball," "The Story of the Man Who Travelled to the Sun." In *Traditions of the Thompson River Indians,* Memoirs of the American Folk-Lore Society, VI, pp. 32–34, 53–54, Boston, 1898.

———. "The Gambler," in "Traditions of the Lillooet Indians of British Columbia, *Journal of American Folk-Lore,* Vol. 25, No. 117, pp. 338–39, July-September 1912.

Ten Broeck, P.G.S. "Manners and Customs of the Moqui and Navajo Tribes in New Mexico," Part 4, 72–94, in *Information Respecting the History, Condition and Prospects of the Indian Tribes of the United States.* Collected and prepared under the direction of the Bureau of Indian Affairs; edited by Henry Rowe Schoolcraft for the series Ethnological Researches Respecting the Red Man of America. Philadelphia: Lippincott, Grambo & Co., 1853–56.

Thompson, Stith, editor. "The Conquering Gambler" (LXXIII), *Tales of the North American Indians.* Bloomington: Indiana University Press, 1966 [1929].

Tyler, Hamilton A. *Pueblo Gods and Myths.* Norman: University of Oklahoma Press, 1964.

Tylor, Edward B. "Backgammon Among the Aztecs," *Macmillan's Magazine,* vol. 39, 1878, pp. 142–150. London, 1878. In *The Games of the Americas: A Book of Readings,* edited by Brian Sutton-Smith. New York: Arno Press, 1976.

———. "On the Game of Patolli in Ancient Mexico and Its Probably Asiatic Origin," *Journal of the Anthropological Institute of Great Britain and Ireland.* Vol. VIII, 1878, pp. 116–31, London. In *The Games of the Americas: A Book of Readings,* edited by Brian Sutton-Smith. New York: Arno Press, 1976.

———. "The History of Games," *The Fortnightly Review,* London: Chapman and Hall 25, n.s., Jan. 1–June 1, 1879, pp. 735–47. In *The Study of Games,* edited by Elliott M. Avedon and Brian Sutton-Smith, pp. 63–76. New York: John Wiley & Sons, Inc., 1971.

———. "On American Lot-Games, as Evidence of Asiatic Intercourse Before the Time of Columbus," Supplement to *International Archives for Ethnographie* 9, 1896, pp. 56–66. In *The Study of Games,* edited by Elliott M. Avedon and Brian Sutton-Smith, pp. 77–93. New York: John Wiley & Sons, Inc., 1971.

van Buitenen, J.A.B, editor and translator. *The Mahābhārata: The Book of the Beginning.* Chicago: University of Chicago Press, 1973.

van Buitenen, J.A.B, editor and translator. *The Mahābhārata: The Book of the Assembly Hall; The Book of the Forest.* Chicago: University of Chicago Press, 1975.

Vivian, Gwinn. "Navajo Archaeology of the Chacra Mesa, New Mexico," thesis from the University of New Mexico, 1960.

Waldman, Carl. *Atlas of the North American Indian.* New York: Facts on File, 1985.

Wetherill, Lulu Wade, and Byron Cummings. "A Navaho Folk Tale of Pueblo Bonito." *Art and Archaeology,* Vol. 14, pp. 132–36, September 1922.

Wheelright, Mary C. *Hail Chant and Water Chant,* Navajo Religion Series, vol. 2. Santa Fe: Museum of Navajo Ceremonial Art, 1946.

White, Leslie A. *The Pueblo of Sia, New Mexico.* Bulletin of the Bureau of American Ethnology, no. 184, Washington: Smithsonian Institution, 1962.

Whitman, William III. *Navaho Tales.* Boston: Houghton Mifflin, 1925.

Wilcox, David R. "Hohokam Social Complexity." In *Chaco & Hohokam: Prehistoric Regional Systems in the American Southwest,* edited by Patricia L. Crown and W. James Judge. Santa Fe: School of American Research Press, 1991.

Williams, Mentor L., editor. *Schoolcraft's Indian Legends from Algic Researches, The Myth of Hiawatha, Oneota, The Red Race in America, and Historical and Statistical Information Respecting the Indian Tribes of the United States.* East Lansing: Michigan State University Press, 1956.

Windes, Thomas C. *Investigations at the Pueblo Alto Complex, Chaco Canyon, New Mexico 1975–1979,* Vol. 1, pp. 20–22. Summary of Tests and Excavations at the Pueblo Alto Community National Park Service, Santa Fe, New Mexico, 1987.

Wyman, Leland C. *The Sandpaintings of the Kayenta Navaho: An Analysis of the Louisa Wade Wetherill Collection,* University of New Mexico Publications in Anthropology, no. 7, Albuquerque, 1952.

York, Frederick. "An Ethnographic Survey of Localities of Significance to the Navajo Population in the Vicinity of the NMGS Impact Area." In New Mexico Generating Station Third-Party Environmental Impact Statement: Cultural Resources in San Juan, McKinley, and Sandoval Counties, New Mexico. Carol J. Condie, editor. *Quivera Research Center Publication,* 39:IV-186. Manuscript on file, Albuquerque District Office, Bureau of Land Management, Albuquerque, 1982.

Zolbrod, Paul G. *Diné bahane': The Navajo Creation Story.* Albuquerque: University of New Mexico Press, 1984.

Index